TOWARDS A GLOBAL COMMUNITY

EDUCATION IN THE ASIA-PACIFIC REGION: ISSUES, CONCERNS AND PROSPECTS

Volume 7

Series Editors-in-Chief:

Dr. Rupert Maclean, *UNESCO-UNEVOC International Centre for Education, Bonn; and*
Ryo Watanabe, *National Institute for Educational Policy Research (NIER) of Japan, Tokyo*

Editorial Board

Robyn Baker, *New Zealand Council for Educational Research, Wellington, New Zealand*
Dr. Boediono, *National Office for Research and Development, Ministry of National Education, Indonesia*
Professor Yin Cheong Cheng, *The Hong Kong Institute of Education, China*
Dr. Wendy Duncan, *Asian Development Bank, Manila, Philippines*
Professor John Keeves, *Flinders University of South Australia, Adelaide, Australia*
Dr. Zhou Mansheng, *National Centre for Educational Development Research, Ministry of Education, Beijing, China*
Professor Colin Power, *Graduate School of Education, University of Queensland, Brisbane, Australia*
Professor J. S. Rajput, *National Council of Educational Research and Training, New Delhi, India*
Professor Konai Helu Thaman, *University of the South Pacific, Suva, Fiji*

Advisory Board

Professor Mark Bray, *Comparative Education Research Centre, The University of Hong Kong, China*; Dr. Agnes Chang, *National Institute of Education, Singapore*; Dr. Nguyen Huu Chau, *National Institute for EducationalSciences, Vietnam*; Professor John Fien, *RMIT University, Melbourne, Australia*; Professor Leticia Ho, *University of the Philippines, Manila;* Dr. Inoira Lilamaniu Ginige, *National Institute of Education, Sri Lanka;* Professor Phillip Hughes, *ANU Centre for UNESCO, Canberra, Australia*; Dr. Inayatullah, *Pakistan Association for Continuing and Adult Education, Karachi;* Dr. Rung Kaewdang, *Office of the National Education Commission, Bangkok. Thailand*; Dr. Chong-Jae Lee, *Korean Educational Development Institute, Seoul*; Dr. Molly Lee, *UNESCO, Bangkok, Thailand;* Naing Yee Mar, *Glocorp, The Netherlands*; Mausooma Jaleel, *Maldives College of Higher Education, Male*; Professor Geoff Masters, *Australian Council forEducational Research, Melbourne*; Dr. Victor Ordonez, *Senior Education Fellow, East-West Center, Honolulu*; Dr. Khamphay Sisavanh, *National Research Institute of Educational Sciences, Ministry of Education, Lao PDR*; Dr. Max Walsh, *Secondary Education Project, Manila, Philippines.*

Towards a
Global Community:
Educating for Tomorrow's World

Global Strategic Directions for the Asia-Pacific Region

Edited by

JACK CAMPBELL

University of Queensland,
Brisbane, Australia

NICK BAIKALOFF

University of Queensland,
Brisbane, Australia

and

COLIN POWER

University of Queensland,
Brisbane, Australia

 Springer

A C.I.P. Catalogue record for this book is available from the Library of Congress.

ISBN-10 1-4020-3960-3 (HB)
ISBN-13 978-1-4020-3960-7 (HB)
ISBN-10 1-4020-4338-4 (e-book)
ISBN-13 978-1-4020-4338-3 (e-book)

Published by Springer,
P.O. Box 17, 3300 AA Dordrecht, The Netherlands.

www.springer.com

Printed on acid-free paper

Printed in the Netherlands.

SERIES SCOPE

The purpose of this Series is to meet the needs of those interested in an in-depth analysis of current developments in education and schooling in the vast and diverse Asia-Pacific Region. The Series will be invaluable for educational researchers, policy makers and practitioners, who want to better understand the major issues, concerns and prospects regarding educational developments in the Asia-Pacific region.

The Series complements the *Handbook of Educational Research in the Asia-Pacific Region*, with the elaboration of specific topics, themes and case studies in greater breadth and depth than is possible in the Handbook.

Topics to be covered in the Series include: secondary education reform; reorientation of primary education to achieve education for all; re-engineering education for change; the arts in education; evaluation and assessment; the moral curriculum and values education; technical and vocational education for the world of work; teachers and teaching in society; organisation and management of education; education in rural and remote areas; and, education of the disadvantaged.

Although specifically focusing on major educational innovations for development in the Asia-Pacific region, the Series is directed at an international audience.

The Series *Education in the Asia-Pacific Region: Issues, Concerns and Prospects*, and the *Handbook of Educational Research in the Asia-Pacific Region*, are both publications of the Asia-Pacific Educational Research Association.

Those interested in obtaining more information about the Monograph Series, or who wish to explore the possibility of contributing a manuscript, should (in the first instance) contact the publishers.

Books published to date in the series:

1. Young People and the Environment:
   An Asia-Pacific Perspective
   Editors: John Fien, David Yenken and Helen Sykes
2. Asian Migrants and Education:
   The Tensions of Education in Immigrant Societies and among Migrant Groups
   Editors: Michael W. Charney, Brenda S.A. Yeoh and Tong Chee Kiong
3. Reform of Teacher Education in the Asia-Pacific in the New Millennium:
   Trends and Challenges
   Editors: Yin C. Cheng, King W. Chow and Magdalena M. Mok
4. Rasch Measurement: A Book of Exemplars
   Papers in Honour of John P. Keeves
   Editors: Sivakumar Alagumalai, David D. Curtis, Njora Hungi
5. Reforming Learning:
   Issues, Concepts and Practices in the Asian-Pacific Region
   Editors: Chi-Hung Ng and Peter Renshaw, *in press*
6. New Paradigm for Re-engineering Education:
   Globalization, Localization and Individualization
   Yin Cheong Cheng

CONTENTS

PREFACE

This book is the outcome of a global project undertaken on behalf of the World Education Fellowship (WEF) in collaboration with UNESCO. Stage 1 of the project involved the analysis of vision statements from leading Australians and the results of the 1998 WEF World Conference in Tasmania (see Campbell, W.J (Ed.) *Creating Our Common Future: Educating for Unity in Diversity*. Paris: UNESCO-WEF-Berghahn Books, 2001).

Towards a Global Community: Educating for Tomorrow's World describes the outcomes of the more comprehensive study undertaken under Jack Campbell's leadership on behalf of WEF. The first three chapters of this book provide a picture of the type of community that leaders from a diversity of nations and cultures, mainly but not exclusively from the Asian-Pacific region, see as preferred global futures, and the attributes that need to developed through education "to empower young people to live well both as individuals with unique potentials worthy of fulfilment, and as responsible members in a very diverse and restless global community."

In the second part of the book, the focus shifts to the ways in which education can contribute to the development of the attributes deemed to be essential to the realisation of the type of global community sought by participants in the WEF study. Colin Power focuses on a quality basic education for all as an essential pre-condition for the creation of a just and peaceful global community, while Margaret Henry emphasises the importance of attending to the developmental needs of young children in getting the foundations right. Then Abraham Blum provides an overview of education for sustainable development, while Richard Bawden shows what is and needs to be to provide a secure and sustainable source of food for all. One of the key issues raised in this study is the need to educate for social justice, an issue taken up by Diva Lopes de Silveira. She ends with a message of hope, describing social justice programs in a developing country. Judy Lawley gives practical examples from the Living Values project in New Zealand of the ways in which schools are seeking to create a global community. Then David Woolman provides an account of conflict theory and educational programs for conflict resolution. Jakar and Lucas pick up the challenge of educating for conflict resolution in a troubled region, providing case studies of effective programs. The final Chapters help draw the treads together as we seek to helping our students to become effective and responsible citizens not only of their own nation, but also of the Asia-Pacific region and the world. Rob Gilbert maps the curriculum requirements and challenges in educating for world citizenship, and Joe Le Bianco explores the ways education for citizenship and "effective personal literacy" are being redefined and can contribute to realising the vision of a more humane world.

All credit for the conceptualization and direction of the project described here goes to the late Professor Jack Campbell. However, the project would not have been possible without the valued input support and encouragement provided by Jack's wife Dr. Elizabeth Campbell, especially so during his serious illness. Our thanks, also, goes to the informants from 36 countries who so willingly participated in the project to investigate possible educational pathways 'Towards a Global Community'. It is clear that Professor Campbell supported the view held by Beatrice Ensor, who founded the New Education Fellowship in 1921 (later to be re-named: World Education Fellowship), that it was of little use in trying to work in one country alone in order to change education's impact. The movement needs to be regional and global if all nations in the Asian-Pacific region are to be contribute effectively to the building the type of preferred future set out in this book.

The UNESCO Conference on Education for the 21st Century in the Asia-Pacific Region (Melbourne, 1998) stressed that the major danger facing the region is that of a gulf opening up between a minority of people who are capable of finding their way successfully in a competitive global knowledge economy, and the majority who feel that they are at the mercy of events and have no say in the future of society. This book seeks to highlight strategic directions for education in the Asia-Pacific region, building on experience on expertise of educators and education systems in the region and beyond to address this danger.

Nick Baikaloff and Colin Power

INTRODUCTION BY THE SERIES EDITORS

Education for international understanding, and for learning to live together in peace and harmony, is being increasingly addressed by education policy makers, researchers and practitioners in countries throughout the world, regardless of the particular countries level of socio-economic development.

This is to be expected since in this rapidly changing age of globalisation, tensions are becoming increasingly apparent both within and between countries along racial, ethnic, religious and socio-economic lines. This is occurring to such an extent that reference is now frequently made by social commentators to there being 'a clash between civilizations'. In addition, many commentators claim that our age is experiencing such a crisis of values, that they fear the collapse of all that gives meaning to our actions and to our lives.

Education may be seen as providing an essential means to address and help rectify these categories of problems. As the Report to UNESCO of the International Commission on Education for the Twenty-first Century (UNESCO, 1996), *Learning: The Treasure Within*, so aptly points out, one of the four pillars of education in the Twenty-first Century is 'learning to live together; learning to live with others'. The authors of the report note:

> 'In confronting the many challenges that the future holds in store, humankind sees in education an indispensable asset in its attempt to attain the ideals of peace, freedom and social justice. The Commission affirms its belief that education has a fundamental role to play in personal and social development. The Commission does not see education as a miracle cure or a magic formula opening the door to a world in which all ideals will be attained, but as one of the principal means available to foster a deeper and more harmonious form of human development and thereby to reduce poverty, expulsion, ignorance, oppression and war.' (p. 13)

This book is most timely, addressing as it does how education can contribute to promoting a true global community, where countries, communities and individuals can leave in harmony, and where cultural diversity is not seen as a threat but as grounds for celebration. As the authors of this book put it, the challenge is to provide education and schooling which 'empowers young people to live well both as individuals with unique potential worthy of fulfilment, and as responsible members in a very diverse and restless global community'.

The book is the outcome of a global project undertaken by the World Education Fellowship in collaboration with UNESCO. Amongst other things it reports on the views of community leaders from 36 countries concerning their vision about preferred global futures, and on what needs to be done to have a world where the needs of the group as well as the needs of individuals can be adequately accommodated.

The International Decade of Education for Sustainable Development (DESD), for which UNESCO is the Lead Agency, was launched at the United Nations in New York on 1 March 2005. The study reported upon here has much to tell us about what can and needs to be done through education to achieve conflict resolution and peace building, and so sustainable development, on a global basis.

Rupert Maclean
Director of the UNESCO-UNEVOC International Centre
Bonn, Germany
and
Ryo Watanabe
Director, Department for International Research and Cooperation
National Institute for Educational Policy Research (NIER) of Japan,
Tokyo

Part I

Chapter 1

INTRODUCTION

Jack Campbell

The study reported here is concerned with developing educational curricula that will empower young people to live well both as individuals with unique potentials worthy of fulfilment, and as responsible members in a very diverse and restless *global* community. The curriculum exercise is undertaken transnationally, and involves, inter alia, research data pertaining to (a) features of desirable future human worlds and (b) attributes needed by individuals if they are going to contribute to the creation of those worlds.

The study shares with many other exercises in curriculum-remaking an instrumental element concerned with preparation for futures, but the futures, in this case, are *preferred*, rather than *forecasted*, ones, and the preparation is primarily concerned with ensuring that the young people develop the attributes needed to create *for themselves* worlds in which they want to live. As Edwards (2001, p. 119) has said:

> [E]ducation should help young people acquire the necessary under-
> standings, skills, dispositions and values to construct for themselves
> identities that will enable them to live their lives meaningfully, pur-
> posefully and co-operatively amidst the change and uncertainty
> they will increasingly encounter.

We share with Edwards (2001) some discomfort with the notion of one generation, however knowledgeable, foisting upon future generations *its* view of desirable human worlds—'To do [this] is an affront to personal autonomy and an infringement of the basic principles of democratic living'. Nevertheless, we concede that what we have done in this study is not free of this sin! Curriculum construction almost inevitably involves some judgements by one generation of what the succeeding generation will require in the way of 'understandings, skills, dispositions and values'.

In espousing an education that will encourage young people to identify themselves as members of a world community, we are not denying the importance of affiliations to the family, neighbourhood (schools, churches, clubs, etc.), and then more inclusive units up to, and including, nations. On the contrary, we accept that these are vital for the development of healthy personalities, and helpful in fostering the wider identification that we seek. The position taken here, however, is that senses of responsible membership in families, neighbourhoods and nations, although necessary, are not sufficient for living well in the 21st Century—a sense of membership in the global community is also needed.

Conventionally these days, a study such as this would fall within the discourse of educating for world (or global) 'citizenship'—witness the following publications:

3

J. Campbell et al. (eds.), Towards a Global Community, 3–12.
© 2006 *Springer. Printed in the Netherlands.*

Citizenship Education and the Modern State (Kennedy, 1997); *Educating World Citizens: Toward Multinational Curriculum Development* (Parker, Ninomiya and Cogan, 1999); *Citizenship for the 21st Century: An International Perspective on Education* (Cogan and Derricott, 2000); *Citizenship through Secondary Geography* (Lambert and Machon, 2001). In view of the seminal nature of these publications, and the debt that we owe to them, it behoves us to explain briefly why we have not followed their lead by locating the study within the citizenship domain.

More than 2300 years ago, Aristotle declared, 'The nature of citizenship... is a question which is often disputed: there is no general agreement on a single definition' (Barker, 1946). The situation has changed little since the days of Aristotle. If disagreements have been reduced, it has been at the expense of simply adding new definitional components to satisfy the emphases of competing interests. As Slater states (2001, p. 48), 'The changes in the meaning of citizenship which have taken place over the [20th] century demonstrate the "emptiness" of the concept. We load it with meaning, and change those meanings as groups in society put forward their competing beliefs and aspirations'. It can be argued that there is nothing in this that is unusual or cause for concern. As Malouf writes in the *Foreword* to the *Third Edition of the Macquarie Dictionary* (1997):

> Language in its daily use ... is a keen receptor of change: of the way we, as individuals, grow into new apprehensions of the world and seek new terms, or extend the meaning of old ones, to accommodate them; of the way society at large keeps readjusting the light in which we view and learn to live with one another, or view ourselves.

During the 20th Century, there have been major changes in relation to how 'we view and learn to live with one another, or view ourselves', and one would expect the concept of citizenship to keep pace with these changes. The problem from the point of view of this study is simply that our concerns still do not fit comfortably within the concept.

At the core of many definitions of citizenship is the Marshallian idea of a status bestowed on persons who are full members of a community (usually a nation state), and who are equal with respect to the rights and duties with which the status is evidenced (Marshall, 1950, p. 84). In its minimalist form, the essential ingredients of this definition are: membership of a political state; a legal status; 'negative' rights associated with freedom of speech, movement, association and assembly; 'positive' rights associated with accessing resources, income, health care, education and welfare; duties and responsibilities; and inclusion and exclusion—i.e. *legal* or *formal* citizenship. To this definition has been added the resurrected Aristotelian notion of a citizenry which is politically literate in the knowledge, skills and attitudes necessary to understand and influence political decisions—i.e. *substantive* or *participatory* citizenship—an emphasis on values, and a focus on identity. According to Isin and Wood (1999), what was once a unitary and homogeneous political or legal concept has become a multidimensional and plural one, comprising 'political, civil, economic, diasporic, cultural, sexual and ecological' aspects. In the process, it has inevitably become subject to multiple interpretations arising from social and cultural perspectives (Albala-Bertrand, 1995; Goodman, 1994).

As Lynch (1994, p. 15) and Linklater (1998, p. 24) point out, whereas the current concept of *national* citizenship is still clear enough, in a strict definitional sense that of *world* citizenship has always been, and remains, a logical contradiction. This latter judgement stems mainly from the fact that there is, as yet, no world state to which citizenship can be attached. Others (e.g. Colley, 1996; Edwards, 2001; Moretti, 1999; Said, 1995) target the pervasive presence of *exclusion* within definitions of citizenship, and imply that the retention of this element makes citizenship an inappropriate concept under which to consider the notion of *total inclusiveness* inherent in world perspectives, affiliations and responsibilities. If the cardinal principle is that humanity is indivisible, it is oxymoronic to retain elements of 'us' and 'them'.

It might be argued that both of the strictures immediately above are somewhat 'precious' but, considered together with the disparate nature of elements included in the concept, and the diverse meanings attached to them in different cultures, they suggest that *citizenship* carries too much 'baggage' for purposes of this study, and could be an impediment, rather than a help, to the deliberations. Moreover, as Gilbert points out (1997, p. 73), the discomfort is probably two-sided: 'Promoted as they are by nation states, and historically grounded in such a strong tradition of grand narratives of progress through the story of the nation, programs in education for citizenship will surely find the concept of world citizenship difficult to accept and even more difficult to reconcile with the nationalist agenda'. For reasons such as these, there would be merit in defining citizenship strictly in its legal sense, and developing some other term to explain the various elements with which this study is concerned.

1.   TOWARDS 'ONE GLOBAL COMMUNITY'

During the 18th and 19th Centuries, the world of humans on planet Earth was typically divided into nation states that were considered to be the culmination of a natural evolutionary movement in cultural and political structures. By the beginning of the 20th Century, however, we find such units being described, not entirely cynically, as societies united by a common error as to their origins and a common aversion to their neighbours (Huxley, Haddon and Carr-Saunders, 1939). Moreover, throughout that 20th Century, some nations were made and unmade, if not at the drop of a hat, by somewhat arbitrarily drawing lines in the sand. The result has been that, in the Balkans, the Soviet Union, the Middle East and Africa, in particular, changing boundaries have confused national affiliations and weakened the sense of national loyalties. In some cases, as the Russian social scientist, Kon (1993), reports, this void created in the national consciousness is being filled by a retreat into narrower ethnic or religious identities. Looked at across the spectrum, however, processes of tentative transnational community building, loose regionalisation, and somewhat aggressive localisation are proceeding concurrently (Giddens, 1999). Lo Bianco (2001) states, 'Indeed there are different kinds of nations, different ways for nations to be organised into states that can reduce, share or otherwise modify sovereignty, and plural states, with complex amalgams of national feeling and post-national sentiment, co-exist with kinds of nationality that are exclusive and excluding'.

In addition to the flow of structural changes alluded to above, nations have become more 'porous' with respect to *economic activities, challenges to sovereignty* and *movement of populations*. Ohmae (1996) believes that the globalisation of markets, involving both the production and consumption of goods, is making territorial borders redundant and nation states obsolete. It has to be said, however, that despite their prominence in the current discourse, the precise nature and effects of economic globalisation are not yet fully charted, and it could be premature to assume the demise of the nation state on these grounds. Although acknowledging that economic trends are connecting economies and economic elites in all countries in new ways, Porter (1997, p. 82), for example, reminds us that 'Most world economic activity remains domestic not international, even in the United States, and the imperial empire of Great Britain probably involved more international integration than developing globalisation ... '

Trade alignments are most advanced within the European community and there is some evidence to suggest that they are being broadened into cultural and political responsibilities. This view is held by Heiberg (1995) who writes enthusiastically, 'In Europe, sovereignty is being transformed by a process of transnational community building, linking local communities into broader associations, breaking the monopoly of the territorial state, making the latter less all-encompassing and less sovereign, creating multiple identities also across borders, transforming relations between citizens and societies, societies and states'. On the other hand, Power (2001, p. 27), writing as Deputy Director-General of UNESCO, reminds us that the task of creating a European identity has proved to be difficult, and he implies that it would be naive to believe that we can sit back and expect economic globalisation to achieve a world identity for us.

Some (Crook, Pakulski and Waters, 1992; Featherstone, 2000) see evidence of developing political globalisation in the establishment of supra-national agencies, often aimed at protecting the sovereign immunity of the individual. Frequently mentioned in this respect are the UN Commission for Human Rights; UN High Commission for Refugees; the International Court of Justice; International Criminal Court; Amnesty International; alliances of indigenous people; women's movements; Christian Aid; ecological organisations such as Greenpeace; and a range of other organisations that refuse to halt their concerns at the borders of nation states. There is, however, a long way to go before significant measures of national sovereignty are transferred to these agencies. Declarations from the UN, for example, signal an international democratic direction, but are not easily, if at all, enforceable. When writing of attempts by the UN to preserve the earth's fragile ecosystems, Power states (2001, p. 21):

> The Rio Conference tried to stem the destruction, but in an intensely competitive world, few nations have been willing to take the steps which most people acknowledge are fundamental to our common future. Two timid conventions were signed, the words sustainable development and Agenda 21 were brandished about, but little happened.

Moreover, in recent Australian papers we find this item:

> The International Criminal Court will start on July 1, 2002, and deal with war crimes, crimes against humanity and genocide. The Australian Government will ratify the court, but with the condition

that it could veto any charges against an Australian. France has already invoked a clause that gives its citizens exemption from war crimes charges for seven years after joining. But the [Australian] Government is tipped to go even further, declaring as a condition of ratification that no Australians could be tried by the court without Government approval. Otherwise, Australia risks losing its sovereignty. According to [the Prime Minister], the US had 'danced a number' of impressive arguments for its refusal to ratify the court.

A third strand to the globalisation phenomenon is the diversity of populations which is to be found now in almost all nations. To cite Lo Bianco (2001):

At no stage in history has the population diversity of nations been so great as now. World population movements are greater than at any previous stage in history. The poor and the displaced move across borders in increasing numbers, but so do the rich and powerful. Recruited labour migration goes to countries of former emigration, countries of immigration also host massive out movements of people; student mobility is vast in a globally connected education marketplace, and the movement of elites in vast numbers gives rise to hybridising cultures everywhere.

The influx of persons from other cultures brings with it new ideas of rights and responsibilities, of relations between God and people, citizens and state, and sets in train processes of acculturation, integration, conflict and the like. All of this can herald the emergence of a pluralistic world society, if not a global community, but it can also lead to a backlash of hyper-nationalism, reflected in acts of 'ethnic cleansing', as in Kosovo, Rwanda and other places within recent years.

Perhaps chief amongst the forces fostering a sense of a single community have been common threats as a result of over-population, inappropriate use of resources, climatic change, ozone depletion and desertification, as well as the intervention of military weapons that make a mockery of national boundaries. Ellyard (1991, p. 14) writes, 'For centuries fear has divided humanity, now it is uniting it. Around the world this fear of major global ecological problems is beginning to enforce further cooperation between nations'. The focus on ecological hazards has, in the opinion of many, generated a sense of common destiny, new understandings of the place of humans in nature and new considerations relating to rights, political expressions and shared values (Gilbert, 1997, p. 74).

The forces towards a global community that have been discussed above all contain a strong element of 'reaction', but there remains one that does not fit that categorisation, namely, a growing recognition amongst reflective persons from many countries that the richness and diversity of the world's cultures provide a marvellous repertoire of strategies for common well-being that cannot be matched by any one national culture. As Degenhardt (1982, p. 82) stated, '[One's own culture] may carry a picture of the world that is accurate or distorted, informed or ignorant. It may guide us to better or worse moralities, it may open up to us real possibilities for conceiving the world and conducting our lives, or render us blind and hostile towards whole realms of human awareness and endeavour'. In similar vein, Hedley Beare writes (1991, p. 3), 'Once born, all of us, with and without help, begin to spin around ourselves a web of meanings, which allow us to interpret our world and also to protect ourselves from its ravages. In the one process, we can ensure our survival, our fulfilment as a creature in the cosmos, and, paradoxically, our imprisonment—enclosed within a world-view and a social fabric which are of our own making and which prevent us from experiencing reality in its wholeness'. Finally, Barbara Lepani writes (1999, p. 12), 'The second type of ignorance that gets in the way of learning is our culturally informed world-view, encoded in language, values and assumptions. As wonderful as the richness of [one's culture] is, it is a prism on the world which can all too easily become a prison'.

2.   NATURE OF THE STUDY

The ultimate goal of the study is to contribute to the extension of personal identities and commitments beyond the national level to the global one, and this is to be achieved by asking a small number of curriculum specialists to develop school curricula based on the responses of transnational 'learning communities' to two questions:
1. *Tier 1*. What are highly desirable features of global futures that, given the will, could be achieved in the foreseeable future?
2. *Tier 2*. What attributes would individuals need if they are to create those desirable global futures?

(Although these questions are structurally similar to those addressed by Parker, Ninomiya and Cogan, 1999, they differ substantially in that Parker and colleagues were concerned, primarily, with *forecasted challenges and crises*, whereas we are concerned with *preferred futures*.)

Taken together, the two research questions suggest a commitment to vision-driven educational planning: one begins by specifying preferred futures, and then proceeds to identify the kind of human attributes needed to realise those futures.

Of the four main types of 'future' studies—*science-fiction, extrapolative, predictive* and *normative*—this one is of the last kind. We accept that science-fiction scenarios, extrapolations from the present and predicted futures are interesting and valuable, but we have chosen a normative approach on two main grounds: (a) we believe that education should lead society by helping to create preferred futures, and not just respond to demands to prepare students for futures that happen to be forecasted; (b) in recent times, forecasted futures have proven to be notoriously wide of the mark—how many people, for example, predicted the sudden re-unification of Germany, collapse of the USSR, events in South Africa or the September 11, 2001 terrorist attacks in the USA?—whereas, by exercising moral choices relating to what a good society should be, we can help to shape the future and convert our visions into reality.

We are aware that some people will contest the claims above, and dismiss 'vision-driven' educational planning as will o' the wisp, wish-list stuff, which should be re-placed by hard-nosed pragmatism. We believe, however, that visions are perceptions of our best possibilities, of how things morally ought to be, and that they generate creative, persistent and targeted powers, which enhance the chances of fulfilment.

Martin Luther King's 'I-have –a-dream' inspired millions of people throughout the globe, and became a key element in the world-wide campaign to obtain justice and dignity for all; Nelson Mandela's vision of a free South Africa resulted in the dismantling of apartheid much more rapidly than would have occurred through evolution or incrementalism; Mahatma Gandhi's vision of unity in diversity was an inspiration to all who sought to oppose violence and to mobilise culturally different groups; President Kennedy's vision of an American walking on the moon by the end of the 1960s led to a massive marshalling of resources which ensured the success of the venture; the UNESCO-sponsored Jomtien Conference of March 1990 re-formulated a commitment to provide basic education for all which resulted in a spectacular turn around of the decline evident during the 1980s.

Leonard Cheshire VC (1981) wrote, 'We need a vision, a dream. The vision should be the oneness, the essential and organic solidarity of the human family. The dream, that we each in our own way make our personal contribution towards building unity and peace among us'. Patricia Williams, in the Reith lecture of 1997, said, 'I do believe that to a very great extent we dream our worlds into being: an optimistic course might be charted if only we could imagine it'. (cited in Wade, 2001, p. 180). Finally, Njuguna (2001), a Kenyan youth delegate to the 40th International Conference of World Education Fellowship, 1999, said, 'Remember, if you can imagine it, you can achieve it. If you can dream it, you can become it' (cited in Campbell, 2001).

Because the Tier 1 question in the study encouraged participants to respond in terms of *societal* features, at first glance it might be thought that we are adopting a Plato-ean approach, namely, design the ideal State through whose educational policies the ideal individual could be developed, rather than a Roussea-ean one, namely, educate the ideal individual through whom the ideal society might come to realization. This, however, would be a misreading of the study. The society has been placed up front because we believe that most problems are anchored there, requiring attention to economic and political structures, to poverty, forms of social injustice and the like. This belief was reinforced early on in the study by an educationist from Jamaica who responded to our invitation to take part in the study by expressing reservations about the usefulness of it:

> Because I live in the developing world where we suffer trade imbalances and inequities of trade agreements, where it is mainly some countries that have the power to define the terms (for example, what is protectionism versus social support mechanisms), I am feeling very pessimistic about our global future. The future lies in these structural changes. But if we begin by talking about educating world citizens, we may focus on attitudes and values and miss the point.

By concentrating first on the societal features, and placing these clearly on the table, it was hoped to ensure that they were not marginalised. We have no difficulty acknowledging the need to address matters such as poverty, inadequate health care, over-population, conflict, social injustices and the like and, at the same time, accepting that a major path towards their solution lies through the full development of individuals. In the final resort, changes to society's structures are dependent upon the sensitivities, knowledges, values, attitudes and action-competencies of human beings acting individually or collaboratively. Thus, at Tier 2, after deliberating on the characteristics of the 'good society' in Tier 1, we turn to a consideration of what human attributes are needed. Moreover, at Tier 2, we consider individuals as ends-in-themselves, as well as means to social ends. Considered as a whole, the study has a closer affinity to the thinking of Rousseau than to that of Plato.

The overarching methodology at Tiers 1 and 2 involved establishing transnational 'reference groups'. It might be argued, perhaps, that participants at *Tier 1* should all have been reflective *young* people, but many of the youth whom we approached expressed reservations about their ability to envisage desirable futures without input from more mature and more worldly wise mentors. As a result, of the 183 persons who contributed visions at Tier 1, all but 35 were chosen, with the help of consultants, on the basis of criteria formulated by Parker, Ninomiya and Cogan (1999):

- Future orientation as demonstrated by the ability to envision changes and opportunity in the future.
- Leadership as demonstrated by speeches, writings, esteem amongst peers.
- Interest in civic affairs as demonstrated by participation in civic groups.
- Knowledge of global issues and trends.
- Balance in gender, ethnicity and disciplines as far as possible.

The majority of these 183 had 'track records' as leading thinkers on the issues with which we are concerned, and they included persons from aesthetic arts; agricultural science; community development; economics; education; geography; history; human relations; industry; industrial relations; languages; law; mathematics; medicine; microbiology; multiculturalism; psychiatry; psychology; religion; social work; social analysis; sociology; town planning; UNESCO administration; and veterinary science. The 35 young persons, aged between 14 and 25 years, were, in the main, leading members of youth associations within UNESCO and World Education Fellowship with a demonstrated interest in global unity.

The 36 countries from which the Tier 1 participants were drawn were Australia; Belgium; Brazil; Cambodia; Canada; China; Czech Republic; Denmark; Finland; France; Germany; Greece; Hungary; India; Indonesia; Israel; Jamaica; Japan; Kazakstan; Kenya; Netherlands; New Zealand; Nigeria; Norway; Pakistan; Philippines; Portugal; Russia; Samoa; South Africa; Sri Lanka; Sweden; Switzerland; Thailand; United Kingdom; United States.

It will be noted that, of the commonly-identified geopolitical regions—Australasia, Asia (South-East and South-West), Europe (Western and Eastern), Latin America; Middle East, North America, and sub-Saharan Africa—all but the Middle East were reasonably well represented at Tier 1. The failure to attract participants from that last region can probably be explained in terms of timing (the study was launched on September 8, 2001—as it happened, 3 days before the terror attacks in the US); the subsequent war in Afghanistan; and an escalation of the on-going Israeli/Palestinian confrontation. Several prospective participants from the Middle East did, indeed, indicate preparedness to take part but failed to return submissions. (Amongst the participants, however, were several of Middle East origin living elsewhere.)

At Tier 2, where the concern is with the attributes needed by individuals to realise the visions of Tier 1, we 'retreated' to those participants (64) from the Tier 1 'community' who, in addition to being visionary, were experts in social-science disciplines—psychology, psychiatry, sociology, community development, human relations, multiculturalism, social work, social analysis, town planning and education. These 64 participants were drawn from 29 of the 36 countries represented at Tier 1.

Within each of Tiers 1 and 2, there were two research 'steps': first, an invitation to participants to respond in an open-ended manner to the questions and second, an invitation to assign ratings of 'desirability' to the issues that had emerged at the first steps. The findings of Tiers 1 and 2 form Part I of this report, and provide the basis upon which the curriculum is developed.

At Tier 3, there was a further contraction of participants to educationists who had track records as curriculum developers relating to the issues that had emerged through the study. These educationists were invited to take on board the findings from Tiers 1 and 2, to which they had contributed, and report in a specific manner on the curricula that were required to develop the attributes identified as likely to contribute to the realization of the Tier 1 visions. The submissions by the educationists form Part II of this report.

3. REFERENCES

Albala-Bertrand, L. 1995. The need to reinforce citizenship education worldwide: a conceptual framework for research. *Education Innovation and Information 82*, 2–9.

Barker, E. (Trans.). 1946. *Aristotle: The Politics of Aristotle*. Oxford: Clarendon Press.

Beare, H. 1991. The womb and the cocoon: some observations on parenting and schooling. *New Horizons in Education 85*, 2–15.

Campbell, J. (Ed.). 2001. *Creating Our Common Future: Educating for Unity in Diversity*. Paris: UNESCO Publishing.

Cheshire, L. 1981. *The Hidden World*. London: Collins.

Cogan, J.J. and Derricott, R. 2000. *Citizenship for the 21st Century*. London: Kogan Page.

Colley, L. 1996. *Britons: Forging the Nation, 1707–1837*. London: Vintage.

Crook, S., Pakulski, J. and Waters, M. 1992. *Postmodernization: Change in Advanced Society*. London: Sage.

Degenhardt, M.A.B. 1982. *Education and the Value of Knowledge*. London: Allen and Unwin.

Edwards, G. 2001. A very British subject: questions of identity. In: Lambert D. and Machon P. (Eds.) *Citizenship Through Secondary Geography*. London: Routledge Falmer, p. 119.

Ellyard, P. 1991. Education for the 21st century. *New Horizons in Education 84*, 2–17.

Featherstone, M. 2000. Technologies of post-human development and the potential for global citizenship. In: Nederveen Pieterse J. (Ed.) *Global Futures: Shaping Globalisation*. London: Zed Books.

Giddens, A. 1999. *The Reith Lectures*. London: BBC.

Gilbert, R. 1997. Issues for citizenship in a postmodern world. In: Kennedy K. (Ed.) *Citizenship Education and the Modern State*. London: Falmer Press.

Goodman, D.S.G. 1994. How high's a barricade? *Australian Book Review 162*, 24–31.

Heiberg, M. 1995. Building Cohesion in the Wake of the Israeli–Palestinian Conflict: The Question of Sovereignty. Unpublished paper, delivered Sydney.

Huxley, J., Haddon, A.C. and Carr-Saunders, A.M. 1939. *We Europeans*. Harmondsworth: Penguin Books.

Isin, E.F. and Wood, P.K. 1999. *Citizenship and Identity*. London: Sage Publications.

Kennedy, K. (Ed.). 1997. *Citizenship Education and the Modern State*. London: Falmer Press.

Kon, I.S. 1993. Identity crisis and post-communist psychology. *Symbolic Interaction* 16(4), 395–410.

Lambert, D. and Machon, P. (Eds.). 2001. *Citizenship Through Secondary Education*. London: Routledge Falmer.

Lepani, B. 1999. *Flexible Delivery of Education and Training: What does the Future Hold?* Lateral Solutions (Aust) Pty Ltd., The Australian Centre for Innovation and International Competitiveness Ltd., University of Sydney.

Linklater, A. 1998. Cosmopolitan citizenship. *Citizenship Studies* 2(1), 23–41.

Lo Bianco, J. 2001. Talking globally: challenges for foreign language education from new citizenship and economic globalisation. *Forum for Modern Language Studies* 37(4), 456–479.

Lynch, J. 1994. *Education for Citizenship Education in a Multi-cultural Society*. London: Cassells.

Malouf, D. 1997. Foreword. *Macquarie Dictionary* (3rd ed.). Sydney: Macquarie Library.

Marshall, T.H. 1950. *Citizenship and Social Class*. Cambridge: Cambridge University Press.

Moretti, F. 1999. *Atlas of the European Novel: 1800–1900*. London: Verso.

Njuguna, P. 2001. In: Campbell J. (Ed.) *Creating Our Common Future*. Paris: UNESCO Publishing, p. iii.

Ohmae, K. 1996. *The End of the Nation State*. New York: Free Press.

Parker, W.C., Ninomiya, H. and Cogan, J. 1999. Educating world citizens: toward multinational curriculum development. *American Educational Research Journal 36*(2), 117–145.

Porter, P. 1997. Knowledge, skills and compassion? Education research and the universities. *The Australian Educational Researcher 24*(1), 79–96.

Power, C.N. 2001. UNESCO's response to the challenge of establishing unity in diversity. In: Campbell J. (Ed.) *Creating our Common Future: Educating for Unity in Diversity*. Paris: UNESCO Publishing.

Said, E. 1995. 'Afterword' in *Orientalism: Western Concepts of the Orient*. Harmondsworth: Penguin.

Slater, F. 2001. Values and values education in the geography curriculum in relation to concepts of citizenship. In: Lambert D. and Machon P. (Eds.) *Citizenship Through Secondary Geography*. London: Routledge Falmer.

Wade, R. 2001. Global citizenship: Choices and change. In: Lambert D. and Machon P. (Eds.) *Citizenship Through Secondary Geography*. London: Routledge Falmer.

Chapter 2

TRANSNATIONAL VISIONS OF DESIRABLE FUTURES

Jack Campbell and Nick Baikaloff

For I dipt into the future, far as human eye could see, Saw the vision of the world, and all the wonder that [could] be.
Alfred Tennyson, Locksley Hall

1.   STEP 1: OPEN-ENDED VISION SUBMISSIONS

Kofi Annan's acceptance speech for the Nobel Peace Prize, Oslo, December 10, 2001, includes a statement that encapsulates the main message of this chapter, and we feel justified in citing it at the outset because several of the participants forwarded it in support of their submissions:

> Today, in Afghanistan, a girl will be born. Her mother will hold her and feed her, comfort her and care for her—just as any mother would anywhere in the world. In these most basic acts of human nature, humanity knows no divisions. But to be born a girl in today's Afghanistan is to begin life centuries away from the prosperity that one small part of humanity has achieved. It is to live under conditions that many of us in this hall would consider inhuman.
>
> I speak of a girl in Afghanistan, but I might equally well have mentioned a baby boy or girl in Sierra Leone. No one today is unaware of this divide between the world's rich and poor. No one can claim ignorance of the cost that this divide imposes on the poor and dispossessed who are no less deserving of human dignity, fundamental freedoms, security, food and education than any of us. The cost, however, is not borne by them alone. Ultimately, it is borne by all of us—North and South, rich and poor, men and women of all races and religions.
>
> Today's real borders are not between nations, but between powerful and powerless, free and fettered, privileged and humiliated. Today, no walls can separate humanitarian or human rights crises in one part of the world from national security crises in another. Scientists tell us that the world of nature is so small and interdependent that a butterfly flapping its wings in the Amazon rainforest can generate a violent storm on the other side of the earth. This principle is known as the 'Butterfly Effect'. Today, we realise,

J. Campbell et al. (eds.), Towards a Global Community, 13–38.
© 2006 Springer. Printed in the Netherlands.

perhaps more than ever, that the world of human activity also has
its own 'Butterfly Effect'—for better of worse. (Annan, 2001)

Although not all participants were prepared to argue that human individuals are
equal in all respects, they accepted as axiomatic that, *by virtue of being human,
all are entitled to be treated with respect and dignity.* Humanity is indivisible: a
human life is a human life, is a human life, and that life is entitled to nurturance
sufficient, not only for its maintenance but, also, for its full human development. In
the few instances where justification of this proposition was felt necessary, recourse
was most frequently made to the perspective of God ('God makes no distinctions,
and neither should we'—Indian participant), an appeal to common species, if not
common ancestry ('Every human being should be able to see the similarities of all
humans ... Thus, "I am in you and you in me"'—Indonesian participant), or to the
'awe-inspiring' nature of humankind:

> Human identity, individual as well as collective, can be probed by
> the simple expedient of allotting us our proper place on a graph
> representing the structure of the natural world. We all exist at the
> nexus of time and space, and our provenance can be traced back on
> the eternal chain of time across the infinite realm of space to the
> distant moment when life began. Is it not awe-inspiring? (Japanese
> participant)

Given this philosophical perspective, and underlining its significance for them,
several participants proceeded to deplore instances where human lives were perceived
to be assigned *unequal* respect and dignity. Thus, one Canadian participant wrote:

> The future, however defined, has to promise more possibilities for
> sharing—for sharing our humanity across shameful disparities and
> painful divisions. One and all, sharing responsibilites for eliminat-
> ing the causes that dehumanize each one of us. What we need most
> of all is an openness to be able to acknowledge dehumanization
> wherever (and however) it occurs. (Canada)

In addition to the moral argument that all humans should be treated as equal in
dignity and worth, there was the pragmatic one, namely, that, 'for better or worse',
the fate of humanity in the future will be a common one. Participants made frequent
reference to common threats, hybridisation of ideas, interdependency of almost all activities and decline of national sovereignty. It was considered that modern-day nations
are increasingly becoming pluralistic groups, characterised by internal ideological
differences and interacting with other pluralistic groups at a whole host of points, not
only economic and political ones. It is no coincidence that some of the most serious
threats to global well-being are now *within* nations, rather than between them.

Having accepted the principle that all humans should be treated with dignity
and acknowledgement of worth, participants went on to spell out what this means in
terms of specific 'entitlements': basic food, shelter and health care; basic security;
social justice; participatory democracy; and retention and development of diversity.
Although extreme 'poverty' in any of the five features was judged to be unacceptably

'dehumanising', most participants considered that distinctions could be made among them. In particular, those features judged to be 'essential for survival' (food, shelter and health care; security) were ascribed priority over those judged to be 'very highly desirable', but whose 'frailty', or even absence, would seldom be directly life-threatening (social justice; participatory democracy; and retention and development of diversity). To a large extent, this was a recognition of differing levels of urgency among human needs, as in Abraham Maslow's hierarchy, and attention was drawn to this by several participants. One from India said:

> For millions of people, violence has become a fact of life. One of the striking reasons for this is that a majority of the world population does not have access to basic and essential needs of life. Here, Abraham Maslow's need-hierarchy model holds good, as most of us are still at the base of the pyramid of needs—physiological needs. Man cannot digest heavy ideals on an empty stomach. For the upliftment of morality and spirituality, it is essential that all world citizens get an opportunity for a decent livelihood.... Nobel Prize winner, Amartya Sen, has rightly emphasized the need for the universal provision of basic amenities.

Another participant, this time from Australia, wrote:

> There are many countries in which poverty is so extreme that the populations have no choice but to sacrifice the futures of themselves and their children in order to survive in the present. Hungry, diseased and destitute people rarely concern themselves with 'understanding life with compassion and love'. And so care for ecological integrity, for example, will only come when appetites are satisfied, poverty eliminated.

1.1. An Overview of Challenges and Pointers to Better Futures

A reading of the 183 submissions suggests that most participants concentrated on what they, personally, regarded as the most salient features of desirable futures, and they left it to others to respond with their own choices. A minority, however, succeeded in referring to an amazingly comprehensive coverage of 'challenges' and approaches to solving these. As an introduction to a more detailed discussion, the following 'Preamble' from an Australian participant, for example, fleetingly canvasses many of the major issues raised by the participants as a group, and provides what might be a useful overview of Sections III and IV.

Preamble

> I flux from pessimism to guarded optimism in my thoughts about the feasibility of 'better futures'—and then back again. I especially think about the present events and the reactions to them in the context of other events and reactions that I have witnessed over my three score years or so as I have shuffled about this planet. It

is always illustrative to think about the past when musing about the future—to think about the desired futures and achievable ends that others, in earlier times, have previously believed were possible when pursued in good faith.

The world human population has doubled in my lifetime to a level which many would argue, based on the extent and rate of the degradation of the bio-physical environment of the globe, has reached, if not exceeded, its 'carrying capacity'. Together we live now in what is sometimes referred to as a risk society—an age of reflexive modernity where we have not only become victims of our own excesses on a global scale, but seem unable to work out what it is we should do next in terms of more sustainable futures.

I have lived through the times of Adolf Hitler and Josef Stalin, of Pol Pot and Idi Amin, and countless other despotic tyrants who seem to emerge with despairing repetition—one after the other—in so many different parts of the world. And, wave after wave, still they come; the ethnic cleansers, the freedom repressors, the human rights abusers, the public purse robber barons, the guardians of terrorists, etc. There are but a few people on earth yet who enjoy those political, religious, cultural, economic, and educational freedoms that we ascribe to democracy. And even where those freedoms do exist, they are often both fragile and abused in the absence of the responsibilities and accountabilities that should be central to their establishment and maintenance. It is such a lack of responsibilities and accountabilities that continue to fuel the staggering size of the global narcotics 'trade', of other internationally organized crime, and the continuing expanding disparity between those who can afford to entertain the lifestyle that they desire, and those who cannot. And to all of this we must add the terrible pervasion of poverty and hunger, and the devastation of disease that prevail in so many parts of the world.

The challenge is even more profound when we face the nature of human nature itself. There is little to suggest that several millennia or so of civilization has led thus far to much accommodation of difference, nor much increased appreciation, particularly of the ethical and spiritual potential of humanity.

None of this bodes well for the achievement of better global futures—on any scale. What hope is there for democracy under such conditions? What hope can there be for freedoms of speech and act, for economic well-being or human rights or social justice or ecological integrity? What hope for political, cultural and religious freedom, or transformative education, or, most crucially, peace?

Well, in spite of all the evils that abound, there is cause for hope.

In my lifetime I have seen an extended pause in world warfare, the collapse of the ideologically inflexible Soviet Union and its satellites, the dissolution of apartheid in South Africa, and the installation of forms of democratic government in some Latin

American, Asian and African nations. I have seen the smallpox and bubonic plague viruses virtually extinguished and the beneficial impacts of antibiotics on a host of bacterial infections across the globe. I have witnessed an extraordinary shift towards the appreciation of the fragility of the bio-physical environment, and some impressive attempts to reduce environmental degradation and institute restoration. I have seen the wealthy nations proffer huge sums of money and technical expertise to help other less well-endowed nations with their processes of development. I have seen the United Nations come of age as a global institution that has promoted peace and freedom, and equitable development, and the role of education in all of this. I am currently witnessing the trial of at least one erstwhile political leader for war-crimes against humanity at an international court of law. And finally I have witnessed the phenomenal growth of the 'electronic media' and their extension into virtually every corner of the world. By their very nature, and increasing accessibility, these media are able often to transcend local and national restrictions on the freedom of the press, while illustrating and promoting the benefits of participation and open communication.

1.2. The Nature of the Challenge

The intention in this section is to present mainly a small representative selection of verbatim excerpts on the five highly desirable global features which were considered to be achievable within a 'foreseeable future'. These will be presented in turn, and then, in Section IV, attention will switch to the measures that participants in the study saw as necessary to realise the preferred futures.

1.2.1. Provision of Basic Food, Shelter and Health Care to All

Several sources, including participants in this study, have estimated that there is close to a billion people in the Third World living in chronic poverty, and current global population trends indicate that to this number will be added the population of India every decade. Food, population and the environment combine to form a spectre that is monumental in size and, if ignored, could bring complete ruin to both the rich nations that have separated themselves from the pack, and the poor ones who have been unable to escape the poverty trap.

> You will recall that I began my address with a reference to the girl born in Afghanistan today. Even though her mother will do all in her power to protect and sustain her, there is a one-in-four risk that she will not live to see her fifth birthday. Whether she does is just one test of our common humanity—of our belief in our individual responsibility for our fellow men and women. But it is the only test that matters. (Annan's acceptance speech for the Nobel Peace Prize, Oslo, December 10, 2001—cited by several participants in this study).

One cannot kill an idea through killing its carrier or its origi-
nator. In order to eliminate dangerous ideas one has to change the
factors in the real world that make an idea—an abstraction—root
itself and grow. [Among these factors] are poverty, bondage and
lack of life chances. ... In absolute numbers there have never been
so many people living in poverty. ... The eleventh of September
clarifies with stark brilliance that the problems of the poor are also
our problems. ... (Sweden)

Another feature that has to be faced courageously and immediately is famine. There are many people, especially children, starving
to death, whereas in other countries there is a great surplus of food.
There are countries which destroy food, in order to maintain the
prices at a high level, non-concerned that other people are starving
to death. It is desirable to develop a sense of shared responsibility
of all people for the common good. This is one of the features for
which UNO is going to be held responsible, through shared plans
of all countries integrating UNO. It is a shame that this powerful organization is not able to face effectively hunger, illiteracy, sickness,
and underdevelopment in the world. (Brazil)

South Africa is a place where children are roaming around
the streets looking for food and something to make them warm.
This is so cruel and it breaks my heart to see such kids because
there is no good that can come out of what they are doing. (South
Africa—youth participant)

World-wide, the AIDS virus is growing. Unfortunately, in spite
of science having advanced so much that people are now talking of
taking a vacation on the moon, there is no vaccine around which
can cure AIDS. Let us hope that in the near future our scientists
will work towards*this* goal. It will be a blessing for mankind. Let
us all on World Aids Day (1st December) take this vow that we will
free the world of this killer disease. (India)

1.2.2.   *Removal of Global Threats to Security: Collaborative Peace*

This study was launched just three days before the traumatic events of September
11 in the United States, and it was inevitable, then, that issues of global security would
feature prominently in the visions of a better world. Participants reported that they
were more conscious of (a) the need to solve the problems of violent conflict; (b)
the difficulties of doing so; (c) the threats of religious fundamentalisms and (d) the
urgency, at this time, of a mature, non - retaliatory response to acts of terrorism.

Tensions and subtensions between people are human reality. Increasingly there is a greater appreciation of the need to resolve
them, but that does not in itself create the will for doing so. It is
usually political or economic pressures which bring about the will
to negotiate. The reason for this is that the world is not, and is not
likely to be, an idealised place. It is important to accept that power,

richness, greed, crime, stress and violence will always remain in some form or another and in some volume. What is important is to seek to create symbioses between differences and different needs—ways to accommodate that set of tensions between ideologies, beliefs and loyalties to them. (United Kingdom)

A cooperative peace. This entails the various nations of the world working together cooperatively to resolve their conflicts constructively with the help of international and regional agencies. It also involves working together to solve problems common to many nations, such as disease, poverty, pollution, the depletion of natural resources, lack of education for living in a peaceful world, global warming, and so forth. (United States)

The current practice of using religious commandments to control people behaviour is a vicious circle, as we can see in the example of conflict in Northern Ireland between Protestants and Catholics, where human beings turn into wild animals, capable of exploding bombs on the children's way to school. (Czech Republic)

I was in the throes of preparing my response to the Tier 1 question when those devastating terrorist attacks occurred here in the USA. I have delayed responding until now (a) to allow me time to assimilate the possible relevance and impacts of those horrendous events to what I believe could be achieved in the 'foreseeable future' in terms of 'highly desirable futures'; and (b) to observe the response of the government here, governments elsewhere, the people of the US and the rest of the world's population as a gauge of global reaction to the truly terrible events. There would be no greater irony (or tragedy) than a terroristic response to terrorism—a response in which as many innocent victims or more were killed as those in the original terrorist attack. A brutal engagement with all the technologies of modern warfare against imputed 'enemies' who live in caves and tents in an impoverished land, and through which many hundreds if not thousands of such innocent victims would die, is neither a sensible nor responsible reaction. (Australian participant, temporarily resident in the US)

There is a rising cry ringing from America and throughout the world to stamp out such unforgiveable acts of inhumanity. The United States of America is preparing to use its military power to attack the terrorists and their bases as well as countries that aid or harbor them. There is no question that terrorism must be eradicated. But can it truly be eradicated by such means? Even if we are able to remove the master-minds of the terror and destroy their bases of operation that would not mean that we have eradicated the future possibility of similar crimes. (Japan)

If you are looking through the same window as I am at the moment, the world has never seemed or been a smaller place. It was as if I was there with the Americans in New York last week when the terrorists struck. I saw the horror and the devastation. I saw a present through that window that I don't want to see through the window to the future. It is a world in which one country grieves the loss of innocent victims and is preparing to seek revenge for the violent actions which claimed those lives by perpetrating more acts of violence which will cause the loss of ten-fold more innocent lives and displace millions more. So, while much about the events of the last week in New York bear the hallmarks of a new world, or at least a new way of unleashing force, there is much about it that is old—old fears, old injustices, anger, hatred, lurking below the surface and, indeed, old ways of reacting. (Australia—youth participant)

Those guilty of the monstrous crimes committed on September 11 ... must be found, networks broken up. The evilness must be brought to justice. But, in parallel, the work for a new order for a more just and safer world must be intensified. Neither evilness nor democracy can in this hour be compromised. ... Tony Blair pointed out in his speech to the Labor Party Congress the historical opportunity that actually has arisen: 'This is a moment to seize. The kaleidoscope has been shaken. The pieces are in flux. Soon they will settle again. Before they do, let us re-order this world around us'. (Sweden)

1.2.3.   Social Justice

Many of the calls for social justice in this section relate to *intra*national behaviours—citizen rights of a legal kind, absence of discrimination on the basis of gender, ethnicity, and the like—but an important section concerns non-exploitation of workers in the 'powerless' countries. Several participants commented that globalisation, as conceived and practised in the world today, favours a few rich countries, and completely fails to come to grips with the challenges, rewards and potentials inherent within it. It was not claimed that all individuals have a right of access to everything (there may, for example, be limited opportunities, or prior conditions to be met), or that there need be equal proportions of all groups engaged (different groups may have different preferences, if not abilities—witness, women in front-line battle units). Rather, the argument was that there should be no selection on *irrelevant* criteria, and that, when preconditions feature, 'affirmative' programmes should be available to ensure that 'disadvantaged' groups experience genuine equity.

If one examines the various forms of justice (procedural, distributive, retributive and reparative, and scope), it is evident that there is a massive injustice in all the forms of justice throughout the world, within nations and among nations. (a) Procedural justice. We want all categories of people to be treated with politeness, dignity and respect by judges, police, teachers, parents, employers, and others in authority. We want all to have voice and representation, as well as adequate information, in the processes and decisions that affect them. (b) Distributive justice. Gross disparities in the distribution of the benefits, costs and harms to different categories of populations within and among nations should be eliminated. I refer here to such benefits as income, education, health care, housing, water supplies, and police protection, and such harms as accidents, sickness imprisonment, physical attacks, premature death, rape. (c) Retributive and reparative justice. Are crimes for different categories of people less likely to be viewed as crimes, to result in arrest, to be brought to trial, to lead to punishment, imprisonment, or the death penalty? Is there a reasonable attempt to repair the community by reparative treatment for both the victim and the offender? (d) Scope of justice. Are all people no matter what their race, religion, ethnic group, sexual orientation, intelligence, etc. included in the moral community so that they are entitled to be treated with justice and care? (United States)

Another trajectory of future society should be based on human rights. The right to live in a dignified manner so that one can contribute significantly to the progress of humanity is the basis on which the future society has to be constructed. Thus there is no room for gender inequality, communal or caste/class inequality and regional inequality. Of course these principles have been enshrined in every nation's constitution, but now the effort has to be made to implement them. Flowers cannot bloom where one half remains in the snow and the other half gets all the light. In fact, the time has arrived when we have to move from morality of submission, pity, dole to morality of justice, dignity and social concern. (India)

Wealth distribution is an important course of action, but it is not the most important one. Being concentrated in the hands of a few people, money is not always transferred into new jobs for the poor. [Advantages] are, very often reserved to individuals from middle class and elite. (Brazil)

Ending global labor exploitation by multi-national corporations is also needed. Alternatives to child labor that reduce levels of adult unemployment and interferes with education of future generations are also necessary. (United States)

On one hand, we have nations preaching global ethics, and, on the other hand, in order to support their own economies, the same nations bully the other less powerful and developing nations to strengthen their hands of inhuman activities. (India)

Today's systems for food production are not designed to solve the problems of the poor countries. In that sense they are not global. They are designed out of now ailing national and regional perspectives. The agriculture policy of the EU has only one goal: to feed the people of the EU. Period. This policy of the EU leads to hunger and lack of work opportunity in the surrounding Muslim countries. (Sweden)

Creating a more balanced global division of resources. For example, by creating additional industries and workplaces where they are most needed and not only most convenient. Also, prevent the exploitation of weaker sections of the world in the form of under-aged working children, underwaged working women, old people, new immigrants. (Israel)

1.2.4.   Participatory Democracy

This section can be regarded as an extension of the social *justice* one above, in as far as the concept of 'citizen' has been extended from the notions of *status* and formal legal *rights* and *obligations* (*formal* equality), to equality in terms of *participation*, *recognition* and *representation* (*substantive* equality). This extension acknowledges a shift from mono-cultural citizenship to pluralistic citizenship, which is increasingly becoming the norm. As an Australian participant explains, 'The meaning of citizenship is no longer confined to a passive view of rights as a "bearer of rights", but includes an "active citizenship" as a democratic activity embodying a notion of the citizen as a political agent pursuing the criteria of "good citizenship". For this reason, *participation*, *recognition* and *representation* are central to a pluralistic citizenship as they serve to enhance the status of citizenship and strengthen one's membership and belonging to a political community'.

In Cambodia during the past, Pol Pot came to be a leader by civil war, by violence. Therefore, in order to keep his power, he ordered his soldiers to kill intellectuals, savants, political men, teachers of other political parties. Citizens did not have the freedom to express their views about government with constructive ideas. Therefore Cambodian people want to choose the leader through democratic, fair and free elections, and not by force like Pol Pot. (Cambodia)

Given our shrinking world, democratic ideals must be interpreted for all of the planet's diverse cultural contexts. I have in mind Dewey's notion of 'democracy as a moral way of living'. From this normative perspective, the question then becomes how democratic 'morality' can be understood in the context of a wide range of moral/ethical traditions. (United States)

Government at all levels will be democratically elected directly by the citizens affected by their decisions. A world where individual citizens have greater accountability for their actions. This will be at the local, national and international level, and could be for large actions like the commission or perpetration of genocide, or for small actions like the purchase of a product produced through child labour. (United Kingdom)

It is my vision that democracy as a governing principle and a way of living is maintained, promoted and invested in. Constitutions, elections and representative democracy are the essential basics. People should be encouraged to participate in democratic non-governmental activities and organisations to actively learn and develop their understanding of their society and world. This is both essential to compensate for the short-comings of representative democracy and to allow people to feel ownership and partnership of the world and the developments of their societies. (Denmark—youth participant)

1.2.5. Retention and Development of Diversity

To a small number of participants, just as a human life is a human life is a human life, so a culture is a culture is a culture, with each worthy of equal respect. To most, however, a culture is a worldview and a way of life which must earn respect within the context of human rights, such as those in the Universal Declaration, and Rights of the Child. Several participants mentioned flagrant breaches of those rights, especially relating to the treatment of women and children, in a number of (named) cultures, and claimed that in such cases the appropriate reaction was not approval, acceptance or indifference, but condemnation in the name of humanity. Thus, while retention and development of diversity clearly qualified as a major feature of desirable futures, not all participants were prepared to support it without reservation in areas of global significance or personal rights.

> Slowly it is being realised that the recognition of individual and cultural diversity is required by democratic principles of equity, human rights and self-determination. Slowly, too, cultural diversity is being seen as an asset, rather than a liability, in as far as, like biological diversity, it provides the basic elements for adaptation and survival in times of change or crisis. We need to replace the melting pot model by a mosaic, rich in diversity, but, nonetheless, having a clear, unifying pattern based on 'global ethics'. Can this be achieved? Long ago, one of my heroes, Mahatma Gandhi, gave us an answer: 'I do not want my house to be walled in on all sides and my windows to be stuffed. I want the culture of all lands to be blown about my house as freely as possible. But I refuse to be blown off my feet by any'. (Australia)
>
> In the areas of art, music and literary culture, preservation of diverse traditions both of majority and minority peoples is essential. Cultural violence that degrades the traditions of any people must be resisted. It is also necessary to resist the homogenisation associated with global commercialization of particular mono-cultures such as the process of Westernization that strives to base cultural legitimacy on one general style of life, i.e. economic consumerism. The creative energies of all people need to be encouraged as an alternative to the trend of mass mercantilism. (United States)
>
> Having one's own identity individually, and collectively as a nation, is essential for living in a global community. Each nation and people has a unique history, culture and thought. Culture and thought are deeply rooted in a nation's geographical climate and geographical soil. Also the soil and climate of the human relations among which one is raised, and the character of the community one

lives in must all combine with these external influences to produce the inner individual and collective culture of the nation. (Japan)

Cultural diversity, with the accent on 'unity in diversity' would be recognised as a source of richness rather than an encumbrance. Limitations on cultural expression would be required only where they impinged on the cultural life and well-being of others. Religious tolerance would be universal, but fanatical excesses and virulent fundamentalism interfering with the rights of others would not be allowed—e.g. triumphant Protestants 'marching' through Catholic areas in Northern Ireland; amplified 'prayer-calling' from minarets in non-totally-Islamic communities; aggressive TV 'selling' of Christianity as currently adopted in US television channels, etc. Minority languages would not be discriminated against, and minorities would have the opportunity to acquire the language of their country of residence to facilitate their participation and the protection of their rights. (United Kingdom)

1.3.   Pointers to Better Futures

Participants in this project identified five major measures which they believed would, over the long haul, put us on the path to a better world. These were: controlling global population; sustaining environmental resources; redistributing some wealth and resources; relinquishing some nation-state sovereignty to supranational entities; and establishing caring and humane connections at all levels.

1.3.1.   Controlling Global Population

The matter of population control received somewhat different treatment from participants in the developed countries than from those in the developing ones. The former drew attention to the fact that, as a result of scientific advances in irrigation systems, inorganic chemical fertilisers, weed and pest control, new plant varieties and agronomic practices, global food production increases achieved since 1965 have been spectacular. They acknowledged the force of the law of diminishing returns, the need for a still higher production to meet the needs of those currently undernourished as well as those as yet unborn in impoverished countries, but they considered that, given a global will, the burgeoning populations could be adequately fed, clothed and housed. On the other hand, participants from South-West Asia, in particular, argued that population growth had the capacity to destroy humanity.

Few contemporary issues have as far reaching implications as the problem of world population growth. According to the United Nations, more than 90% of the expected population increase [in the foreseeable future] will be concentrated in developing countries. (India)

The burgeoning population has a great impact on the quality of life, fertility being highest among the underdeveloped countries. In fact, population problem is the cause of world's ills—hunger, disease and poverty. Food production lags behind population growth in many countries. In India, whatever progress is achieved, is not visible because of overpopulation. It is the women when educated who will bring desired results in controlling population. (India)

The greatest block that humanity all over the world faces today and in the foreseeable picture is increasing population. The ever increasing population gives rise to varied problems like food shortages, environmental disasters, corruption, terrorism, gender discrimination and deterioration of health services. Population is the root cause of them all. This is particularly true for instance in Africa, Tanzania and Ethiopia, and in Asian countries like India, Bangladesh, Philippines and Afghanistan. Life on earth is being threatened. The world's population today is over 6 billion, and is rising by about 1.4 percent each year. If this rate of growth continues, the population will reach about 10 billion by the year 2030. (India)

The rapidly accelerating global environmental crisis makes efforts to control population growth essential to the preservation of civilization and human survival. This means education for birth control, limitation of family size and alternatives to self-reproduction, such as adoption of orphans, homeless people, refugees and abandoned children should be encouraged with incentives. (United States)

1.3.2. *Sustaining Environmental Resources*

A second practice aimed at alleviating the dehumanising effects of extreme poverty, and one that was thought to involve fewer moral dilemmas than population control, was sustainment of the environment—i.e. ensuring that one people's use of environmental resources does not jeopardise the environments and well-being of others, or destroy the capacities of future generations to satisfy their reasonable needs and wants. It was argued that never before in the history of this planet has its thin life-supporting surface been subject to such diverse, novel and potent agents, and a continuation of current treatment of the environment would eventually destroy the fitness of the planet for human life. It was acknowledged that 'poor' populations were in a Catch-22 situation: while '[n]o long-term strategy of poverty alleviation can succeed in the face of environmental forces that promote persistent erosion of the natural resources upon which we all depend, no environmental protection programme can make headway without removing the day-to-day pressures of poverty that leave people little choice but to discount the future so deeply that they fail to protect the resource base necessary for their own survival and their children's well-being'. (Dodswell, 1995)

Sustainable development to me does not represent a specifically desirable future as much as a prerequisite for having a future at all. (Denmark—youth participant)

The drive for economic security and a competitive edge in the world market has led many countries to subordinate long-term ecological concerns to short-term economic goals. All countries face this dilemma. But the poorest countries, especially those that have borrowed heavily from international banks and agencies to finance economic development programs are especially pressured. (India)

Today, as perhaps never before, it is necessary to secure practical realization of the triad—ecological upbringing—ecological enlightenment—ecological education. All the parts of this triad are closely interrelated. They constitute the basis for cultivation of an ecological world outlook in the population based on awareness of the need to preserve the vital environment for humankind, which is now, in effect, the entire biosphere of the Earth. (Russia)

Environmental objectives, including: reductions in the emissions of greenhouse gases, and gases which endanger the ozone layer; reductions in the pollution of waterways and river catchments; progress in the preservation of endangered species of plants and animals; the restoration of the quality of the soil, the reduction of salinity problems, and the preservation of optimal water tables; the safe management and treatment of waste, especially nuclear waste; the preservation and regrowth of native forests. (Australia)

Deforestation occurs in rainforests and sub-tropical areas. These places are the homes of many animals, and if we destroy their homes they will have nowhere to go, and eventually there will be no more of them left. By destroying the environment, we are destroying ourselves and our children, because it will affect us later. (South Africa—youth participant)

We must secure Earth's bounty and beauty for present and future generations. There is the obvious shift from non-renewable to renewable resources, and from destructive processes to regenerative ones. In this regard there is a whole host of 'alternative technologies' that are much more ecologically benign than current ones, that are beginning to become available. Natural resources are most exploited when there are no seeming alternatives to such exploitation. Many, often romantic, notions abound with regard to the care and compassion that indigenous peoples are often stated to have for their bio-physical environments. This may well be so when there are no other pressures upon them. But this is rarely the case anywhere in the world anymore. (Australia)

1.3.3. Redistributing Some Wealth and Resources

In the long-term, population control and sustainability of environmental resources were seen as the major direct practices likely to improve the lot of humanity on this planet, but, in the short-term, a number of practices were considered likely to provide alleviation. Among these was financial assistance from affluent countries to enable poorer ones to get themselves closer to a position of self-sufficiency.

Alongside the developments in *global* economics designed to alleviate poverty, there was considered to be a need to provide funds for the invigoration of *local community* and *neighbourhood* enterprises. Remenyi (1990) explains: '[This] strategy is founded on the philosophy that the solution is in the community of consumers that make up the poor. Among the poor there are literally hundreds of so-called "micro-enterprises" that service the daily needs of the poor. The skills needed to set up are those that are learnt in the household, because it is the daily need for food, clothing, transport, shelter, health, education, sanitation, etc., that these enterprises supply. The solution lies in finding ways to increase the income and employment generation capacity of these mini-firms sufficiently to provide a viable alternative to present environmentally destructive survival activities'.

Advanced countries should provide assistance to developing countries so that the gap between countries can be lessened. All nations should learn that unrest situations often occur when people of some 'poor' countries are in need of help. (Thailand)

A more just and humane international economic and trade system: reform World Bank, IMF, WTO so that the poor benefit from globalisation; set up international assistance programmes run by UN and funded by a tax on profits of multilateral companies, international financial transfers, on arms deals; cancel debts of LDCs in exchange for poverty alleviation programmes; insist on all developed countries providing 0.7 GNP for aid; freeze funds being laundered by arms and drug barons, and corrupt heads of state. (Australia)

'The reduction of poverty' should cease to be a meaningless phrase in Aid documents. Instead, it will become the basis of actions of courage and commitment to improve the life chances of most of humanity. All third world debts should be written off, all financial institutions should provide 30% of their annual profits for homes, food and learning opportunities for those in need, and Aid projects should be sustained and devoted to practical projects, rather than hit-and-run ones. It is hypocrisy to continue to fund, in the name of diplomacy, the corrupt leaders who steal millions of Aid money. (Samoa)

We need banks, businesses, and investors that understand how to create profitable markets out of the most destitute social environments. The local and global business community must play an essential role in the conquering of the future for peaceful coexistence—privileged and non-privileged. (Sweden)

At the same time as global economics are expanded, there should be community-based initiatives designed to create economies (mostly smaller than national entities), consisting of both city and rural sectors, dedicated to local production, employment, cultural life, and civic improvement. These would operate at a high level of self-sufficiency alongside the global economic systems which are relied upon to provide cheaper mass produced goods at the high-tech end. (Australia)

1.3.4.   Relinquishing Some Nation-State Sovereignty to Supranational Entities

To many participants in this study, progress towards a better world, particularly in relation to human rights of individuals, will be dependent on the creation or revitalisation of supranational entities. Participants, however, were under no illusions concerning the difficulty of establishing effective supranational agencies; with the experience of a committed United Nations behind them, they thought that progress would be painstakingly slow. Comments featured with respect to global governance, human rights, avoidance of violent conflict, arms control, terrorism, poverty alleviation, refugees and displaced persons.

> It is desirable to work towards the establishment of a true representation of the peoples of the world at the global level. A UN Parliamentary Chamber representing the peoples of the world will need to be established in the long term. This goal can be achieved gradually by individual country members of the UN which should include within their delegation to the UN, at least on a consultative basis, representatives of civil society (NGOs) or parliamentarians. (Switzerland)
>
> The realistic answer to what is going on—processes that have been in the works for decades—is to seriously initiate supranational institutions and processes that with executive powers (the Hague Court is a beginning) and on democratic footing can support a development of shared value for all cultures and nations based on: the principles of democracy and the rule of law; the principles of human rights; the principles of sustainable development and biological diversity; the principles of effective and honest market economy. These principles are more important than the constitutions and legal traditions of individual countries, and, under continuous debate and development, could form the basis for policies that see to the wholeness that the globalising world in reality is becoming. (Sweden)
>
> After the tragic events of 11th September, 2001, it is difficult to discuss 'ideal world futures', to examine variations on this theme, and to decide which initiatives may lead to realisation. The terrorist actions have left no way out and have pushed the world to immediate collective action against this unprecedented threat. The International Security Council has specific powers to investigate the slightest signs of danger coming from any criminal or secret organisation anywhere in the world, from religious fanatics to whole totalitarian regimes. Under the same international control, effective swift-acting mechanisms have to be developed to quell these acts at their origins. (Russia)
>
> The United Nations should remain a vital institution for leading the worldwide efforts at peace building and socio-economic development. However, if it is to be effective, it must be strengthened with more powers for intervention to protect human rights,

make peace and assist with equitable distribution of basic needs. (United States)

1.3.5. Establishing Caring and Humane Connections at all Levels

Mutually supportive relationships were seen by many as basic to the health and survival of the human group. These 'deep connections' could be initially established within families, schools, local communities, and, with the aid of modern communication technology, extended within national and global networks.

> There has to be eagerness for the development of world community based on unity in diversity. Let many minds and many points of view find their own harmony seeking to regenerate what Mahatma Gandhi once described as 'the conscience of the world'. As is cited in *Reg-Vida*: 'Meet together, talk together/May your minds comprehend alike/Common be your action and achievement/Common be your thoughts and intentions. Common be the wishes of your hearts/So there may be union among you'. (India)
>
> What is the most effective means for achieving positive globalisation that brings about desirable futures? Although individual citizens may have only small power, human networks supported by partnership and cooperation will exert great influence. (Japan)
>
> I believe that there should be a rebuilding of a sense of community. Families need to be strengthened by becoming embedded within the fabric of a supportive community. In a society of the future there will need to be social planners who are seeking new ways to prevent social isolation and engender this return to a sense of community. (Australia)
>
> Without unnecessary references to recent developments, visions must be elaborated about how to provide safety in a global environment. Sustainable safety cannot be achieved through power balances or international agreements, but only through knowledge, understanding and tolerance between and among the people of the world. I hope that greater efforts will be done to provide especially young people with opportunities to visit and stay in other cultures, and encourage them to participate in societal, cultural and educational activities and structures, to develop understanding and empathy for other cultures and for cultural differences as such. (Denmark—youth participant)
>
> If human beings are to survive and prosper in a peaceful, safe global environment, 'world citizens' should have a larger presence and acquire recognition on a broad basis. It is of growing importance to foster 'world citizens' who are able to think globally, and to build up their networks. It is also significant for individual citizens to be conscious of their role as members of the global community, to have deep insights into various happenings and phenomena across the world, and to address global problems.

Cooperation of such citizens, as well as the build-up of their networks, will have a large impact on the future course of society. (Japan)

We are increasingly a 'networked global society', able to share good and bad news alike with each other on an unparalleled scale at an unparalleled pace. We are also able to share values and world-views and paradigms and present circumstances—even if, until now, we have done far too little of this. (Australia)

This is a future where the growing realisation that the interdependence between communities within and across countries of the globe is a fact of life that may destroy our world as we know it today. But it is also a future where this growing realisation can create an interdependence of positive connections that will see, finally, a wake-up call for 'okay' communities and nations to invest heavily in the 'not-so-okay' for the survival of both. (New Zealand)

2.   STEP 2: RATING-SCALE RESULTS

A perusal of the visionary statements submitted by the 183 participants suggested that 68 themes occurred frequently among 'highly desirable' features for the future. These were subsequently grouped, as items, under the categories already identified in Step 1. Thus: *Provision of basic food, shelter and health care* (e.g. extreme poverty, which denies many humans access to the basic necessities of life, to be eliminated); *Removal of global threats to security: collaborative peace* (e.g. nations and other collectives to work cooperatively on programmes to solve common problems—poverty, disease, drug trafficking, asylum-seeking); *Social justice* (e.g. all individuals, irrespective of gender, race, religion, ethnic group, sexual orientation, intelligence, to be treated with dignity, justice, respect and care); *Participatory democracy* (e.g. individuals to have a voice and representation, as well as adequate information, in the processes and decisions that affect them); *Retention and development of diversity* (e.g. celebration of cultural diversity to take place within the human-rights norms developed by the global community); *Sustainability of planet Earth* (e.g. there is to be a general recognition of humankind's responsibility within the ecological structure to sustain a fragile planet); *Supranational entities* (e.g. there is to be respect for international treaties and organisations); *Caring and humane connections at all levels* (e.g. knowledge to be generated not as a personal or national possession, but as a globally available asset for the benefit of all).

Participants were asked to consider each of the 68 items and assign ratings ranging from: *Essential* (5) through *Highly Desirable* (4), *Desirable* (3) and *Somewhat Desirable* (2) to *Undesirable* (1). For purposes of analysis, participants were classified as males (55) and females (45), and into categories A (43) (Asia—South East and South West; Latin America; sub-Saharan Africa), and B (57) (Australasia/Pacific; Europe—Eastern and Western; North America). The substantial drop in participants, from 183 at Step 1 to 100 at Step 2 will be noted: this can be explained almost entirely by the fact that, unfortunately, the rating scale was forwarded in May, 2002 and coincided with long vacations in all regions except Australasia/Pacific. ('Even learned Homer sometimes nods'!)

2.1. Selected Findings

Table 2.1: Percentages of Respondents Rating Items as 'Essential' or 'Highly Desirable'

	All	Male	Female	Cluster A	Cluster B
	(N = 100)	(N = 55)	(N = 45)	(N = 43)	(N = 57)
Provision of basic food, shelter and health care					
1. Extreme poverty, which denies many humans access to the basic necessities of life, to be eliminated	96%	98%	94%	97%	96%
2. The divide between the 'haves' and 'have nots', with respect to basic necessities, to be reduced	84%	81%	88%	83%	84%
3. Over-consumption, waste and misuse of the world's resources of basic necessities, to be controlled internationally	68%	69%	67%	69%	68%
4. Production, development and consumption of scarce resources to be coordinated internationally	55%	56%	55%	48%	59%
5. Financial assistance programmes to be available for countries lacking adequate resources	71%	73%	67%	69%	71%
6. Robust and sustainable economic initiatives to be undertaken by affluent countries as a global commitment for the benefit of destitute countries	74%	71%	79%	72%	75%
7. Neighbourhood and regional-based economic initiatives, operating at a high level of self-sufficiency alongside the global economic systems, to be encouraged throughout the globe	78%	77%	79%	76%	79%
8. Unsustainable population growth to be controlled by means of incentives and education	78%	83%	70%	79%	77%
9. Corruption relating to basic necessities to be eliminated within countries receiving aid	85%	83%	88%	86%	84%
10. All people to be guaranteed access to healthy life-style and health care	85%	75%	100%	93%	80%
11. Research programmes, aimed at eradicating some diseases and drastically reducing others, to be vigorously undertaken as a global commitment	78%	71%	88%	90%	71%
12. Adequate support to be given to world health organisations to raise the standard of health care in many parts of the world	79%	73%	88%	90%	73%
13. The supply and use of drugs of addiction, such as heroin, cocaine, tobacco, etc. to be tightly controlled	72%	73%	70%	86%	64%
Removal of global threats to security: collaborative peace					
14. Relations between nations to be regulated by international law, not force	88%	92%	82%	83%	91%
15. Acts of ethnic cleansing within nation-states to be acknowledged to be crimes against humanity, and the perpetrators held accountable before the International Criminal Court	91%	90%	91%	86%	93%
16. International acts of terrorism to be acknowledged to be crimes against humanity and the perpetrators held accountable before the International Criminal Court	93%	94%	91%	86%	96%
17. In addition to the united global determination to bring the perpetrators of violent conflict to justice, the complex conditions (economic, social, cultural political, historical, religious) that generate the conflict to be addressed	79%	79%	79%	79%	79%
18. Nations and other collectives to work cooperatively on programmes to solve common problems—poverty, disease, drug trafficking, asylum-seeking	87%	87%	88%	90%	86%
19. Differences of viewpoint to be settled by discussion and, if necessary, arbitration	74%	75%	73%	86%	68%
20. The sense of nationalistic elitism to be replaced by a more secure, less threatening and less exclusive pride in belonging to a number of collectives	66%	63%	70%	69%	64%
21. Deeply entrenched historical narratives and myths to be re-examined, in order to establish a new base for cooperation between, and within, nations	56%	54%	61%	69%	50%

(continued)

Table 2.1: Continued

	All	Male	Female	Cluster A	B
	(N = 100)	(N = 55)	(N = 45)	(N = 43)	(N = 57)
22. Religious fundamentalism to be replaced by inter-faith understanding, and a search for a 'common ethic'	**72%**	73%	70%	72%	71%
23. The human right to freedom of religion to be understood in the context of other human rights	**74%**	71%	79%	79%	71%

Social justice

24. All individuals, irrespective of gender, race, religion, ethnic group, sexual orientation, intelligence, to be treated with dignity, justice, respect and care	**92%**	88%	97%	97%	89%
25. Differential treatment, by way of affirmative actions, to be available to the substantially disadvantaged, the marginalised, the excluded and the vulnerable	**71%**	67%	76%	76%	68%
26. Gross disparities in the distribution of the benefits, costs and harms to different categories of populations to be eliminated	**79%**	77%	82%	83%	77%
27. Within nation-states, perpetrators of crimes to receive substantially the same punishment, and victims of crimes the same reparation, irrespective of who they are	**74%**	67%	85%	76%	73%
28. Opportunities for all people to be able to engage in work that is meaningful and satisfying	**85%**	83%	88%	86%	84%
29. Individuals to gain just rewards for their work, free of exploitation	**87%**	83%	94%	90%	86%
30. Every person, whether unemployed, under-employed or employed, to be guaranteed a wage that is adequate to sustain acceptable standards of living	**68%**	65%	73%	69%	68%
31. Global labour exploitation by multi-national corporations to be eliminated	**80%**	83%	76%	79%	80%
32. Increased parts of national budgets in affluent countries to be allocated to establishing a more balanced division of resources throughout the world	**67%**	63%	73%	86%	57%

Participatory democracy

33. Individuals to have a voice and representation, as well as adequate information, in the processes and decisions that affect them	**80%**	77%	85%	79%	80%
34. Governments at all levels to be democratically elected directly by the citizens affected by their decisions	**79%**	81%	76%	79%	79%
35. All nations to adopt democratic institutions which allow people freedom to develop in their own independent ways, freedom to express themselves, and gain information useful to their welfare	**74%**	69%	82%	83%	70%
36. The meaning of citizenship to be extended from a passive view of rights and obligations, to include actions associated with participation, recognition and representation	**78%**	77%	79%	79%	77%
37. Certain national powers to be devolved to local government so that individuals can be more involved in decisions that affect their immediate living circumstances and localities	**59%**	58%	61%	79%	48%
38. The nation to be made up of a host of democracies each small enough to express the spirit of neighbourhood and personal acquaintance	**48%**	46%	52%	66%	38%
39. High priority to be given in social planning to the development of small and vibrant local communities which provide a wide range of congenial leisure and work programmes, depending on collaborative participation of all within them	**52%**	48%	58%	55%	50%
40. Provision to be made from local to global levels for the democratic addressing of major issues, such as the challenges, rewards and potentials of globalisation, itself	**58%**	60%	55%	66%	54%

(continued)

Table 2.1: Continued

	All	Male	Female	Cluster A	Cluster B
	(N = 100)	(N = 55)	(N = 45)	(N = 43)	(N = 57)

Retention and development of diversity

	All	Male	Female	A	B
41. There is to be an overarching reverence for life in all its forms	**82%**	82%	83%	83%	82%
42. There is to be recognition of the interdependency of all life forms	**80%**	79%	83%	83%	79%
43. There is to be protection and, in as far as possible, enhancement of bio-diversity	**80%**	79%	82%	76%	82%
44. Diverse world-views to be generated and carefully examined as potential sources of inspiration	**69%**	69%	70%	72%	68%
45. Individual and cultural diversity to be acknowledged as providing a valuable context within which solutions to common problems may be found	**84%**	81%	88%	90%	80%
46. Economic and political decisions, and the development of information and communication technology, to enhance the expression and development of cultural diversity and minority rights	**74%**	69%	82%	83%	70%
47. Celebration of cultural diversity to take place within the human-rights norms developed by the global community	**78%**	71%	88%	86%	73%

Sustainability of planet earth

	All	Male	Female	A	B
48. The global environment to be recognised as a complex web of social, cultural, economic and political, as well as geo- and bio-physical, components	**88%**	87%	91%	93%	86%
49. There is to be a general recognition of humankind's responsibility within the ecological structure to sustain a fragile planet	**96%**	98%	94%	97%	96%
50. The use of environments and resources by one group of people is not allowed to jeopardise the environments and well-being of others, including future generations	**91%**	90%	91%	93%	89%
51. There is to be a shift in usage from non-renewable to renewable resources . . . non-renewable ones to be used sparingly, and renewable ones sustainably	**86%**	92%	76%	83%	88%
52. There is to be a shift from destructive processes (polluting emissions of various kinds, salinity, etc.) to regenerative ones (restoration of soil quality, preservation and re-growth of native forests, etc.)	**91%**	92%	88%	90%	91%
53. The development and use of technology to be governed by ecological ethics and not by short-term economic and financial benefits; values are to monitor and influence the growth and direction of these developments	**91%**	88%	94%	93%	89%

Supranational entities

	All	Male	Female	A	B
54. Exclusive state sovereignty within territorial boundaries to give way to some shared arrangements with supranational institutions	**52%**	56%	45%	41%	57%
55. The current concept of citizenship to be extended beyond national boundaries	**68%**	77%	55%	76%	64%
56. There is to be respect for international treaties and organisations	**89%**	94%	82%	86%	91%
57. International laws and powers of intervention to be strengthened and to include key rights of individuals, as well as global issues such as wars and threats of wars between and within nations, manufacture of weapons of war and torture, international crimes including arms dealing and drug trafficking, international acts of terrorism, political corruption and degradation of the environment	**84%**	85%	82%	86%	82%

(continued)

Table 2.1: Continued

	All	Male	Female	Cluster A	B
	(N = 100)	(N = 55)	(N = 45)	(N = 43)	(N = 57)
58. The fragmented approach to dealing with displaced persons, refugees and asylum-seekers to give way to a compassionate global policy aimed, primarily, at ensuring the security, sustenance and safety of people in their own countries	**74%**	77%	70%	79%	71%
59. Further work to be undertaken towards the establishment, at the global level, of a true representation of the peoples of the world	**76%**	77%	76%	79%	75%
60. The United Nations to be developed into a more effective agency with respect to leading worldwide efforts at peace building and socioeconomic development	**87%**	90%	82%	86%	88%
61. The process of transnational community building, which is occurring in regions such as the European Union, to be encouraged and extended	**72%**	77%	64%	76%	70%
Caring and humane connections at all levels					
62. Families to be strengthened by becoming embedded within the fabric of supportive communities	**67%**	65%	70%	72%	64%
63. Interdependence between communities within and across countries to be encouraged	**74%**	75%	73%	83%	70%
64. Global projects, involving the participation of peoples from all regions to be encouraged	**65%**	60%	73%	83%	55%
65. Forums to be established at both regional and international levels where ideological issues, such as religions, can be addressed graciously and common ground sought	**65%**	65%	64%	76%	59%
66. 'Learning communities' to be established on a wide scale to accelerate individual and group capacities and to provide a counter to national injustices	**79%**	81%	76%	90%	73%
67. New tools of internet, e-mails, web-sites and e-linkages, which provide opportunities for individuals to become significant participants in shaping communities from local to the global, to be established	**65%**	60%	73%	79%	57%
68. Knowledge to be generated, not as a personal or national possession, but as a globally available asset for the benefit of all	**76%**	85%	64%	83%	73%

2.2.   Discussion of Selected Findings

As indicated in the Table 2.1 title, the focus here is on the percentages of respondents rating the items as essential or highly desirable, and it will be noted that these are almost universally high. In view of the fact that all the items had been drawn from submissions of 'highly desirable features', this finding is not surprising—it suggests that there is considerable consensus among participants concerning such features and, perhaps, that the analysis accurately reflects the content of the submissions.

The measure of consensus can be further highlighted by identifying items for which 75% or more of participants from *all* four groups (males, females, Cluster A and Cluster B) assigned ratings of essential or highly desirable. These items ($N = 32$) appear in shaded form within Table 2.1 above. As an overview, it can be noted that *sustainability of planet Earth* attracted most support, with all its six representative items meeting the criteria, and that, within the concern of this study, *caring and humane connections at all levels*, was judged to be least essential.

Table 2.1 reveals eight items that were rated unusually high by participants in all sub-groups:

Item 1: Extreme poverty, which denies many humans access to the basic necessities of life, to be eliminated (overall, 96% of participants assigned ratings of five or four to it).

Item 49: There is to be a general recognition of humankind's responsibility within the ecological structure to sustain a fragile planet (overall, 96%).

Item 16: International acts of terrorism to be acknowledged to be crimes against humanity and the perpetrators held accountable before the International Criminal Court (overall, 93%).

Item 24: All individuals, irrespective of gender, race, religion, ethnic group, sexual orientation, intelligence, to be treated with dignity, justice, respect and care (overall, 92%).

Item 15: Acts of ethnic cleansing within nation-states to be acknowledged to be crimes against humanity, and the perpetrators held accountable before the International Criminal Court (overall, 91%).

Item 50: The use of environments and resources by one group of people is not allowed to jeopardise the environments and well-being of others, including future generations (overall, 91%).

Item 52: There is to be a shift from destructive processes (polluting emissions of various kinds, salinity, etc.) to regenerative ones (restoration of soil quality, preservation and re-growth of native forests, etc.) (overall, 91%).

Item 53: The development and use of technology to be governed by ecological ethics and not by short-term economic and financial benefits; values are to monitor and influence the growth and direction of these developments (overall, 91%).

An alternative way of looking at the rating-scale data is to 'raise the bar' by identifying those items that attracted 50% or more of *essential* ratings. (50% was chosen as the benchmark because of the clear natural break that occurred in the data at this point.) Twenty-four of the items qualified and, ranked in order of percentages, these were:

Item 1: Extreme poverty, which denies many humans access to the basic necessities of life, to be eliminated. (82% of all participants assigned a rating of *essential*.)

Item 24: All individuals, irrespective of gender, race, religion, ethnic group, sexual orientation, intelligence, to be treated with dignity, justice, respect and care (77%).

Item 50: The use of environments and resources by one group of people is not allowed to jeopardise the environments and well-being of others, including future generations (64%).

Item 48: The global environment to be recognised as a complex web of social, cultural, economic and political, as well as geo- and bio-physical, components (61%).

Item 52: There is to be a shift from destructive processes (polluting emissions of various kinds, salinity, etc.) to regenerative ones (restoration of soil quality, preservation and re-growth of native forests, etc.) (61%).

Item 15: Acts of ethnic cleansing within nation-states to be acknowledged to be crimes against humanity, and the perpetrators held accountable before the International Criminal Court (61%).

Item 16: International acts of terrorism to be acknowledged to be crimes against humanity, and the perpetrators held accountable before the International Criminal Court (60%).

Item 49: There is to be general recognition of humankind's responsibility within the ecological structure to sustain a fragile planet (58%).

Item 10: All people to be guaranteed access to healthy life-style and health care (58%).

Item 51: There is to be a shift in usage from non-renewable to renewable resources—non-renewable ones to be used sparingly, and renewable one sustainably (57%).

Item 33: Individuals to have a voice and representation, as well as adequate information, in the processes and decisions that affect them (56%).

Item 17: In addition to the united global determination to bring the perpetrators of violent conflict to justice, the complex conditions (economic, social, cultural, political, historical, religious) that generate the conflict to be addressed (55%).

Item 35: All nations to adopt democratic institutions which allow people freedom to develop in their own independent ways, freedom to express themselves, and gain information useful to their welfare (55%).

Item 42: There is to be recognition of the interdependency of all life forms (55%).

Item 43: There is to be protection and, in as far as possible, enhancement of bio-diversity (54%).

Item 9: Corruption relating to basic necessities to be eliminated within countries receiving aid (54%).

Item 8: Unsustainable population growth to be controlled by means of incentives and education (53%).

Item 18: Nations and other collectives to work cooperatively on programmes to solve common problems—poverty, disease, drug trafficking and asylum-seeking (52%).

Item 53: The development and use of technology to be governed by ecological ethics and not by short-term economic and financial benefits; values are to monitor and influence the growth and direction of these developments (52%).

Item 34: Governments at all levels to be democratically elected directly by the citizens affected by their decisions (51%).

Item 56: There is to be respect for international treaties and organisations (51%).

Item 2: The divide between the 'haves' and 'have nots', with respect to basic necessities, to be reduced (50%).

Item 27: Within nation-states, perpetrators of crimes to receive substantially the same punishment, and victims of crimes the same reparation, irrespective of who they are (50%).

Item 31: Global labour exploitation by multi-national corporations to be eliminated (50%).

3.   CONCLUDING STATEMENT

Several participants mentioned that, although they were presenting their visions, challenges and solutions in something like a 'shopping list', in reality these exist within a single 'suprasystem'—a complex web of disparate personal, social, cultural, economic, political as well as geo- and bio-physical components. As a 'simplified' example of this systemic complexity, one quoted the UNESCO-EPD report (1997, p. 14):

> Sustainable development is widely understood to involve the natural sciences and economics, but it is even more fundamentally concerned with culture: with the values people hold and how they perceive their relations with others. It responds to an imperative need to imagine a new basis of relationships among people and with the habitat that sustains life.

Given the complexity of the interdependencies, the fact that the phenomena are disparate and not all subject to the same laws of understanding, that both environments and persons are unstable, and that, once initiated, change is difficult to predict or control, it becomes extraordinarily difficult to determine where to intervene effectively. Even the most positively motivated intrusions into suprasystems can lead to all kinds of unanticipated effects, many of which are unpleasant and pernicious. An Hungarian participant wrote of interventions in these terms:

> It is hard to recognise in what direction and to what extent change, either as a single or as a complex occurrence, shifts processes from their stable situations and hitherto followed directions, and it can hardly be foreseen where they will end up. It is particularly difficult to answer what impacts drive certain processes to follow new courses, whether it is a result of their inner self-organisation or the influence of external forces. The strength of man's conscious interference is not easily, if at all measurable. ... [We need greater understanding] of how sensitive to change the processes are on the one hand, and what ability and power to shape the future do individuals and social institutions representing different values possess on the other hand.

An Australian participant quoted from the German scientist, Brunswik (1955, p. 686), '[Within the realm of human behaviour] the traditional nomothetic search for strict [explanatory] laws becomes an insolvable task, and even an omniscient infinite intellect ... would have to adopt a probabilistic approach'.

A second feature of the co-existence of visions, challenges and solutions within a suprasystem was identified as inevitable tensions and conflicts among elements. Indeed, these tensions were seen by some to be essential to the functioning of the suprasystem. Examples mentioned were: the entitlement of all humans to the basic necessities of food, shelter and health care *versus* preserving, if not enhancing, the environment for future generations; population control *versus* protecting the rights of individuals in such matters as procreation, freedom of choice and self-determination; robust economic initiatives *versus* ecological ethics; reducing the divide between the 'haves' and the 'have nots' *versus* allowing 'successful' nation-states to retain a 'lighthouse' status as an incentive to others; condemnation of violent conflict *versus* refusal to ignore heinous crimes being committed against humanity; celebration of diversity among cultures *versus* flagrant breaches of human rights, especially relating to treatment of women, children and minorities; equal treatment of individuals *versus* the need for unequal treatment of members of disadvantaged groups—typically women, children, the excluded, minorities and the handicapped.

As several participants said, in the 'real world' it often becomes a matter of striking a balance among a number of claims, many of which can be shown to have some legitimacy. The upshot is that, on occasions, one might have to tolerate 'customs and mores that are, strictly speaking, inferior to a global ethical consensus'.

4.   REFERENCES

Annan, K. 2001. Acceptance Speech for the Nobel Peace Prize, 10 December 2001, Oslo.
Brunswik, E. 1955. The conceptual framework of psychology. *International Encyclopaedia of United Science*, Vol. 1, Part 2. Illinois: University of Chicago Press, p. 686.
Dodswell, E. 1995. *Our Planet*. Paris: United Nations Environmental Programme.
Remenyi, J. 1990. Food, population and the environment. *New Horizons in Education*, Pub. WEF Australia, 82, p. 12.
UNESCO-EPD. 1997. Educating for a sustainable future: a transdisciplinary vision for concerted action. *Background Paper, International Conference, Environment and Society: Education and Public Awareness for Sustainability*, Thessalonnica, 8–12 December 1997.

Chapter 3

TRANSNATIONAL JUDGEMENTS OF REQUIRED HUMAN ATTRIBUTES

Jack Campbell, Nick Baikaloff and Colin Power

1. STEP 1: OPEN-ENDED VISION SUBMISSIONS

Chapter 2 was concerned with a preferred global *community* considered almost without reference to the nature of the persons within it—as one participant said, 'It seems to be a study of missing persons'! By way of contrast, in this chapter the focus shifts to somewhat idealised *individuals*, as desirable elements within that global community, as worthy ends in their own right, and as means to the social ends identified earlier. It is here that the comment of Brian Hill (1992) is taken on board:

> ...the health of society depends on the development of flexible, multi-competent and satisfied individuals, not merely cogs for the social machine ... The development of the human individual is the hub of the enterprise. A warped self will warp all other levels of interaction and subvert the goals of social reformers.

An Australian participant outlined some of the challenges facing individuals as they seek to live exemplary lives and create better worlds for themselves and others:

> Sectarian civil wars persist with ghastly ferocity even as we 'cele-brate' the end of the super power cold war. Hunger and starvation persist amongst so many millions even as surplus food elsewhere is dumped, and people elsewhere die from obesity. Human rights remain severely abused and democracy remains scarce, even as we pay homage to global consciousness of social justice. And environments continue to be degraded and despoiled at a frightening rate, even as ecological quality assumes centre stage on the international development agenda. Is it that we don't have the intellectual capacity to deal with these persistent human failings? Are they just too complex for us to understand? Or is it that we won't actually turn our attention to them because of the implications of doing so might disturb the established order?
>
> Moreover, *it is* not enough for individuals to know how to deal with the complex behaviour of the world as *it is*; they must now turn to issues concerned with how we believe the world *ought to be*. None of the new technologies are neutral in their outcomes for they all come embedded in huge questions of ethics and morality

J. Campbell et al. (eds.), Towards a Global Community, 39–68.

and aesthetics with which we must learn how to deal. When is bio-engineering 'right', and when is it 'wrong'? What are the ethics of genetic engineering? And are we prepared for the possibility of micro-machines permanently displacing hundreds of thousands of people from jobs that no longer need to be done by human beings? What will that mean in terms of the aesthetics of human satisfaction? And what will this do for social justice—will there be an ever-increasing disparity between those who can work and those who have been displaced? What risks are we prepared to take in supporting nuclear energy options? Whose rights must we consider here? And with communication systems being so potentially pervasive and intrusive, what will this do to the rights of individuals? Or, indeed, to the organization of nations?

Some participants argued that, if individuals are to cope successfully with the kinds of challenges outlined above, they will need to achieve new heights of human development:

Individuals need a capacity to seek for, and create, new ways of living, establishing relations with oneself and between individuals, and new solutions at micro (e.g. day-to-day situations) and macro (e.g. governmental) levels. From the new solutions proposed, new professions, new technologies and new philosophies would emerge. If better futures are to be created by the individuals, these latter must have productive and creative imaginations. (Brazil)

Human beings have evolved through continuous learning and adaptation. And new human learning is constantly necessary because of continuous changes and adaptation in the larger community of life of which we are a part, and on which our own lives and the lives of future generations utterly depend.... As Kenneth Boulding asserted, if humanity is to survive it will have to change more in the next 25 years than in the last 25,000. We are not talking about the physical development of a new brain, but about a new mind, a new way of seeing and being, of learning to be in the world as responsible creative members of the community of life, with co-responsibility for the next stages of planetary evolution. (India)

Projecting the evolutionary process that has so far borne us to a stage we carelessly call *Homo sapiens*, we must, I believe, go on to rid ourselves of our ignorance and infantile desires, and gradually to realize our potential to become worthy members of *Homo creatus*, when we shall have awakened to the true wisdom for which we were created. (Japan)

People have proved maladjusted to the new rate of civilisational development. Spanish philosopher Ortegay Gasset remarked on this circumstance in 1930 by saying, 'Today catastrophe is visiting Man himself who has become incapable of keeping step with his civilisation. Growing civilisation is nothing else than a painful problem. The greater the achievements, the bigger the danger of civilisation'. Seventy years later one can say that Ortegay Gasset's diagnosis has been confirmed many times over. Our knowledge has come to resemble a kind of 'Pandora's Box' from which disasters come out flying and spread around the world. [Transformation of] personalities is the main imperative of the present century. (Russia)

Before proceeding to present a summary of submissions relating to the required human attributes, we shall attempt to clarify the main focus which participants have adopted. Although it is difficult to maintain a clear distinction, the concern has been less with the various interpretations of a 'good education' for living in specific cultures, and more with globally shared understandings of personal attributes needed to create better worlds for all. In a sense, the concern here may be regarded as superimposed on the usual components of a 'good education'. A United Kingdom participant put it this way: 'Individuals should have the "usual" components of a good education—what I have in mind is the broad set of skills, knowledge and attitudes which are taken to characterise the educated adult around the globe. I take these as necessary but not sufficient. Because they are not specific to this exercise, and could lead to endless, irrelevant debate, it is probably idle to articulate them in detail here'.

A second introductory explanatory comment might be useful. A number of participants asked us if, when concerned with individuals, they should be thinking of *all, some, most* or *whatever*. They argued that, however desirable it might be for some individuals to possess a certain attribute, it might not be necessary for all individuals to possess it. Thus, it is important for societies to have some persons who are brain surgeons (perhaps even some who are professors of education!), but not everyone need have that skill. Perhaps more cogent than this analogical argument was one stating that, given the variations in life circumstances, opportunities, and the like, it is unrealistic to expect *all* humans to develop specified attributes, however desirable these are. A Greek participant wrote: 'I believe that there's not just one "recipe" for all, as individuals vary not only in character or nature, but also in conditions of living. It would be easier if there was a starting point common to all, but a lot of people must surpass certain difficulties in order to be in a position of contributing at all to any future'.

Although acknowledging the force of the two arguments above, most participants thought in terms of attributes that have *universal* relevance with respect to responsible global involvement, even although the relevance will vary, at a given time, from country to country, and the exact nature of the attributes in operation will always be cloaked in cultural dress. The result is the emergence here of somewhat 'idealised' images of individuals, and this was a concern to a small number of participants. On the other hand, most participants considered that there were merits in putting 'on the table', as it were, idealised images towards the development of which efforts can then be directed.

2.   THE BASES OF EFFECTIVE INDIVIDUALITY

Several participants argued that both the intrinsic well-being and the instrumental effectiveness of individuals were dependent upon the satisfaction, to a substantial degree, of *fundamental human needs*, especially love, trust, a sense of 'connection', autonomy and initiative. Consistent with the view of Erikson (1950), some saw the development of these attributes as being especially critical in the early years of childhood, but others, drawing upon the United States' study of Hess (1971) and the Australian one of Henry (1996), concluded that, throughout life, individuals seek and require satisfaction of some, if not all, of these needs.

> The first encounter for every human being is the one between mother and child in the mother's womb. From the time it spends in the womb as a foetus until infancy, a child's relationship with his mother is so intimate that they really are not separable. The foetus spends its first months of life suspended in the warm amniotic fluid, listening to the soothing rhythm of its mother's pulse and protected by the wall of the womb. After birth, the infant sucks its mother's milk and listens to the beat of her heart, receives her loving look and tender ministrations. It continues to grow in perfect safety with her loving attention and care: thus it unconsciously continues to share with her these undivided human relationships between mother and child. 'The love for nothing' must be the highest form of love intrinsic to the bond between mother and child. The satisfaction of the biological needs of the child incapable of speech during its early months will ensure its warm sensitivities and capacity for intellectual growth and creativity. If a love freely given between mother and child is the prototype of all human relations, it suggests that love is the most effective factor in ensuring good relations throughout life. With the loss of love, trust and unity, the qualities essential to human existence, it is small wonder that individuals are losing their humanity, and the fabric of our societies is threatened. (Japan)
>
> I see the needs for trust, autonomy and initiative as developmental. First, they occur in sequence: trust provides the feeling of ease (goodness-of-fit) which allows humans to act more freely in exploring and influencing the changing environment, exploration opens up the limitless discovery of new ideas to be found in the environment. Secondly, and in the same sequence, to every human undergoing this process, new capacities become available. First, the individual who feels confident has a greater capacity to act. Broadening one's scope of action brings one in contact with new things to think about. Meeting these three successive fundamental and continually recurring needs enhances the totality of human functioning: feeling, activity and thought. The outcomes of not meeting these needs extend throughout communities and globally: child and adult abuse of many kinds, for example, bullying, exploitation, vindictiveness, cheating, crime, cruelty of various kinds, terrorism. Such behaviours are carried out by people who instead of trust exercise mistrust, instead of autonomy, aggression, instead of exploration of their own ideas, the imposition of ideas. (Australia)
>
> Connectedness. The successful development of every child must depend on the growth of a set of four vital types of

connectedness: *connections to one's self* (the sense of soul, spirit or identity and love of oneself); *connections to the people of one's inner circle*—to the people that are necessary for learning about love, trust and all the virtues without which no person can develop to be a wise human being; *connections to the wider society of mutual influence in one's life*—without some sense of connection to a sphere wider than one's immediate family, the bonds of responsibility we need for a positive future will be too weak to be useful; *connections to the natural environment of our planet*. It is feelings of connection that lead to respect and responsibility within each of us. And unless feelings of respect and responsibility drive our values and actions in regard to the four areas of connection—self, others, society and the environment—we will fail to develop the strength of character and leadership that will literally 'save our planet'. (New Zealand)

Belonging. This embraces the longing for connectedness/relatedness that is the hallmark of all human communities. It refers to the essence of our identity, in terms of our family histories, our culture, our ancestry. We learn who we are in relation to others. While Western values have placed high value on individualism and personal autonomy, this can breed attitudes of self-interest and selfishness. Our sense of inter-dependence has been eroded in the process. Our need for connectedness has been better understood by many of the world's indigenous cultures, where people gain their sense of belonging from being a part of the extended family or tribe. (Australia)

3.   INDIVIDUALS AS POSSESSORS OF INTRINSIC WORTH

In support of the notion of individuals having *intrinsic* as well as *instrumental* worth, several participants cited the Faure report, *Learning to Be* (UNESCO, 1972), where it is written (p. 6), 'The aim of development is the complete fulfilment of man, in all the richness of his personality, the complexity of his forms of expression and his various commitments'. Others cited the UNESCO (1996) Delors report, which states (p. 23), 'In the twenty-first century everyone will need to exercise greater independence and judgement combined with a stronger sense of personal responsibility for the attainment of common goals. Our report stresses a further imperative: *none of the talents which are hidden like buried treasure in every person must be left untapped*' (emphasis ours).

Implicit in the excerpts in the previous section is the notion that the denial of such needs as trust, autonomy and initiative can have a harmful effect upon (among other things) the development of 'universal virtues'. These later featured quite prominently in the submissions. An Australian participant referred to the 13th Century theologian, St. Thomas Aquinas, 'who listed the seven deadly sins as pride (self-centredness), envy, avarice (greed), wrath (anger, violence), gluttony, sloth (apathy) and lust; the seven cardinal virtues as faith, hope, charity (compassion), prudence (good sense), temperance (moderation), fortitude (courage, perseverance) and religion. Others widely regarded as virtues include patience, honesty, fidelity and forgiveness. Modern Western culture has turned this value system on its head: virtues become vices and vice-versa'.

Several participants sought a return to those traditional virtues, or to similar ones appropriate to the well-being of humanity. The truly autonomous individual was to be an integral element within the social fabric, holding it together by the threads of personal morality.

> We have to change radically the way of our thinking and our behavior. The following features can be stated to avoid the catastrophic situation and to get highly desirable global futures: overwhelming majority of humankind accepting a less selfish life; love—not only tolerance—towards each other and towards the whole of nature by the overwhelming majority of humankind; restriction of the antihuman minorities by healing rather than punishing them. (Hungary)

> An enlightened world citizen would be a person of integrity who walks the straight and narrow path of Truth and Non-violence; has the courage to stand up to wrong: colour, class, caste or creed of fellow human beings would not matter to him; God-fearing and good-natured, compassionate, unselfish and public spirited, he would not covet the wealth of others. (India)

> More important than any other formal or informal learnings are my beliefs about kindness compared to cruelty, honesty compared to manipulation, and the many other ways that people's lives, and, therefore, the very lifeblood of our entire planet, are affected when non-virtuous behaviours take precedence over virtuous behaviours. (New Zealand)

> Ideal characteristics of personal identity: unselfishness; solicitude and responsibility; sincerity, integrity and rightfulness; flexibility and open-mindedness. (Finland)

> Each individual should value the concepts of honesty; justice; humility; altruism; love; forgiveness; truth; integrity; patience; moderation; responsibility. (United States)

Somewhat as an extension of the above, other participants argued on philosophical grounds that, in developing individuals to the full, special attention should be given to *distinctive* human attributes. Just as it is demeaning for a proud elephant to spend its life doing circus tricks, and for what could have been a majestic tree to be confined as a bonsai in a small pot, so it is demeaning to deny a human individual opportunities for full and distinctive development. Reference was made to the *'human spirit', moral responsibility, concern for the common good, caring, empathy, future orientation, strategic thinking, creative discourse or dialogue, holistic thinking* and *aesthetic appreciation.*

The *'human spirit'* was variously defined but, following Capra (1988, p. 113), some reference was usually made to a mode of consciousness in which one feels connected to the cosmos as a whole, a search for meaning and purpose in life on this planet, a sense of wonder. A New Zealand participant made reference to 'spirituality', but quickly went on to quote Palmer (1999, p. 6): 'By "spiritual" I do not mean the credal formulations of any faith tradition, as much as I respect those traditions and as helpful as their insights may be. I mean the ancient and abiding quest for connectedness with something larger and more trustworthy than our egos—with our own souls, with one another, with the worlds of history and nature, with invisible winds of the spirit, with the mystery of being alive'.

> For an advanced spirit, I mean a transcendental consciousness of the roles we should play in the planet. The advanced spirit lives in the planet, not as a mere consumer ('things are there, why not have them'?), or as a worker who works merely to make money to buy things, and/or to have/maintain power. Differently, the advanced spirit is someone who could be a consumer, a worker, etc., but at the same time, a world transformer. In the process of living, he/she would raise ideas, thoughts, and values, internalize attitudes, and externalize behaviour, which would transcend the materiality of "things", and of life itself. If so, individuals would never die, for their contributions would remain, as it has happened with Socrates, Mozart, Galileo, and many others. (Brazil)
>
> Sacredness. This has little to do with institutionalised religion, and more to do with our spirituality. It refers to the deepest respect for humanity, its qualities and the environment in which we live. It embraces the stories we tell which help us make sense of our lives, and our place in the universe—the stories which inspire resolution and hope. It is the opposite of religious fundamentalism, which is threatening the modern world by its rigid intolerance. (Australia)

A sense of *moral responsibility for both one's own actions and the welfare of societies*, local and global, featured prominently in the submissions:

> Postmodern society [has] demolished the grand narratives, universal creeds and institutional authority that [have] in the past been the regulator of values and beliefs about the world. It [has] thus left people morally adrift, but it [has] also provided them with the opportunity to be truly moral beings for the first time, exercising genuine moral choice and accepting responsibility for the consequences of their choices. Critically, this responsibility applies not only to people's personal lives but also to their social roles. (Australia)
>
> We have new powers over life and death never dreamed of by our ancestors. But there has been a tragic lag in our development. We have not yet developed the spiritual vision, moral maturity or ethical system to use our new powers in ways that will enhance rather than diminish the prospects of life for our children and grandchildren. (India)
>
> Moral responsibility—internal and external accommodation to established ends, ideals, customs (and the like), which are relevant to regulate social life in the community, the nation or the planet as a whole. Such moral accommodation would not mean alienation to

things/situations on the part of individuals. It means a concrete concern and development to criticise and conform correctly to things
democratically considered valid for mankind's welfare. (Brazil)

We have a choice: we can choose to feel powerless and accept
that the future-affecting decisions being made now will be our
reality tomorrow. But, as author Arnold Mindell says in his book,
The Leader as Martial Artist, 'Today, world problems and politics
are not only for the rich and educated to solve. On our magical
little planet, where the atmosphere can no longer be controlled by
scientists, politicians, witch-doctors or priests, the world's situation
is everyone's task. We cannot afford to leave it to others'. Our world
grows more disturbing and mysterious, yet to what can we turn?
I say, we turn to ourselves. We are the new wisdom teachers. We
create the miracles. Perhaps when I look at world events at large,
any ideal may seem unreachable. But when I look at the reality of
each individual, and on each single fact on the ground, it seems to
me that I discover that it all depends on the decisions, minutely set,
and actions of single individuals. It is then that I get encouraged, that
I see how in fact things can change, one individual at a time . . . . We
need to believe that individual responsibility for global mindedness,
awareness, thinking and action, rests with all of us in our spheres
of influence. (Australia—youth participant)

Individual excellence was seen by several participants as a continuum that cul-
minated in a commitment to fostering the *'common good'*. One quoted Nunn (1920),
'Individuals are never more themselves, never more masters of their own fate, than
when they recognise that they are part of a greater whole, from which they can draw
inspiration and strength, and to which they can give inspiration and strength'.

It is the world and ourselves that we need to want to improve,
to change what was and what is to what could be and should be
from the perspective of that which is in the common good and is
ultimately ethically defensible. (Australia)

New departures in philosophy should strive to build perspectives that integrate multicultural conceptions of being or pluralism.
One focus for this is the connection of individual existentialism
with global awareness that could be actualized by service to humanity and the environment wherever critical needs exist. In terms
of self-actualization this would involve building the capacity to perceive one's own being in ways that come into relationship with the
diversity of being-ness in the world. (United States)

We need to strengthen our understanding of our common well-
being, and of how our future is clearly connected to all parts of
the world. We are interdependent and we need to recognize more
fully the nature of our interdependence. People need to recognize
the connections between their small (micro) decisions and the way
these impact on larger (macro) issues. (United States)

Included in many of the submissions were references to *care and compassion culminating in action*. Mention was made by some to Buddhist philosophy where *doku* (feeling the suffering of another) must develop into *bakku* (eliminating the cause of suffering). One participant quoted Albert Schweitzer: 'I don't know what your destiny will be. But this I do know: the only ones among you who will ever be truly happy are those who have sought and found how to serve others'.

> Caring for each other must be the major interest and characteristic of people. People must live in awareness that we share in one big family, and damage in one part is felt by the other parts of the family. War, diseases, calamities, social unrest, or any disaster in society, will cost others. People must live in cooperation with each other regardless of their political values and orientation, and religion. People must be eager to communicate with each other and develop understanding of each other's strengths and weaknesses, honour the characteristics of the other, accept and view the differences as necessities and treasures, without which life is worthless, colourless, no challenge for creativity and innovation. People must share advantages they have in knowledge, education and technology which are useful for the betterment of others living, without any prejudice or arrogance. (Indonesia)

> Each world citizen [must] be responsible for each other and care for each other. Meaning, the development of mutual responsibility and caring between all world citizens, beyond national and particular issues and interests. This would imply, for example, developing a global policy aimed at taking care of the needy from every point of view, not only by giving material, moral and psychological assistance but also by helping many of them build a new life and future. (Israel)

> Central to this picture of desirable futures is an assortment of people who have something in common. These are people who care—people who *care about themselves*, who *care about other people*, and who *care about the earth* on which we all live. People who care about themselves are concerned about preserving and nurturing the human spirit and body, and take action appropriately. The people within this world-view also care about others. These folk know how to talk with people. They take time, or make time, to stop and talk and they know how to develop conversations about important issues. They see themselves as global citizens, connected with people beyond their immediate environment, and are prepared to use a collaborative wisdom to solve problems. People who care about this planet of ours respond to early warning signals and have the foresight and wisdom to take action. (New Zealand)

> Indifference is the most insidious cause of dehumanization, because it eludes identification or naming. Anything that helps oppose indifference is a highly desirable feature of a global future. This opposition is not merely a change of attitude, but entails a

> critical engagement with and interrogation of the choices and aspi-
> rations that shape our lives as individuals, and also the lives we lead
> through our ever-widening circle of relationships within families,
> communities, workplaces, nation-states. (Canada)

Sometimes linked with care and compassion in the submissions, but containing a stronger cognitive element, was *empathy,* which one participant defined as 'understanding how other people are feeling, what they are thinking, why they act as they do and how they are conceptualising the world'.

> Individuals need to have empathic judgement—to be able to under-
> stand and value how others view the world and why they think and
> act as they do. This necessitates the ability to suspend judgement
> long enough to examine issues objectively and to enter the hearts
> and minds of others—to put one's ego on hold, so to speak. Empathic
> individuals are responsive also to the need for the next generation
> to find their own solutions to problems, rather than fencing-in the
> thinking of younger minds by referring only to established ways
> of thinking and doing. Allowing young minds and imaginations
> to fly freely is liberating for both younger and older generations.
> (Australia)
>
> In this world view, we need people who are able to reposition
> themselves and look at themselves and the world through different
> eyes. People who can talk about 'self' and 'other' and recognize
> themselves as 'the others'. People who see themselves as global
> citizens, connected with people beyond their immediate environ-
> ment, and who are prepared to use a collaborative wisdom to solve
> problems. (New Zealand)

Several participants reported that the creation of better futures is dependent, basically, upon more people having their innate *future-orientation* developed and directed towards what is desirable:

> *Future orientation* is the characteristics and capacity, unique to hu-
> man beings, which enable thinking to be regulated by the past and
> present, but also to reflect continuously assumptions and expecta-
> tions regarding the future. Human beings are informed not only in
> space, in the present and immediate future, like many other living
> creatures, but are also constantly aware to a certain extent of what
> can be expected beyond their immediate environment and over a
> long-range time-horizon. Humankind has a historical view and also
> has a future attitude, which is expressed in future orientation. The
> decisions and actions of future-oriented persons are guided more
> by their intentions, goals and desires for the future than by their
> experiences of the past. The future inspires the driving force of
> human activity. (Hungary)
>
> Essential parts of future readiness are futures thinking and
> future consciousness. *Futures thinking* is considered an individ-
> ual's way of communicating with the environment and a means of

acquiring, defining and evaluating information regarding the future. *Future consciousness* is value-rational understanding of how everyday decisions and choices affect the formation of the future. The view of future and its formation are central for the development of future readiness, as the view of the future has a two-way meaning for the individual: on the one hand, it is created in order to define the goals that are set for actions, and, on the other, actions based on it in the present create future. (Finland)

> There are many dreams and expectations I have from this world of mine. I have been blessed with a mind that tells me that my desired future is possible if I work towards it, since I am the future of this world. There are a billion children of my age and younger who are blessed with a lifetime each to bring about these changes in the foreseeable future, so that our souls can peep from amongst the clouds of heaven and see a new generation, and a new world of colours, lights and happiness. (India—youth participant)

An essential element of futures thinking, in the opinion of several, was *strategic thinking*, defined as reflection—action—reflection. According to Rahman (1993, p. 195), 'Only with a liberated mind, which is free to enquire and then conceive and plan what is to be created, can structural change release the creative potentials of the people. . . . liberation of the mind is the primary task, both before and after structural change'. McMeniman (1991, p. 38) describes this kind of thinking by referring to the task of composing text: 'This very non-linear process involves writers in consideration of the purpose of the piece of writing and the audience; consultation of their own background knowledge; allowing ideas to "incubate"; planning; and backtracking continually and re-reading to keep a check on whether the piece of writing is conceptually "on track" and is getting its message across'. Vygotsky suggested that the basis of all learning is 'internal conversations' in which we constantly shift between 'two planes of learning'—intermental and intramental—and between two planes of enactment—individual and collective. Through continuous progression around these cycles, we adapt and remake learning for ourselves, our own purposes and circumstances.

> Idealism—a body of attitudes taking the spirit, consciousness, ideas, will and other subjective aspects as fundamental data from which the individuals would reflect and act in the world. Not rarely, the idealism hides the origins and conditions of social, economic and technological advancements, showing them as abstract situations. Thus, my opinion is that the idealist individuals would contribute to better futures by critically seeking/analysing subjective realities and placing them before and in straight relation with practical considerations. (Brazil—shades of Paulo Freire's transformative strategy).
>
> Individuals are inevitably caught between the competing claims of freedom, on the one hand, and belonging on the other. Between the desirable goals of self-empowerment and meaningful participation. This calls for heightened forms of self-consciousness

whereby every individual strives to find his or her own unique balance. There is no social formula for what constitutes the ideal balance, because every individual context is unlike any other. Therefore the attributes that I would seek to nurture through educational
initiatives revolve around capacities for self-examination and self-
interrogation. The sensitivities, attitudes, values, knowledges and
'action competencies' that will serve as engines for moving toward desirable futures will always remain aspirations fraught with
paradoxes between the competing ideals of individualism and com-
munalism. Yet it is the full consciousness of the paradoxes within
these ideals that will serve as the first step towards making the
futures not only desirable but also realizable. (Canada)

Somewhat linked with strategic thinking was *creative discourse or dialogue*:

I see communicative skill, and its underlying cultural and spiritual
disposition, as an indispensable attribute. This critical attribute is
the ability to engage in effective communicative dialogue, not simply talk, which I see as different. This kind of communicative dialogue presupposes two crucial claims. First, that knowledge is
generated in the process of iteration between two or more subjec-
tivities (these being individuals, cultures, faiths, or other kinds of
human dualism). Dialogue in this view produces knowledge, and
therefore is always indispensably part of the process of its generation, transfer, and the gaining of commitment to what it implies.
Second, the centrality of communicative dialogue presupposes that
all forms of talk are the basis on which all the values, desires, hopes
and claims that are comprised in the present project foreground. Dialogue is enhancing of human cooperation and collaboration and
critically part of all other endeavours, including the creation and
sharing of knowledge. (Australia)

If individuals are to contribute to better futures, they should,
among other things, develop knowledge, skills and attitudes towards dialogue (reflection and action) with themselves and others
about relevant everyday situations, such as social justice, environmental issues, corruption, oppression, drugs traffic, egalitarian education, etc. They could then democratically make decisions to
change where appropriate. (Brazil)

The specifically human need (because of our brain potential)
to exchange new ideas with one another through language, through
published experiment, through discussion, means that we do not
have to kill ourselves trying out options that the environment will
not reinforce. Satisfying the need to exchange ideas with others, as
Karl Popper remarked, 'permits our hypotheses to die in our stead'.
(Australia)

Several participants referred to the need for learners to become *holistic* or *multidimensional* thinkers, capable of combining feeling with thinking, valuing with

knowing, acting with reflecting, and able to gain fundamental insights through exploration of the distinction of differences among them. Although their models differed a little, that by Bawden (2001) may be taken as an example of what is meant by these descriptive concepts. Bawden's model involves thinkers being able to handle four *forms* of knowledge (propositional, practical, experiential and inspirational), three *orders* (the forms, meta-knowing and epistemic–knowing), *a process of development* (from 'objective dualism' to 'contextual relativism') and *world-views*. Although the forms, orders, process of development and world-views can be separated for purposes of discussion, Bawden sees them as sub-processes (dynamic sub-systems) inextricably integrated in a 'glorious synergy' within a coherent whole learning system (p. 84).

> Society has reconciled itself to the existence of a 'one-dimensional' man, narrow occupational training, and a limited and lop-sided world outlook. The kind of differentiation and socialization that are allegedly dictated by the logic of scientific progress are, in fact, pushing the world to the brink of catastrophe. (Russia)
>
> Letter sent by the principal of a school in the USA to his teachers: I am the survivor of a concentration camp. My eyes saw what no man should witness: gas chambers built by learned engineers; children poisoned by educated physicians; infants killed by trained nurses; women and babies shot and burned by high school and college graduates. My request is: help your students become human. Your efforts must never produce learned monsters, skilled psychopaths, educated Eichmanns. Reading, writing, arithmetic are important only if they serve to make our children more human. (United Kingdom)
>
> In the future, the human nature in a social context of the new millennium is assumed to be multiple, as a technological person, economic person, social person, political person, cultural person, and learning person in a global village of information, high technology, and multi-cultures. Both individuals and the society need multiple developments in the technological, economic, social, political, cultural and learning aspects. (China)
>
> Individuals need to be fully human, complete persons who have developed all the dimensions of their humanity in a holistic manner, their human faculties and powers: physical, intellectual, moral aesthetic, socio-cultural, economic, political and spiritual. They must possess knowledge and understanding that lead to insight and wisdom; values and attitudes that enable them to love and appreciate themselves and others; skills, competencies and behaviors to translate knowledge and values into action. (Philippines)

Aesthetic appreciations, often linked with creativity, featured occasionally in the submissions:

> Beauty –expressed through the arts (music, art, drama, dance, architecture, crafts, etc.), also the acceptance of the individual's right to

reflect artistically his/her perception of reality, concept of dreams, etc. (United States)

On a lighter, but serious note, people need to know how to have fun—how to nurture the inner self. We need to recognise problems and imbalances within our own lives and, given the knowledge and the will, hopefully we can think creatively and come up with some simple and inexpensive solutions. (New Zealand)

Creativity—by experiencing the skills and thinking involved with creativity in the fine, practical and literary arts, people will understand better the importance of the contribution of creativity to quality of life. (New Zealand)

All should be able to appreciate and/or participate in the arts— those things that enable us to perceive and illustrate different perspectives of the reality of the world and to offer different expressions of joy and beauty. (United States)

4.   INDIVIDUALS AS KEY AGENTS FOR CHANGE

It will be recalled that, in addressing the issue of creating better worlds, the Tier 1 findings highlighted the need for attention to be given to eight main matters: *sustainability of planet Earth; provision of basic food, shelter and health care; removal of global threats to security: collaborative peace; social justice; retention and development of diversity; supra-national entities; participatory democracy* and*caring and humane connections at all levels.* The last of these has been discussed in the previous section, and the intention in this section is to take each of the others in turn and discuss responses which participants submitted with respect to individuals' attributes of *awareness, attitude, value, knowledge* and *'action competence'*. At the level of *awareness*, individuals are sensitive to the existence of certain phenomena; *attitude* involves adoption of a position with respect to an issue and a willingness to respond; *valuing* involves ascribing worth to, cherishing, preferring, willingness to act on the basis of, ideas, principles, conventions, procedures and the like; *knowledge* involves specifics of various kinds as well as cognitive abilities to undertake higher-order actions, judging in terms of evidence, criteria, etc.; *action competence* involves possession of the wide range of skills needed to participate successfully in community actions that are aimed at bringing visions into effect.

Although distinctions among these categories are blurred—awareness, for example, contains an element of knowledge—the first three might be regarded as *affective* attributes, the fourth as *cognitive* and the fifth as *skill*. More important, the five categories may be regarded as constituting a hierarchy, beginning with *awareness* (e.g. being aware that people differ with respect to worldviews), passing through *attitude* (e.g. being tolerant of cultural patterns exhibited by individuals from different groups), *value* (e.g. acknowledging that diversity is potentially worth cherishing), *knowledge* (e.g. being well informed on specifics relating to cultural patterns) to *action competence* (e.g. engaging effectively in policies and programmes to sustain and develop diversity). In this hierarchy, action competence is the culmination of the others and, without it, the others, however valuable, would be incomplete. Thus

Overarching all the others is a willingness to act in order to move towards the ultimate goal. For it is relatively easy to agree that something needs to be done, but much more difficult to do something about it, especially when economic forces and political immobility make action difficult. (United Kingdom)

To actualise the vision for a preferred world society, requires that individuals and groups (communities, voluntary organisations, etc) behave in ways consistent with the values they espouse, and that they also develop effective strategies for pressuring governments, authorities and corporations to act in ways which are consistent with the vision set out in the Tier 1 exercise. For example, while 96% of those completing Tier 1 want to eliminate poverty, and 84% want to reduce the gap between rich and poor, to do so requires that all individuals (especially the rich and powerful), corporations and nations actively strive to reduce poverty by supporting programmes for the poor (e.g. meeting their ODA obligations, paying rather than avoiding taxes, supporting welfare policies and charities, paying a fair price for commodities from developing countries, supporting debt swaps, etc.). Over 90% in Tier 1 support the operation of an International Criminal Court in cases of crimes against humanity. But what if powerful nations like the US insist on protecting their own citizens from being accountable? Individuals (especially US citizens) must pressure governments to act in ways that promote collaborative peace. It is not just that individuals need to possess an appropriate set of "personality" attributes, the entire culture of societies and corporations must change as a result of concerted action of individual citizens committed to creating a more just, peaceful and equitable world. (Australia)

4.1. Sustainability of Planet Earth

A number of participants identified the *Tbilisi Declaration* (Intergovernmental Conference on Environmental Education, 1977) as an important landmark in advancing understanding of what is required of individuals, groups and societies if sustainability of Earth is to become a reality. This Declaration received wide and enduring international acceptance, and initiated moves towards the specification of attributes of *awareness*—sensitivity to the interdependence of natural, social, economic and political systems; *values*—concern for issues of sustainability as well as sets of values upon which judgements can be made about appropriate ways of acting individually and with others to promote sustainable development; *knowledge*—an understanding and knowledge, drawn from both traditional and scientific sources, that will enable individuals to think critically about the environment and the effects of proposed actions; *skills*—identification and anticipation of environmental problems, together with an ability to work with others to resolve, minimise and prevent them; *participation*—making and taking opportunities to be actively involved with others in working towards sustainable development (Fien, 2001).

Sustainability of the planet in the future will increasingly rest on the extent to which all individuals understand that human beings are not above nature, and that our collective future depends on respecting its basic laws [*awareness*]. Thus, knowledge of ecological principles and understanding of (short and long term) environmental threats are essential [*knowledge*], plus a deep commitment to sustainable development [*value*]. Individuals will need to consistently act in an environmentally responsible way [*attitude*], to develop the ability to analyse and evaluate options in terms of their environmental consequences [*knowledge*], and to adopt a long-term perspective [*attitude*]. Environmental attitudes and values must translate into environmentally responsible behaviour [*action* competence]. Professionals, technologists, managers and decision-makers must constantly update their knowledge and understanding (life-long learning) [*knowledge/attitude*], think creatively and critically about the environmental and social consequences of proposed lines of action, and make informed and responsible judgements [*knowledge*]. (Australia)

Our primary concern has to be to preserve nature [*value*]. Our responsibility and respect for the elements of nature and environment have to be one of the most vital features of desirable futures [*value*]. Our ancestors viewed the whole of nature as sacred [*value*]. Today we need to return to that reverence [*value*]. The relationship between man and nature has to be defined [*knowledge*]. Efforts have to be made for the promotion of attitudes and behaviour in individuals which are in consonance with human values which help in preserving the place of human beings within the biosphere [*action competence*]. (India)

An attitude of 'reverence for life' in all its forms should inform human activities in relation to the environment [*value*], enabling us to see our role of temporary stewards of life-enhancing global resources which must be conserved and passed on to future generations [*awareness*]. All new technical inventions and discoveries would be evaluated in terms of their potential contribution to sustainable development [*value*], and moral decisions would be required to over-ride short-term economic and financial benefits [*value*]. (United Kingdom)

Individuals need to be concerned with [*attitude*] and involved in the wise utilization of the earth's resources [*action competence*], aware of the interrelationship of human beings with nature [*awareness*], living a simple lifestyle in harmony with sustainable development [*action competence*], caring and preparing for the quality of life of future generations [*value*], possessing global spirituality which respects the sacredness of nature and every human being [*value*]. (Philippines)

Each individual should have basic knowledge of scientific analyses and predictions relative to environmental issues (such

as global warming, pollution, deforestation, depletion of natural resources; alternative development strategies—energy sources,
agricultural practices; distribution and conservation of natural resources [*knowledge*]. (United States)

Individuals should know and understand major natural systems
of the Earth (landforms, soils, water bodies, climate, vegetation) in
order to understand the interaction within and between ecosystems
[*knowledge*]. They should have a concern for the quality and planning of the environment and human habitat for future generations
[*attitude*]. (Germany)

Sustainability of planet Earth. Here individuals need to possess a breadth of knowledge which enables them to understand the
elements which interact within the earth's ecosystem [*knowledge*].
But they also need to understand the network of economic relationships which has resulted in an unbalanced exploitation of the
earth's resources and the consequent dangers posed for the future
of the planet [*knowledge*]. Over and above these understandings,
individuals need to develop an acceptance that the present uneven
distribution of the planet's wealth is unfair as well as dangerous
[*value*]. (United Kingdom)

Individuals need to be sensitive and aware of the global environment as a complex web of components. [*awareness*]. They
should have openness and interest in the discovery of the environment in its totality, natural and man-made [*attitude*]; recognition
of the importance of independent protection of the environment
[*awareness*], and development to this end of attitudes of ethical concern and motivation for the active participation of others
[*attitude*]; making oneself understood in conversations with others
in a foreign language on the necessity to identify, solve or antic-
ipate environmental problems [*action competence*]; following or
rather observing policy formulations and decision making on the
item and assessing them critically within local/national and sub-
regional/international workshops or other encounters, as for example, youth summer camps [*action competence*]. (Germany)

4.2.   Provision of Basic Food, Shelter and Health Care

Participants from the few affluent countries, as well as those from countries that
for ever survive on the brink of famine in terms of food, shelter and health care, called
for a heightened sense of global awareness relating to extreme poverty, followed by a
dedication to provide alleviation at all levels, from the local to the global. Individuals
were asked to develop greater personal responsibility towards over-consumption and
wastefulness, to put their own living standards on the line for the sake of other people
and nations suffering economic deprivation, to live more simply that others may
simply live. It was held that we possess the political, as well as the scientific and
technological power to vanquish poverty, ignorance and disease. What is lacking is
the will to use this power.

The items in this block on which there was high consensus require individuals who are informed about the horrors of extreme
poverty and its causes and effects [*knowledge*]. As well as this
knowledge, there must be deep compassion—an ability and in-
clination to place oneself in the pauper's position, to empathise
with that person, to share the feelings of hopelessness, the physical discomfort and frustration, and the perception of abandonment
and alienation [*attitude*]. Compassion involves more than empathy,
however, for it requires action—there must be a firm resolve to
strive to improve the lot of the pauper [*attitude*]. Such action would
involve acts of generosity through alms-giving, voluntary work for
charitable agencies, demonstrations of friendship, and so on [*action
competence*]. There should also be vigilance in the identification
of discrimination, unfairness, prejudice, corruption, and 'whistle-
blowing' where these are found to occur, together with participation
in welfare-oriented group action [*action competence*]. (Australia)

Once it was stated that, 'There is enough to meet everybody's
needs in the world, but not to meet everybody's greed'. This is very
important in the provision of basic food requirements of people.
The future society should be geared to the development of these
attitudes [*attitude*]. The generations should develop the positive
attitudes and knowledge to prevent pollution, and not to make clean
air, clean water and clean healthy food scarce commodities in the
world [*attitude/knowledge*]. (Sri Lanka)

Awareness and sensitivity concerning the danger of drugs
[*awareness*]; the willingness to consciously deal with the complex
reality of drug abuse and its consequences [*attitude*]; the firm belief
that a personal courageous stand is needed to refuse categorically
and to convince others to abstain from consuming drugs [*value*];
knowledge and deep understanding for dangers emerging from un-
healthy eating habits—too much, too fat, too sweet, no, or not
enough vitamins and mineral substances [*knowledge*]. (Germany)

Essentially, provision of the basics involves an unselfish attitude which accepts the need for richer people to give up some of
their income in favour of those who are less well off [*attitude*] in
order to lessen the disparities between nations as well as within
nations [*value*]. It also requires attitudes of probity so that those in
power do not use their control of the economy to benefit their own
personal wealth to the detriment of the less powerful members of
their community [*attitude*]. (United Kingdom)

4.3.   *Removal of Global Threats to Security: Collaborative Peace*

Several participants quoted from the Constitution of UNESCO where it is stated,
'Since wars begin in the minds of men, it is in the minds of men that the defences of
peace must be constructed'. Others, in a similar vein, stressed the need to understand
the causes of conflict and terrorism and to learn how to critically examine and resolve

conflicts peacefully through negotiation. Although attitude change underpins this shift, 'action competence' emerges here as a crucial attribute.

> Willingness to have a solicitous attitude to the products of human activities and realising that wars are not appropriate as a remedy for conflict resolution [*attitude*]. Willingness to have a respectful attitude to the rights of other human beings to live, and an understanding that nothing should be done to harm other free-thinking individuals [*attitude*]. Capacity to work in cooperation [*action competence*]. (Russia)
>
> Each individual should value the concept of peace—living with all in an atmosphere of peace [*value*]. They should develop action competencies of negotiation, collaboration and cooperation, conflict resolution and mediation skills [*action competence*]. (United States)
>
> Ability to cooperate with others [*action competence*]. This requires a willingness to listen, to talk through issues patiently and flexibly, and to resolve conflicts resourcefully and without rancour [*action competence*]. (New Zealand)
>
> For the development of a peaceful world, individuals need to: respect themselves and others [*value*]; avoid ethnocentrism [*attitude*]; distinguish between interests and positions [*awareness*]; identify common and compatible interests [*knowledge*]; listen attentively [*action competence*]; be alert to the natural tendencies to bias, misperceptions, misjudgments, and stereotyped thinking [*awareness*]; develop skills for dealing with difficult conflicts [*action competence*]; remain a moral person who is caring and just and who considers the other as a member of their moral communities, entitled to care and justice [*value*]. (United States)

4.4. Social Justice

Social justice, as defined by the respondents, includes: notions of fairness, respect for others, tolerance of difference, avoidance of discrimination against minorities, recognition of individuals' rights to participate in social activities. Several participants identified links of attitude to the promotion of social justice, as defined, to knowledge of local laws and international commitment, such as articulated in the UNESCO Universal Declaration of Human Rights.

> A deep commitment to always respecting the inherent dignity of others, their fundamental rights and freedoms as set out in international conventions and declarations [*value*]. A willingness to join with others to combat exploitation of others and corruption, and to support organizations committed to promotion of social justice in all spheres of modern life (social, trade, industrial, family, etc.) [*value/action competence*]. Respect for the rule of law (international as well as national) within a social justice framework

in dealing with others is of fundamental importance [*attitude*]. Once again, this presupposes an understanding of international and national law [*knowledge*], and embracing the values and principles underlying them, as well as support for the development of social justice policies and new instruments to deal with new threats to social justice in the 21st Century (terrorism, discrimination by the State against minority groups and refugees, cultural cleansing, drug abuse, HIV-AIDS orphans, street children, etc) [*value/action competence*]. (Australia)

Sensitive to injustice [*value*]. Willing to seek out and expose social and economic injustices at the local, national and international level, and to work towards removing them [*value/action competence*]. (New Zealand)

Social justice involves the widely recognized notions of fairness and human rights [*value*]. Understanding these principles and issues will enable people to develop justice in their respective countries [*knowledge*]. Preparation of people from young days for responsible life in free society in the spirit of understanding, tolerance and the development of respect for everybody. Develop in people the attitudes and values such as global solidarity and peace [*attitude/value*], which equip man with the knowledge and skills to promote the required values [*action competence*]. (Sri Lanka)

Individuals should have a commitment to promoting human rights and social justice, including a reasonable standard of living for all people [*value*]. They should understand current and past social, political and economic policies and practices which have created inequalities of access to human rights and social justice, including reasonable standards of living [*knowledge*]. They should be able to engage in effective moral and political debate and advocacy for human rights [*action competence*]. (Australia)

This feature is one of the most solid foundations of democracy. There is obviously a need for knowledge and insights [*knowledge*], and a high sense of responsibility and empathy [*attitude*], as well as a resolute and courageous stand on: the historical human rights development and its present and future importance [*value*]; the significance of fundamental and human rights, both for the rights of the individual as well as for the objective principles of society [*value*]. Only a sound knowledge of the administrative decisions and instructions to practically implement or rather apply social justice allows the individual to analyse his situation, his place in the society he lives in and to assess the scope of his rights as well as to evaluate the chances of success of an appeal to be treated with dignity, justice, respect and care [*knowledge*]. (Germany)

A strong concern for social justice [*value*]. I appreciate what Patricia Hill Collins (1998) has written about "visionary pragmatism" which emphasizes the necessity of linking relationships and theoretical vision with informed practical struggle, visionary thinking and pragmatic vision. This points to a vision but doesn't prescribe a fixed end point of universal truth. Rather, current actions can be seen as being part of some larger, more meaningful struggle [*awareness*]. (United States)

4.5. Retention and Development of Diversity

Several respondents seemed to be in agreement with the sentiments expressed in Chapter 1, where it was claimed that the individual's affiliation with family, neighbourhood, other inclusive units, up to the national level was necessary, but not sufficient, for living in the 21st century. A sense of membership in the global community is also needed. But in the pursuit of this, cultural differences cannot, and should not, be cast aside. The gradual drift towards ethnocentrism should be recognised as the precursor to racist attitudes, which have no place in the 'democratic state'. The UNESCO Report 'Learning: The Treasure Within' (p. 22) stresses the requirement of a better understanding of other people, peaceful interchange . . . harmony, which are presently lacking.

Individuals must understand and accept the reality of cultural difference [*awareness*]; be aware that they live in a community, a nation, and a world with people from many different cultures [*awareness*]. People from different cultures may differ in their appearance, dress, behaviour, perceptions, beliefs, preferences, values, history, and ways of thinking about conflict and negotiation. People must learn to understand and accept the reality of cultural differences [*knowledge/attitude*], try to understand the other's culture and try to help the other to understand theirs [*attitude*]. Expect cultural misunderstandings, and use them as opportunities for learning rather than as a basis of estrangement [*attitude*]. (United States)

Intercultural understanding: In order to benefit, rather than suffer, from cultural diversity, it is highly desirable that young people reach a certain level of intercultural understanding [*knowledge*], empathy [*attitude*] and respect [*value*]. These qualities can be best attained through personal exposure to other countries, preferably in a voluntary and organised way. It would additionally be desirable to spread knowledge of economic, environmental, political, health and demographic issues that are consequences of globalisation, or merely globally relevant [*knowledge*]. (Denmark)

Individuals must become sensible towards global integration. They should learn to see their own country as one which is neither superior nor inferior to others, but with specific and relevant characteristics (e.g. culture, knowledge, technology, values, social needs, economic demands, political priorities, etc.) which could be shared with others, without subordination or domination [*attitude*]. (Brazil)

Identifying the "meeting points" between different cultures and subcultures, as well as between religion, science and technology, on those issues where they could be mutually complementary, or have some kind of common denominator [*knowledge*], while, at the same time, accepting the different perspectives as legitimate rights, and also as a source of enrichment [*attitude*]. (Israel)

Individuals should have a good knowledge of at least one culture besides one's own [*knowledge*], and awareness of the diversity of cultures, values and ways of living [*awareness*]. (United Kingdom)

A well developed understanding of one's own culture is necessary [*knowledge*]. If people recognise the values, morals and ethics that underlie their own culture, hopefully they will be better able to understand and respond to the different attitudes and behaviours of others [*attitude*]. It is not intended that people see themselves as giving up their identity and sharing a single culture, but rather working to keep their own cultural identity intact, adding richness to others and being enriched by theirs [*attitude*]. It is possible when cooking, to take a number of ingredients, mix them together and cook them up as a casserole or a stew. The individual ingredients are merged, blended together, and the end result is a tasty dish with one over-riding flavour and one predominant colour. Alternatively, it is possible to take the same ingredients and create a salad, binding them together with a dressing sprinkled over the top. The ingredients retain their intensity of colour, their individual flavours remain intact and enhance the others. The metaphorical salad allows for divisions and diversity, but the dressing provides some unity and cohesion [*attitude*]. (New Zealand)

4.6.   Supra-national Entities

Recent instability at international level, as well as internal upheavals in many countries has raised questions relating to appropriate responses to these events. Many respondents expressed support for an international body to be delegated authority to adjudicate an appropriate solution. Others, while in general agreement, voiced a concern that this might lead to the imposition of an external directive on a sovereign state. The need to learn more about the work of organisations aligned with the United Nations, and how their efforts could be enhanced received support.

The acceptance of the rule of law internationally must be predicated upon the view that decisions of an international body need to be accepted even if one does not agree with the decisions [*value*]. It involves a recognition that the greater good of the global community is better served by such an acceptance than by insisting on individual national sovereignty [*awareness*]. It also involves a belief that one's view or one's nation's view may be wrong in any given circumstance [*awareness*]. (United Kingdom)

Individuals need to know about [*Knowledge*] and support the work of international organizations (the UN family) [*attitude*] and push to ensure that their governments respect the obligations to them and to international norms, work to ensure international practices and policies (including those of international corporations) are just and democratic, and that nation states work within the agreed international frameworks when dealing with each other and with refugees [*action competence*]. Individuals should play an active role in and support international NGOs (e.g. UN Associations, Save the Children, World Education Fellowship, etc.), working to protect human rights, the environment [*action competence*]. (Australia)

4.7.   Participatory Democracy

Our participants pointed to issues such as: poverty, unemployment, denial of education and exclusion from decision-making as factors which inhibit, or would prevent, democratic participation. Within the diverse population inside national boundaries, and beyond them, individuals were seen to share certain fundamental values to be regarded as being 'democratic'. These were identified as: democratic parliamentary processes, respect for human rights and the dignity of all individuals, and for the rule of law. Participants offered several methods of addressing the challenge of a shift in perception and a move to action-competence.

> People will need to cultivate local and global 'habits of the heart' that sustain democracy as the 'moral' basis for living [*value*]. This personal/social 'transformation' challenges most religions and modern transformation. Given our shrinking world, democratic ideals must be interpreted for all of the planet's diverse cultural contexts. I have in mind Dewey's notion of 'democracy as a moral way of living' [*value*]. From this normative perspective, the question then becomes how democratic 'morality' can be understood in the context of a wide range of moral/ethical traditions [*knowledge*]. (United States)
>
> A basic democratic understanding [*knowledge*]. Democracy is a process that must be learned and practised by each new generation. A prerequisite for a functioning democracy is simple knowledge of democratic structures such as organisations, representation, state structures and voting systems [*knowledge*]. Additionally it should be widely understood that the benefits of democracy are accompanied by a responsibility on each individual to inform himself or herself [*awareness*] and, to a certain extent, participate in public life and discussions [*action competence*]. (Denmark).
>
> Individuals need to develop the knowledge [*knowledge*], skill [*action competence*] and value [*value*] essential for effective participation in democratic life (from local to national to international) including the knowledge and skills needed for work in a world of super-complexity, constant change and new information technologies [*knowledge*]. A deep knowledge of the forms and principles of democracy, and the ways in which these have been developed, been

strengthened and threatened over time are important [*knowledge*]. Individuals need to develop democratic competencies continuously by involvement in participatory processes throughout life [*action competence*]. Knowing their rights [*knowledge*] and accepting their responsibilities in a wide range of developmental contexts—family, school, work-place, community, etc [*attitude*]. (Australia)

5.   STEP 2 RATING SCALE RESULTS

The response rate at this 'step' was very good: 62 from 64 social scientists sent in their preferences and the findings are presented in Table 3.1: Percentages of respondents rating items as '*highly desirable*' (Rating 4). In the Table, Cluster A refers to respondents from Asia, Sub-Saharan Africa and Latin America, while Cluster B refers to respondents from Australia, Europe and North America. Shaded items are those receiving highest ratings for desirability.

Because all of the attributes in the rating scale had featured in the open-ended submissions as 'Highly Desirable', it was not surprising that most of them attracted ratings of 4 (highly desirable) when participants were asked to undertake this exercise, and that many were also given 'high educational priority'. Nevertheless, some items stand out as having the widest acceptance from participants as appropriate pegs around which to develop curricula aimed at promoting global consciousness and responsibility. These include

Item 1: Individuals who have senses of trust, 'connectedness' to others, autonomy and initiative, and are able to enter into mutually supportive relationships.

Item 2: Individuals who have commitments to 'universal values' such as un-selfishness, love for others, truth, honesty, integrity, forgiveness, tolerance and the like.

Item 6: Individuals who accept moral responsibility for their decisions and actions.

Item 19: Individuals who are aware that violent conflict, retaliatory attacks and the like are inappropriate ways of resolving disagreements.

Item 27: Individuals who approach nature with a sense of responsibility to the Earth's resources and habitats.

Item 29: Individuals who have a respectful attitude to the rights of others and are prepared to listen to the viewpoints of others.

Item 30: Individuals who have a special concern for the disadvantaged, the excluded, the marginalized, minorities, children.

Item 31: Individuals who are tolerant of diversity in all its forms (social, cultural, economic, political, ethnic, religious, etc.), subject to basic human rights being honoured.

Item 34: Individuals who are committed to human rights and social justice, including a reasonable standard of living for all people.

Item 35: Individuals who have a commitment to sustainability of Earth, caring and preparing for the quality of life of future generations and are willing to change their lifestyles to protect the environment.

Item 37: Individuals who have an over-whelming preference in social and political interactions for conflict resolution through negotiation rather than conquest, denigration or withdrawal.

Table 3.1: Towards a Global Community: Tier 2 Rating Scale Responses. Percentages of Respondents Rating Items as 'Highly Desirable'

	All	Male	Female	Cluster A	Cluster B
	(N = 62)	(N = 40)	(N = 22)	(N = 21)	(N = 41)

1. Individuals as possessors of intrinsic worth

	All	Male	Female	Cluster A	Cluster B
1. Individuals who have senses of trust, 'connectedness' to others, autonomy and initiative, and are able to enter into mutually supportive relationships.	79%	80%	77%	76%	80%
2. Individuals who have commitments to 'universal virtues' such as unselfishness, love for others, truth, honesty, integrity, forgiveness, tolerance and the like.	79%	78%	82%	81%	78%
3. Individuals who have a sense of 'spirituality', which connects them to the cosmos as a whole.	34%	35%	32%	52%	24%
4. Individuals who have a future orientation and faith in their ability to contribute to shaping the future.	47%	43%	55%	71%	34%
5. Individuals who have a commitment to fostering the 'common good'.	66%	63%	73%	71%	63%
6. Individuals who accept moral responsibility for their decisions and actions.	79%	73%	86%	86%	76%
7. Individuals who care, and are committed to eliminating causes of suffering.	66%	68%	64%	76%	61%
8. Individuals who are empathic—understand how other people are feeling, what they are thinking, why they act as they do and how they are conceptualising the world.	58%	48%	77%	76%	49%
9. Individuals who deal effectively with ambiguities, complexities and competing values in a changing world.	50%	50%	50%	57%	46%
10. Individuals who think 'strategically' (reflect—act—reflect), including, importantly, reflecting on themselves as unique beings involved in balancing competing claims.	40%	33%	55%	43%	39%
11. Individuals who engage effectively in creative discourse or dialogue.	39%	35%	45%	52%	32%
12. Individuals who are 'holistic' or 'multi-dimensional' thinkers, who can synthesize science, the fine arts, the humanities, the secular and the spiritual, knowing with feeling, relating, doing and being.	39%	38%	45%	62%	29%
13. Individuals who possess aesthetic appreciations relating to such things as beauty, music, art, drama, architecture, crafts and literature.	27%	25%	32%	52%	15%
14. Individuals who enjoy the simple things in life—laughing with friends, having fun, walking the dog and the like—and take pleasure in being alive.	37%	23%	64%	67%	23%

2. Individuals as key agents in the creation of better world

a. Sensitivities

	All	Male	Female	Cluster A	Cluster B
15. Individuals who have a global perspective and are aware of global problems and solutions.	58%	48%	77%	76%	49%
16. Individuals who are aware of the interrelationship and interdependence of human beings with nature.	66%	60%	77%	86%	56%
17. Individuals who are aware of the misery and deprivation suffered by the poor.	60%	50%	77%	71%	54%
18. Individuals who are aware of the scourge of diseases such as HIV/AIDS	42%	38%	45%	62%	29%
19. Individuals who are aware that violent conflict, retaliatory attacks and the like are inappropriate ways of resolving disagreements	81%	75%	91%	90%	76%
20. Individuals who are aware that social injustice occurs in many societies, and in relationships from the personal to the international.	55%	45%	73%	71%	46%
21. Individuals who are aware that they live in communities, nations and a world with people who hold disparate views.	63%	60%	68%	81%	54%
22. Individuals who are aware of the emerging role of supra-national organisations.	37%	38%	36%	33%	39%

(continued)

	All	Male	Female	Cluster A	Cluster B
	(N = 62)	(N = 40)	(N = 22)	(N = 21)	(N = 41)
23. Individuals who understand that the benefits of democracy are accompanied by a responsibility to inform oneself on relevant issues.	58%	55%	64%	71%	51%
24. Individuals who are aware that policies and programmes for change must culminate in appropriate action.	53%	45%	68%	52%	54%
b. Attitudes					
25. Individuals who consider that, from a global perspective, the current condition of human living is not good enough—there is too much disadvantage.	50%	45%	59%	52%	49%
26. Individuals who have a positive attitude towards global well-being, as well as to self-actualisation.	48%	43%	59%	67%	40%
27. Individuals who approach nature with a sense of responsibility to the Earth's resources and habitats.	76%	70%	86%	76%	76%
28. Individuals who believe that, given the will, extreme poverty, drug abuse, corruption and the like, could be eliminated or substantially reduced.	56%	60%	50%	62%	54%
29. Individuals who have a respectful attitude to the rights of others and are prepared to listen to the viewpoints of others.	79%	75%	86%	90%	73%
30. Individuals who have a special concern for the disadvantaged, the excluded, the marginalized, the minorities, children.	66%	65%	68%	67%	66%
31. Individuals who are tolerant of diversity in all its forms (social, cultural, economic, political, ethnic, religious, etc.), subject to basic human rights being honoured.	69%	73%	73%	71%	68%
32. Individuals who accept that there is a need for strengthening the capacity of supra-national organisations to deal with human rights issues.	34%	38%	27%	29%	37%
33. Individuals who believe that people should have a voice in matters that affect them.	65%	60%	73%	67%	63%
c. Values					
34. Individuals who are committed to human rights and social justice, including a reasonable standard of living for all people.	77%	73%	86%	86%	73%
35. Individuals who have a commitment to sustainable occupancy of Earth, caring and preparing for the quality of life of future generations and are willing to change their lifestyles to protect the environment.	79%	83%	73%	76%	80%
36. Individuals who value a more equitable distribution of basic provisions, and are prepared to live more simply so that others might survive.	61%	63%	59%	76%	54%
37. Individuals who have an over-whelming preference in social and political interactions for conflict resolution through negotiation rather than conquest, denigration or withdrawal.	81%	80%	82%	86%	78%
38. Individuals who recognize the basic worth of all members of society and their right to share equitably in the opportunities and resources of that society.	63%	60%	68%	76%	56%
39. Individuals who value diversity in worldviews as a general stimulant and as a potential source of solutions to common problems.	50%	45%	59%	71%	39%
40. Individuals who, believing in the greater good of the global community, encourage their national governments to accept decisions taken by legally and democratically established supra-national entities, even when, on occasions, these decisions might not be supportive of local interests.	48%	50%	45%	52%	46%
41. Individuals who prefer forms of government which foster shared community values—i.e. democratic government.	63%	60%	68%	76%	56%
42. Individuals who are committed to working collaboratively with others to enhance the well-being of all.	69%	65%	77%	86%	61%

	All	Male	Female	Cluster A	Cluster B
	(N = 62)	(N = 40)	(N = 22)	(N = 21)	(N = 41)

d. Knowledge

43. Individuals who have accurate knowledge of scientific analyses and predictions relative to environmental and ecological matters (global warming, pollution, depletion of natural resources, alternative developmental strategies, energy sources, agricultural practices and the like).	**34%**	38%	27%	38%	32%
44. Individuals who are knowledgeable in matters of food production, health-care, causes and effects of poverty and the like.	**29%**	35%	18%	38%	24%
45. Individuals who understand the causes of conflict and terrorism, and what is known about resolving conflicts peacefully both at the personal and collective level.	**56%**	53%	64%	62%	54%
46. Individuals who understand current and past social, political and economic policies and practices which have created inequalities of access to human rights and social justice.	**45%**	48%	41%	52%	41%
47. Individuals who have a good knowledge of at least one culture other than their own—world-views, philosophical theories, languages, artistic-musical-literary offerings, etc.	**44%**	48%	36%	48%	41%
48. Individuals who know about the need for, and role of, supra-national organisations.	**29%**	28%	32%	33%	27%
49. Individuals who have a knowledge of democratic structures, and how these have been developed, strengthened and threatened over time.	**40%**	45%	32%	48%	37%
50. Individuals who have a knowledge of the causes, effects and nature of the globalisation process and of how the negative impacts and outcomes at the local level might be overcome.	**42%**	38%	45%	67%	27%
51. Individuals who use both own experiences and discourse to generate new knowledge	**47%**	40%	59%	62%	39%
52. Individuals who distinguish between conceptual, empirical and normative statements, and know the respective kinds of validation they involve	**35%**	43%	23%	48%	29%

e. Action competencies

53. Individuals who are able to, and do, collaborate with others—listen, talk through issues patiently and flexibly, and contribute to plans and actions needed to bring these to fruition.	76%	73%	82%	76%	76%
54. Individuals who are able to, and do, help shape and support policies and practices that promote sustainability.	**55%**	53%	59%	52%	56%
55. Individuals who are able to, and do, engage in collaborative democratic exercises to alleviate poverty, counter corruption, ensure equity in distribution of resources, etc.	**68%**	70%	64%	71%	66%
56. Individuals who can, and do, resolve conflicts using participatory democratic processes—collaboration, negotiation, mediation and the like.	73%	68%	82%	67%	76%
57. Individuals who seek out and expose injustices, at the local, national and international levels, and work towards removing them.	**48%**	50%	45%	52%	46%
58. Individuals who work towards protecting and strengthening difference that does not harm others.	**45%**	40%	55%	48%	44%
59. Individuals who encourage their governments to respect international obligations, contribute to international policies and practices, and behave within the agreed international frameworks.	**63%**	60%	68%	62%	63%
60. Individuals who are able to, and do, participate in community and political actions aimed at the betterment of society.	**66%**	65%	68%	67%	66%

Item 53: Individuals who are able to, and do, collaborate with others—listen, talk through issues patiently and flexibly and contribute to plans and actions to bring these to fruition.

Item 55: Individuals who are able to, and do, engage in collaborative democratic exercises to alleviate poverty, counter corruption, ensure equity in distribution of resources, etc.

At first glance, one of the most striking findings is the relatively low ratings assigned to the 'knowledge' items, whether these appeared in the 'intrinsic-worth' category (Items 8, 9, 10, 11 and 12) or the 'key-agents' one (Items 43–52). We interpret this as a rejection of the notion that knowledge, on its own as a private possession, has special merit. Rather, its usefulness lies in being a base upon which to build attributes judged to be more important. As a UNESCO report (UNESCO 1989: 5) stated, 'The new epistemology of knowledge and learning needs to include a change from emphasizing the private benefits of learning, to emphasizing the public benefits of learning. We need to develop a sense of service and to stress community benefit and the advancement of the public good'. Moreover, participants responses indicate that in their view, each of sensitivities, attitudes and values, too, has limited significance until translated into actions, a view also mirrored in the Delors Report (UNESCO, 1996) in its emphasis of 'Leaning to do' and 'Learning to live together'.

Clearly, from these data, it could be argued that the 15 attributes (compared with eight in the study by Parker, Ninomiya and Cogan, 1999) given highest and most consistent ratings for desirability and educational priority need to be given serious consideration as goals in the development of the kind of curricula with which we are concerned.

The core values anchored on human dignity that under-ride the work of the Asia-Pacific Network for International and Values Education (APNIEVE) are remarkably similar: health and harmony with nature, truth and wisdom, love and compassion, creativity and appreciation of beauty, peace and justice, sustainable human development, national unity and global solidarity, and global spirituality. The development of these attributes throughout life is a integrated process:

> The teaching-learning cycle of the valuing process starts with knowing and understanding oneself and others, leading to the formation of a wholesome self-concept, a sense of self-esteem, self-worth and self-confidence, as well as a genuine respect for others. It proceeds to valuing, reflecting, choosing, accepting appreciating and acquiring needed skills, such as communication, decision-making and finally results in action. It seeks an integration of the learner's knowledge, values and attitudes and skills to bring about his/her full development (UNESCO-APNIEVE, 2002).

6.   CONCLUSION

In our earlier Australian study (Campbell, McMeniman and Baikaloff, 1992), participants ascribed overarching value status to the 'human spirit', the quality central for education in the Universal Declaration of Human Rights (the full development of the human personality) and the UNESCO Commissions (learning to be). As Bill Oats (2001) put it

> The human spirit is the element of our inward search for meaning... The clearest evidence of the reality of the human spirit is to be found in the lives of those human beings in whom this spirit has struggled for expression and recognition... our humanity is a marvellous compound of distinctive attributes—reason, creativity, imagination, explorative curiosity, search for meanings, empathy, feelings of compassion, awareness of connectedness with other components of the living planet....In creating our common future, nurturance of the human spirit should loom large among our priorities.

The respondents in this global study are seeking the type of education that will give a much higher priority in our schools, colleges and universities to 'strengthening the human spirit' to the point that young people develop the global values and 'action competencies' needed to create a more peaceful, tolerant, just, equitable and ecologically sustainable global future. Their preferred global future and educational priorities are very much akin to those emphasised by the participants from all regions in the world in the work of UNESCO's International Commission on Education for the 21st Century and its report (Delors, 1996).

But at the same time, the educational 'reforms' being pushed by some of most powerful and wealthy nations place a premium on values and actions deemed to be necessary to succeed in a highly competitive global market. While it has become increasingly evident that many of our most pressing problems (poverty, global warming, terrorism, the drug trade, corruption, HIV-AIDS, etc.) have a strong global dimension, it is to be regretted that when it comes to the crunch, the vested interests of the rich and powerful too often take precedence of the needs and basic rights of the poor. Even in democracies, strong action is being taken by the powerful to drown out the voices of those committed to human rights, social justice, peace and sustainable development. Yet, we do hope for a better future. For the human spirit has 'outlasted all attempts by autocratic tyrants, political ideologists and arrogant materialists to deny or suppress it. It strives for expression, but rebels against dictation or dogma' (Oats, 2000).

While there is a tension at the national level between the type of education priorities emphasised by the participants in this study and those of groups seeking to reproduce or legitimate their power or ideology, there is also evidence to many education reforms are placing considerable emphasis on a set of agreed values, goals and key learning similar to those featuring in this study and the Delors Report. For example, the National Goals for Schooling in the 21st Century in Australia (MCEETYA, 1999) insist that our schools empower all with 'the necessary knowledge, understanding, skills and values for a productive and rewarding life in an educated, just and open society' while countries like Singapore have recognized that our individual and collective future will increasingly depend on our capacity to solve problems, to innovate and to think critically and creatively. Curriculum reforms increasingly are focussing on essential learnings covering desirable global, national and individual futures: the provision of basic human needs and the protection of human rights for food, heath-care and education, collaborative peace, social justice, participatory democracy, development of diversity and sustainable development. In the chapters that follow, we explore the implications of the priorities identified in this study for the reform of curriculum and pedagogical practice.

7.   REFERENCES

Bawden, R.J. 2001. Educating for unity through diversity of knowing: a systemic perspective. In: Campbell J. (Ed.) *Creating our Common Future*. Paris: UNESCO Publishing.

Campbell, J., McMeniman, M.M. and Baikaloff, N. 1992. *Visions of a Future Australian Society: Towards an Educational Curriculum for 2000 AD and Beyond*. Brisbane: Ministerial Consultative Council on Curriculum.

Capra, F. 1988. *Uncommon Wisdom*. London: William Collins.

Erikson, E.H. 1950. *Childhood and Society*. New York: Norton.

Fien, J. 2001. Educating for a Sustainable Future. In: J. Campbell (Ed.) *Creating Our Common Future: Educating for Unity in Diversity*. UNESCO Publishing/Berghehn Books.

Henry, M.B. 1996. *Young Children, Parents and Professionals*. London: Routledge.

Hess, R.D. 1971. Community involvement in day care. *Day Care: Resources for Decisions*. Washington, DC: US Office of Economic Opportunity.

Hill, B.V. 1992. Setting educational goals for the future. *New Horizons in Education* 87, p. 40.

McMeniman, M.M. 1991.The teacher's role in fostering self-determined learning. *New Horizons in Education* 84, p. 31.

Ministerial Council of Education, employment, Training and Youth Affairs (Australian Govt.). 1999.

Nunn, P. 1920. *Education: Its Data and First Principles*. London: Arnold and Co.

Oats, W.N. 2001. Nurturing the human spirit. In: J. Campbell (Ed.) *Creating Our Common Future*. Paris: UNESCO Publishing.

Palmer, P.J. 1999. Evoking the spirit in public education. *Educational Leadership* 56(4) pp. 6–11.

Parker, W.C., Ninomiya, H., and Cogan, J. 1999. Educating World citizens: towards multicultural curriculum development. *American Research Journal* 36(2), pp. 117–145.

Rahman, A. 1993. *People's Self-Development*. London: Zed Books.

UNESCO. 1972. *Learning to Be: The World of Education Today and Tomorrow (Faure Report)*. Paris: UNESCO Publishing.

UNESCO. 1996. *Learning: The Treasure Within (Delors Report)*. Paris: UNESCO Publishing.

UNESCO-APNIEVE. 2002. *Learning to Be: A Holistic and Integrated Approach to Values Education for Human Development*. Bangkok: UNESCO.

Part II

Chapter 4

BASIC EDUCATION FOR ALL

Colin Power

The first three chapters of this book describe the type of global community that the participants in this study see as preferred global futures: they look forward to a more peaceful, just, sustainable and caring world. The participants also indicated a set of priorities for education, that is, the attributes that our formal and non-formal education programs need to develop in individuals if they are to contribute to the creation of these preferred futures.

As we have seen, the Tier 1 findings indicate that in setting priorities for the future, education systems need to give attention to eight issues:

- sustainability of planet earth,
- provision of basic food, shelter and heath care for all,
- removal of global threats to security: collaborative peace,
- social justice,
- participatory democracy,
- retention and development of diversity,
- supranational identities and
- caring and humane connections at all levels.

The Tier 2 findings indicate the sensitivities, attitudes, values, knowledge and action competencies that need to be developed to 'empower young people to live well both as individuals with unique potentials worthy of fulfilment, and as responsible members in a very diverse and restless global community'.

In the second part of this project, we asked a number of leading educators from around the world to reflect on the priorities identified in Tiers 1 and 2, and what they mean for education in the 21st century. They were also asked to provide 'practical case studies' of education programs which have been 'outstandingly successful in coping with the pedagogical challenges involved in seeking to develop the attributes essential if we are to actualise our vision in a world which often seems to be heading in the opposite direction'.

This chapter focuses on basic education for all as a basic human right, being an essential prerequisite for full development of the human personality and for effective participation in daily life and in creating a better future. Chapter 5 is also concerned with getting the foundations right. Margaret Henry emphasises the importance of attending first to basic developmental needs of young children. She explains how they can be helped to learn to trust, and gives examples of the type of learning environments necessary to build the autonomy and sense of involvement deemed essential for children to 'enter into mutually supportive relationships'.

J. Campbell et al. (eds.), Towards a Global Community, 71–80.

Chapters 6 and 7 focus on the issue of sustainable development. As such, these chapters focus on the basic survival needs of the planet and of all its inhabitants (particularly for food, clean air and water) as a fundamental global issue. In Chapter 6, Abraham Blum provides a masterly overview of the history of education for sustainable development (ESD) and the curriculum reforms necessary for the effective implementation of environmental and ESD programs. In Chapter 7, Richard Bawden reminds us that nothing is more important for the future of individuals than the need for a secure and sustainable source of food for all. He questions the dominance of the technocentric world view of development, and indicates the ways in which some education systems are seeking to provide an 'antidote' to the ignorance and indifference in society by developing a deeper understanding of issues like sustainable universal food security and a commitment to assume our responsibilities for others and for an 'improved and inclusive state of well-being'.

One of the key issues raised in this study is that the need for our schools, colleges and universities to educate for social justice, an issue taken up by Diva Lopes de Silveira. Echoing the emphasis given by participants on the need to eliminate poverty and to enable all to live with dignity in a just and caring society, her chapter ends with a message of hope, describing social justice programs in Brazil focussing on poverty reduction, education, housing, agrarian reform, environmental protection and the indigenous population. De Silverira's call for a 'chaotic-solidaristic integration' between conflicting social needs, economic demands and political priorities is taken up by Judy Lawley in Chapter 9. She gives provides practical examples from the Living Values project in New Zealand of the ways in which schools are seeking to create a global community by creating contexts and programs for developing more caring and humane connections among people and with nature.

In seeking to create a more caring, just, tolerant and peaceful world, we cannot ignore the reality that we live in an increasingly unequal, complex and conflicted world. It is crucial that all, young and old, learn to resolve conflicts peacefully. In Chapter 10, Woolman provides an overview of conflict theory and educational programs for conflict resolution. He argues that conflict resolution training strengthens the values and skills needed in the practice of effective citizenship and that students well grounded in the process of peaceful conflict resolution are more likely to demand government adherence to this process in the management of domestic and international relations. In the next chapter, Jakar and Lucas pick up the challenge of educating for conflict resolution in a troubled region, providing case studies of programmes being used in Israel.

Chapters 12 and 13 help draw the treads together as we seek to face the challenge of living in an interdependent global community and to help our students to become effective and responsible citizens not of their own nation, but also of the world. Using the items assigned highest priority by participants in this study, Rob Gilbert maps the curriculum requirements and challenges in educating for world citizenship. In Chapter 13, Joe Le Bianco reflects on the changes accompanying the processes of globalisation, and then explores the ways our concepts of citizenship and 'effective personal literacy' are being redefined and the pedagogical approaches being used to promote intercultural learning.

1. BASIC EDUCATION FOR ALL: AN HISTORIC STRUGGLE

The first written scripts appeared over 5000 years ago, and with that development, human capacity to pass on knowledge from one generation to the next took a quantum leap forward. However, for most of human history, only a tiny elite could read and write, and then, as now, controlling access to knowledge and to elitist forms of education remains one of the principle means through which those in privileged positions in society maintain their power and advantages and pass these on to their children.

The founders of the many newly independent nations and the United Nations (UN) had seen how colonial and totalitarian regimes maintained power either by denying the masses access to basic education and/or by perverting the nature and content of teaching so that education systems became agents of indoctrination by the state. The UN was created to mark a new era in the story of humanity, one in which recourse to force and violence to resolve conflicts would give way to the peaceful and concerted action of Member States. The challenge to the UN remains that of converting that noble idea into practical action. How does one construct the defences of peace in the minds of men and women? How does one lay the foundations for democracy, sustainable development and a more just and non-violent world?

For UNESCO's first Director-General, Julian Huxley, the most immediate challenge for the UN in education was the 'existence of immense numbers of people who lack the most elementary means of participating in the life of the modern world'. One of the first acts of UNESCO was to create in 1946, a Fundamental Education Committee. The report of this Committee published in 1947 was Fundamental Education: Common Ground for All Peoples. The report insisted that 'Fundamental education is ideally a part of democracy and must be education of the people, by the people'. Fundamental education was seen as encompassing not only the three R's (basic skills in reading, writing and arithmetic) but also such basic knowledge as was required for the purpose of economic and social development... the 'kind of minimum and general education which aims to help children and adults who do not have the advantages of formal education, to understand the problems of their immediate environment and their rights and duties as citizens and individuals, and to participate more effectively in the economic and social progress of their community'. The Report both reflected and inspired the thinking of leaders of the then developing world including Gandi, Paulo Freire and Nyerere.

By 1948, basic education was recognized as a fundamental human right, enshrined in Article 26 of the Universal Declaration of Human Rights:

1. Everyone has the right to education. Education shall be free, at least in the elementary and fundamental stages. Elementary education shall be compulsory. Technical and professional education shall be generally available and higher education shall be equally available on the basis of merit.
2. Education shall be directed to the full development of the human personality and ton the strengthening of respect for human rights and fundamental freedoms. It shall promote understanding, tolerance and friendship among all nations, racial and religious groups and shall further the activities of the United Nations for the maintenance of peace.

To this day, ignorance and indoctrination remain root causes of poverty and conflict. While there has been reluctance on the part of some governments to accept their responsibility to meet the basic education needs of all their citizens, we must continue to insist that basic education is an essential human right for all, and that it is the responsibility of governments, individually and collectively, to ensure that this right is met. If that right continues to be denied to millions of people around the world, the preferred futures cherished by the participants in this study will remain a distant dream. Moreover, it is not just any education that will do. Millions of children and adults in both developing and developed countries are provided with education that is of poor quality in terms of length and quality. A second rate education cannot be expected to develop the attributes deemed by most parents, educators and governments to be essential for effective participation society of the 21st century.

We should not forget that the Universal Declaration of Human Rights insists that the purpose of the education to be provided for all is to promote the full development of the human personality, and to promote respect for human rights, tolerance and understanding. Education aimed at the full development of the human personality, education for all without discrimination by sex, age, ethnicity or religion, remains a cornerstone in the historical struggle to lay the foundations for peace and sustainable development in the minds of men and women.

2.   MEETING BASIC NEEDS

In 1950, the estimated number of illiterates stood at about 700 million and the illiteracy rate at 45%. Sadly for most of the 20th century, the spread of literacy and expansion of primary education could not keep pace with rapid population growth, growing poverty and conflict and levels of debt in developing countries. The actual number of illiterates and children out-of-school continued to grow, as did the number of children and adults living in abject poverty and misery. About one in four persons worldwide were struggling to survive on less than $1 per day. Rates of malnutrition and infant mortality remained high, the gaps between the rich and the poor were growing at an alarming rate, and there was an explosion in debt, poverty and violence.

By 1990 (International Literacy Year), the number of children who had never been to school was in excess of 130 million, and over 900 million adults were illiterate. Recognizing that education is the key to sustainable development and peace, the UNDP, UNESCO, UNICEF and the World Bank joined forces at a landmark world conference on Education for All (EFA) in Jomtien, Thailand in 1990. The Conference was attended by 155 governments, 33 inter-governmental and 125 non-government organizations who committed themselves to ensuring that every person should benefit from educational opportunities designed to meet their basic learning needs.

EFA goals include the expansion of early childhood care and development activities, universal access to primary education by 2000, improvement in learning achievement, reduction in adult illiteracy rate to one-half of its 1990 rate with an emphasis on female literacy, expansion of provisions of basic education and training in other essential skills for youth and adults and increased acquisition by individual and families of the knowledge, skills and values required for better living and sustainable development.

The global EFA campaign involved establishing priority action for EFA at the national level, assessing needs and planning action, developing appropriate basic education policies and a supportive policy environment, improving managerial, analytic and technological capacities, mobilizing the media, building partnerships within and between nations in support of EFA and mobilizing the necessary resources. An important feature of the EFA programme was the establishment of an EFA Global Monitoring mechanism and regular national assessments and reporting of progress.

Despite all the obstacles, the EFA alliance was reasonably effective in placing educational for all and literacy on national and international policy agendas during the 1990s. As a result, many developing countries made monumental efforts to tackle their basic education problems and donors and development banks gave a much higher priority to supporting basic education programs in developing countries deemed to be 'seriously committed' to achieving their national EFA goals.

For the first time in history, the absolute number of illiterates begun to decline from its historic peak in the early 1990s and the illiteracy rate has fallen to about 18%. Today, about 3 billion adults are literate, 700 million more than in 1990. At last, the growth of literacy exceeds population growth.

But a great deal remains to be done. Even today, an estimated 113 million children never have been to school and 860 million adults are illiterate. The 2002 EFA Monitoring Report (UNESCO, 2002) reconfirmed the bleak diagnosis given at the follow-up meeting (Dakar, 2000): almost one-third of the world's population live in which will fail to achieve the EFA goals unless strong and concerted efforts are made. It is predicted that 43 countries will miss at least one key EFA target, and 28 are at serious risk of not achieving even one of the millennium development goals for education set at the 2000 UN Millennium Summit by 2015.

Moreover, the level of basic knowledge and skills one need to participate in the knowledge society of the 21st century is infinitely higher and qualitatively different from what it was in the 20th century—given the impact of information and communication technology than in the 20th century. In every society, functional illiteracy has become a major problem, marginalizing an ever larger number of youth and adults. Recent studies show that in most developed countries over 15% of adults in the workforce (OECD, 1997) and about 12% of 15 year olds (OECD, 2001) lack the minimum levels of competence needed to cope adequately with the demands of everyday life and work: they have grave difficulty with the simplest reading and quantitative tasks. Literacy levels were found to be strongly associated with economic life chances and well-being. They help determine employment stability, incidence of unemployment and income. Other studies suggest that levels of literacy in the workforce are reflected in levels of national productivity, and reveal that the social costs of failure to meet the basic educational needs of youth and obsession with privatisation are very high. In sum, about one in four children and adults worldwide lack the basic knowledge and skills needed to participate in the knowledge society of the 21st century. They are 'the prisoners of ignorance', the victims of an unjust and unequal world.

The real costs of the denial of the right of all to education are not only very high in economic and development terms, but also are serious in political and social terms. To cite one example: the Taliban was led by largely ignorant, under-educated but over-indoctrinated mullahs. Terrorism and authoritarian regimes breed on a combination or ignorance and marginalisation. Not surprisingly, faced with high levels of poverty, terrorism and violence, many families are seek an better future for their children by escaping any way they can. If rich nations continue to ignore the growing poverty and despair in poor and marginalized nations and even to abuse the rights of those living under occupation or sanctions, and of refugees, asylum seekers and prisoners-of war, we will add fuel to terrorism and violence as a way of life, and to the racism and xenophobia which lurks within our national psyche. One does not eliminate terrorism by military action or force, but by education, respect for fundamental rights and freedoms, and programs for sustainable human development.

For the individual, not being able to read, write or add is a tremendous source of individual deprivation in the modern world. When people are illiterate, their ability to understand and invoke their rights, to participate effectively in the labour market and in political life and to tackle health problems is very limited. Basic education for all is both a fundamental human right in itself, but also the key to ensuring other rights are actualised. There can be no doubt that for women and girls in particular, literacy and non-formal education programs are a source of empowerment. For all, they are a passport to learning throughout life, the foundation on which the development of higher order problems solving and critical thinking capacities rest.

3.   BARRIERS AND NECESSARY CONDITIONS

The major obstacle to achieving education for all stems from the vicious cycle of poverty, conflict and injustice in which most of the world's poorest countries and people are trapped. Conversely, the necessary conditions for achieving EFA goals include responsible leadership, strong political will, peace and stability and equitable and sustainable economic development.

There is a strong correlation between poverty and illiteracy. Countries like Afghanistan, Angola, Ethiopia, Solomon Islands, Somalia and Sierra Leone are both poor and most of their citizens are illiterate. They also tend to be unstable, both politically and economically. Yet during the late 19th and 20th century, a number of countries that were historically poor and whose citizens were poorly educated suddenly blossomed. For example, shortly after the Meiji Restoration (1868), the Japanese leadership demonstrated a strong public commitment to education, making sure that there was 'no community with an illiterate family, nor a family with an illiterate person', even though Japan was at the time still a very poor country. By 1910, Japan was almost fully literate. The strong political will and sacrifices made to provide education for all heralded Japan's remarkable history of economic development, determining to a large extent the nature and speed of its economic and social progress. Later on, particularly in the second half of the 20th century, South Korea, China, Singapore, Malaysia and other South East Asian countries followed similar routes and firmly focussed on the expansion of education for all. Stability, responsible leadership and a strong commitment to education have been the key to their development.

As the history of the struggle for nationhood and independence also demonstrates, literacy is a necessary condition for effective participation in political and community life, and for the establishment of a stable democracy. For Freire (1976) the process of learning to read and write is necessarily accompanied by the learner's increasing consciousness of his or her existential position and of the possibility of acting independently to change it, a process of empowerment. From this perspective, literacy programs have a 'political' and not merely a technical-pedagogical-economic dimension.

The assessments of progress made towards achieving EFA goals made in preparation for the World Education Forum (Dakar, 2000) confirm that the nations making greatest progress towards achieving their targets were those in which there was strong political leadership from the President/Prime Minister and government as well as at the community level, a commitment backed up by increased priority given to basic education in budget and improved policy, management and training of personnel. Countries falling behind are those that show decreases in education expenditure as a share of GDP and total public expenditure, and a reluctance to tackle measures necessary to improve internal and to ensure quality standards are maintained.

It is also clear that to be successful literacy and other basic education programmes must begin with a careful analysis of the real needs of learners and empower them with the knowledge and skills needed to survive. A good example is the Gobi Women's Project (UNESCO, 1997). With the disintegration of the former Soviet Union, Mongolia was abruptly severed from its exterior financial and technical support creating an acute economic crisis for the country's rural population. The quality life, indeed the very survival of Mongolia's nomadic people, especially girls and women, was at stake. In 1991, UNESCO and the Government of Mongolia launched a non-formal distance education programme. Little by little, the women became confident in articulating their own needs and learning agenda. Their requests were direct, down-to-earth: 'We need a booklet about processing cashmere-wool and how to do it in our present conditions. We'd like to know how to process and dye skins as well. We need to know how to market our products now that the commune has collapsed. We want to know more about the new laws, especially those on herder's rights'. By the end of the century, more than 20,000 nomadic women were taking part in education activities offered through radio, printed materials and the support of visiting teachers. Today, the programme is reaching all adults and youth in Mongolia currently unreached by the formal education system.

Of particular interest are the sub-national programmes upon which so much depends in heterogeneous countries with large populations. For example, in India, District Level Total Literacy Campaigns have resulted in rates of literacy over 80% in an increasing number of districts. This so-called 'campaign-mode' at the village level depends very much on people's participation and low costs, involves non-governments organizations and volunteers and adopts a variety of strategies. The focus on community self-help, voluntary action and a policy of literacy saturation has resulted in major gains in many districts.

Perhaps the most spectacular modern EFA transformation has taken place in China. The combination of political will, reduction in population growth (the education of girls and women is a major factor in reducing population growth, maternal deaths and infant mortality), stability and economic progress has led to a dramatic decrease in the number of illiterates and children-out-of-school. Recent programs have enabled over 200 million illiterates and semi-literates to read and write, and mean that virtually all children now complete a primary education and the majority continue on into secondary schooling. Yet, the challenges facing China are vast. The harsh realities of life in remote rural areas mean that basic education must meet community expectations and demands both urgently and precisely. Located in Manchuria, Jilin Province has suffered from its remoteness and poverty. It has had great difficulty in obtaining sufficient numbers of appropriately trained teachers to meet even the most basic learning needs of its children, and in providing primary schooling in remote locations. Jilin's Comprehensive Rural Primary Education Reform Project (UNESCO, 1998a) set out to meet the learning needs of its children, to improve the quality of schooling, to make it more meaningful to local students and their community's development, and to narrow the gap between actual education and agricultural production. The Project has been 'hugely successful, re-orienting the curriculum to local learning needs, significantly improving achievement and retention rates' and in reaching Jilin's EFA targets.

The international non-government organization, Enda Tiers Mode, based in Dakar Senegal has many EFA facets: street schools for working children, art and music shows for training marginalized youth, income generating activities for prisoners, drugs and HIV-AIDS prevention campaigns for adolescents and young adults (UNESCO, 1998b). Throughout the streets of the crowded capital, in the most deprived slums and with the people most at risk, Enda is providing non-formal basic education programs, redefining attitudes and approaches to learning, work, health and environmental preservation. Strongly attached to the ideal of 'participation' in any developmental project, Edna's teams work closely with local people in elaborating and carrying out programmes. They strongly believe that it is the young and the poor themselves, who normally have no say, who should conceive and carry out their own development strategies. For it is their knowledge and art of survival, despite the lack of resources, that hold the keys to success. Enda is now also active in other parts of Africa, Asia and Latin America. Its alternative approaches to today's world of globalisation, urban expansion, economic instability and fast demographic growth are of particular relevance to those seeking an appropriate and equitable future for the poor for developing countries.

All nations face the problem of coping with the 'new basics' as advances in science, technology and other field of knowledge transform our world, and the types and levels of knowledge and skills required for effective participation in the ever more complex and changing knowledge society world rise and themselves are transformed. OECD estimates of the levels of functional illiteracy suggest that about one in eight schools leavers and workers in developed countries are functionally illiterate. Given low birth rates and globalisation processes, developed countries must also address the literacy and other learning needs of disadvantaged groups (particularly indigenous peoples, refugees and children from dysfunctional families), and provide adequate learning opportunities for youth and adults economically and socially at risk because of their low skills. They must also met their international obligations to support basic education and literacy programmes in developing countries in their region and beyond, or face the consequences of increasing instability and violence in their 'own backyard'.

4.   CONCLUSION

The Convention on the Rights of the Child and the Universal Declaration of Human Rights give added weight to the argument developed in this chapter that meeting the basic learning needs of all children and adults is a top priority in our struggle to move towards the type of future given priority by participants in this study and espoused by world leaders at Summits and by representatives of governments in world forums.

The continuing need for conventions, declarations, monitoring and reports on action taken to achieve EFA goals and targets is 'underlined by factors in the environment that abridge basic rights or undermine their achievement.... Education for all is not only a moral obligation and a right, it is also an investment with very high potential rates of individual and social return' (UNESCO, 2000). Yet so often we find that commitments and pledges made by governments and organizations are not met, and that policies and expenditures on education have not been integrated into the heartland of national and international development plans and strategies.

Education and training need to be seen by governments and employers as investments in the development of our most precious asset, people, rather than as expenses to be trimmed. Oddly, rich and powerful nations can easily and quickly find enormous amounts of money to improve their military might and to mount so-called 'peacekeeping' operations, but they cannot find the funds to provide meet the education, health and other basic needs of all of their own citizens or to fulfil their international humanitarian obligations.

The investments in education currently being made by many governments fall well below the minimum (6% of GDP) recommended by the International Commission on Education for the 21st Century (UNESCO, 1996), and most advanced nations' commitment to Overseas Development Aid falls well below the well-established UN target (0.7% of GDP). The result is enormous and growing inequity and injustice within and among nations, growing levels of corruption, oppression, crime and violence and lost opportunities for development and participation.

We do have the resources necessary to provide a decent basic education for every child and to significantly reduce adult illiteracy. We do have the resources needed to meet many other basic human needs (eliminating many infectious diseases, providing food security, clean water, etc). Our national leaders could adopt policies and programs that contribute much more to our longer-term peace, security and development. But it will take people-power, a politically, socially and culturally enlightened electorate and an actively engaged civil society to challenge the dominant but unsustainable political and economic orthodoxy that is currently shaping our future. And the best way to empower people is to meet their basic education needs.

As the International Commission put it

The Commission does not see education as a miracle or a magic formula ... but as one of the principal means available to foster a deeper and more harmonious form of human development, and thereby to reduce poverty, exclusion, ignorance, oppression and war.

5.   REFERENCES

Freire, P. 1976. Are literacy programs neutral? In: Ballade L. (Ed.) *A Turning Point for Literacy*. Oxford: Pergamon Press.
OECD. 1997. *Literacy Skills for the Knowledge Society*. Paris: OECD.
OECD. 2001. *Knowledge and Skills for Life*. Paris: OECD.

UNESCO. 1996. Learning: the treasure within. *Report to UNESCO of the International Commission on Education for the 21st Century (Chair: J. Delors)*. Paris: UNESCO Press.

UNESCO. 1997. In the Green Desert. *No 12 Education for All Innovation Series*. Paris: UNESCO.

UNESCO. 1998a. The head of the dragon. *No 13 Education for All Innovation Series*. Paris: UNESCO.

UNESCO. 1998b. Working and inventing on the streets of Africa. *Innovations for Youth No 1*. Paris: UNESCO.

UNESCO. 2000. Education for all 2000 assessment: global synthesis.*Report for World Education Forum, Dakar*. Paris: UNESCO Press.

UNESCO. 2002. EFA global monitoring report 2002: education for all is the world on track. Paris: UNESCO.

Chapter 5

EDUCATING TO MEET DEVELOPMENTAL NEEDS

Margaret Henry

From around the world, respondents to this study have strongly endorsed the view that those who are likely to help bring about desirable futures for the planet will be people who have:

> senses of trust, 'connectedness' to others, autonomy and initiative, and are able to enter into mutually supportive relationships (Item 1, Tier 2 Rating Scale).

The basic tenet of this chapter is that the resources on which respondents have placed such high priority—that is, trust, autonomy and initiative—are built up as developmental needs are met, and, further, that it is only through the meeting of these fundamental developmental needs that we have the prospect of a desirable future—indeed any ongoing future—on this planet.

The chapter will explore this statement by discussing in turn

1. the relationship of trust, autonomy and initiative to developmental needs;
2. how humans meet developmental needs;
3. how educators help or hinder the meeting of developmental needs;
4. an educational example of the meeting of developmental needs across cultural boundaries.

1.   THE RELATIONSHIP OF TRUST, AUTONOMY AND INITIATIVE TO OUR DEVELOPMENTAL NEEDS

The high priority that participants in this study have given to trust, autonomy and initiative, indicates that we intuitively recognise how fundamental are our needs for these three internal resources.

The notion of resources should be clarified at the start. Resources are not needs. Rather, resources are what we acquire as we meet our needs. Some of these needs humans share with other species, some are particular to ourselves. All species have a fundamental need for some material resources, for example a life sustaining environment, air, food, water, shelter. But beyond the material resources, we have other fundamental needs which, when we meet them, give us essential internal resources.

The fundamental needs of a species are those whose fulfilment (at least to a reasonable degree) provides resources that lead to the long-term survival of that species, and what I shall be attempting to show in this section is that the meeting of our fundamental human needs is a developmental process, a subset of the evolutionary development of the whole range of life on earth. I see the meeting of these

81

J. Campbell et al. (eds.), Towards a Global Community, 81–93.
© 2006 *Springer. Printed in the Netherlands.*

fundamental human needs as a manifestation of the processes of evolution through natural selection. These processes of natural selection are

- − differential fit with the environment
- − variation
- − replication

(Darwin, 1859, p. 127; Dennett, 1995, p. 343).

To understand how the meeting of our fundamental needs is simply one example of the ongoing processes of natural selection (see Henry, 2004), we may consider the following sequence. First, if they are to thrive, all species, including our own, need a goodness-of-fit between themselves and their immediate environment (survival of the fit). Second, all species, including our own, need to be able, as they change or mutate or their immediate environment changes, to engage in self-initiated action, exploring/influencing in diverse ways (variation) the many properties of the options offered by their environment. Third, many species, including our own as well as mammals, birds, reptiles and fish, are able to and need to preselect the behavioural options worth repeating (replication), and here our own species moves to a different plane because of the flexibility and capacity of the human brain both to give and to get insights about the environment and to share those insights with others. As our expanded insights feed in to an enhanced goodness-of-fit with the environment, the process begins again.

The three processes of natural selection identified by Darwin: fitness, variation and replication are all clearly to be seen in the sequential aspects of human development that the developmental theorist Erik Erikson (1950) has described taking place in the first half-dozen years of a child's life. Erikson calls these aspects challenges; I am calling them fundamental human needs. Thus Erikson sees 1-year olds hard at work affirming a sense of trust or confidence, in themselves and in their world. (In terms of natural selection, babies are consolidating the *fit* between themselves and their immediate surroundings.) Next, Erikson describes toddlers attempting to 'do their own thing', to build up autonomy. (In terms of natural selection, toddlers' self-initiated action means trying out the great *variation* of possible explorations accessible as they become increasingly mobile. A challenge to parents and carers!) And in the preschool years Erikson sees a great explosion of new ideas as young children talk, begin to create, ask questions and carry these ideas through in what he calls initiative. (In terms of natural selection, it is the carrying through of these ideas–often by means of language and child–child or child–adult exchange—that constitutes the *replication* that adds to human insights.) Erikson believes that each of these phases needs to be at least substantially fulfilled if the child is to move on to the next. That is, as one internal resource is acquired it provides the means towards acquiring the next. Referring back to the previous paragraph, one sees Erikson's phases precisely mirrored in the brief account given there of human evolution, at every point emphasising the relationship between the organism and the immediate environment (i.e. between genes and experience, Magnusson and Cairns, 1996). Setting out the parallels in italics, infants building *trust*/confidence are acquiring a sense of 'goodness-of-fit between themselves and their environment'. Toddlers building *autonomy* are engaging in 'self-initiated action, exploring in diverse ways . . . the options offered by their environment'. In building *initiative* preschoolers are demonstrating the 'capacity of the human brain both to give and to get insights about the environment'.

While Erikson's theory of human development proposes that over our lifetime we all encounter five further challenges (resulting, if fulfilled, in outcomes of industry, identity, intimacy, generativity and integrity), I believe that an amendment of his theory would see his first three challenges covering the whole of the lifespan, as would their outcomes, the internal resources of trust, autonomy and initiative. Already a variety of habituation experiments (Werner and Lipsitt, 1981) have shown that babies from birth onwards are not only consolidating trust but are avidly interested (emerging autonomy) in watching, listening, tasting and smelling and can also discriminate (initiative) between different sights, sounds, tastes and odours. Turning to later age-groups, the very composition of industry, identity and so on may be conceived as a mix–in each case in varying proportions—of trust, autonomy and initiative. For example, industry in the school age child may be thought of primarily as a confluence of activity and new ideas, emerging from a bed of trust/confidence. The mutual relationships that make up intimacy may have as primary ingredients trust (in each other), confirmed by self-initiated activity (towards each other) and the exchange of ideas (with each other). At every age, as change occurs, adults may have to find, or re-find, ways of meeting their fundamental needs for the internal resources of trust, autonomy and initiative.

Thus the fulfilments of these basic human needs are developmental in two quite precise ways. First, they occur in sequence, in the order given: trust provides the feeling of ease (goodness-of-fit) which allows humans to act more freely in exploring and influencing the changing environment, exploration opens up the limitless discovery of new ideas to be found in the environment. Secondly, and in the same sequence, to every human undergoing this process, new capacities become available. The person who feels confident has a greater capacity to act. Broadening one's scope of action brings one in contact with new things to think about. Meeting these three successive fundamental and continually recurring needs enhances the totality of human functioning: feeling, action and thought.

Meeting the need for new ideas—the need that education is specifically concerned with—occurs, as we have seen, as the needs for trust and autonomy are first met, and met in that order, opening up the capacities just described. But if we, as adults, missed out when we were young on adequately meeting our needs for trust or autonomy, the developmental nature of these processes across the lifespan means that we may have more chances to meet them later on in our lives.

2. HOW DO WE MEET OUR DEVELOPMENTAL NEEDS?

In this section we explore the propositions that:
— adults continue throughout life to attempt to meet the three developmental needs for the internal resources of trust, autonomy and initiative;
— adults can help to fulfil these needs in both adults and children by exercising particular, and very ordinary, behaviours;
— adults who exercise these behaviours increase the internal resources not only of other adults and children, but of themselves.

The first of these propositions has been dealt with very briefly in the last section, and wherever we are in the world we have evidence of it every day as we (and other adults) ceaselessly try to feel comfortable or more comfortable in our situations, try to do our own thing/s and try to think of new and better ways of carrying those things through. It is when we even moderately fulfil these needs that we are in a position to help others to do the same.

Chief among those who purposefully set out to do this with young children are parents and other early childhood educators. When Robert Hess in 1969 and 1971 looked at the US studies up to that time which linked parental behaviours in the very early years with children's emotional, social and intellectual performance in the first years of school, he identified ten adult behaviours which continue to emerge in subsequent Western studies of facilitative adult–child (not just parent–child) interactions (Amato, 1987; Ochiltree and Edgar, 1995; Pierrehumbert et al., 2002; Schaefer, 1981). In assessing positive child outcomes, raters in the Hess studies referred to children's happiness, ability to act/interact and to operate intellectually at potential—three sets of characteristics that reflect the reasonable fulfilment of the developmental needs discussed earlier, and the acquisition of the internal resources of trust, autonomy and initiative.

In my own work with parents, adult student teachers and child care providers (Henry, 1996), the 10 adult–child behaviours identified by Hess (1969, 1971) have proved equally effective in adult–adult interaction. A later section of this chapter will provide some substantiation.

In Table 5.1 below, I set out the 10 behaviours identified by Hess (but in a different order from his) within three behavioural dimensions that summarise our connections with one another through feeling, acting and thinking. I call these three dimensions responsiveness, control and involvement. Table 5.1 also includes the internal resources, trust, autonomy and initiative, that result when these behaviours are exercised at the positive poles of the dimensions.

Table 5.1 shows how ordinary human beings can—and do—put the principles of natural selection into action. Note, in particular, that the table shows the promotion of trust, autonomy and initiative occurring developmentally, that is, in sequence. Promoting—and enabling—trust allows the promotion of autonomy allows the promotion of initiative. As suggested in Section 1, this sequence is a subset of the working of the processes of natural selection among human beings in general, where the establishment of goodness-of-fit with the environment leads us to be able to explore and

Table 5.1: How do adults help children and one another to meet developmental needs?

We adults can:
Promote trust in children and in adults through our *responsiveness*, by
    relating warmly to them
    expressing a high regard for them
    being attentive to and engaged with them
Promote autonomy in children and in adults through our *control* methods, by
    encouraging their independence
    explaining *why* some things have to be done
    being as consistent as we can
Promote initiative in children and in adults through our *involvement*, by
    encouraging them to achieve
    talking *with* rather than *to* them
    engaging in 'by the way' teaching
    having interesting resources around for them

thence to consider the new ideas made available by that exploration. Observations of very young children (Henry, 2004) make this developmental sequence readily apparent:

> In young children one may see the sequence proceeding as one need after another is met. Babies who have had their trust needs reasonably met, so they do not feel threatened by scarcity of emotional resources (Crittenden, 1985), grow into toddlers who are able to extend some of their resources to their peers. An example was the 18-month old girl I saw, with a piece of cake in each hand, offering one piece to a fellow toddler. Very often, though, as physical powers increase, the need for autonomy—to do one's own thing—produces struggles over ownership of objects. Although these struggles are uncomfortable for all concerned, they are an important part of exploring the properties of the world:
>
> 'Rather than being a sign of selfishness, early struggles over objects are a sign of developing selfhood, an effort to clarify boundaries between self and other...The ability to distinguish self from other also permits young children to learn how to resolve disputes and share (Berk, 1998, p. 425)'.
>
> Once toddlers learn (from the feedback—new ideas—they receive from others) what belongs to them, they can know what belongs to someone else. Empathy and cooperation—sociable independence—become possible. Shared feedback, among children and adults, about rights and responsibilities, is thus an essential factor in 'the creation of a more equitable society' (Lubeck, 1996, p. 159).
>
> Collaboration, then, can be seen not as a practice that can be taught in itself, but as the culmination of the meeting, to a reasonable degree, of the three fundamental needs: for trust, for autonomy and for initiative (Henry, 2004, p. 307).

A similar sequence applies among adults (as will be shown in an example at the end of this chapter). Participants in this study seem to have understood this, in endorsing Item 1 Tier 2. We agreed with Campbell, who framed the item that global citizens will have:

> senses of trust, 'connectedness' to others, autonomy and initiative, and [be] able to enter into mutually supportive relationships (Item 1 Tier 2 Rating Scale).

Why, in this item, are 'trust, autonomy and initiative' bracketed with 'mutually supportive relationships'?

Because they are bracketed in life. When two or more adults engage in two-way (mutually supportive) relationships by applying the behaviours listed in Table 5.1 towards each other, the processes of natural selection come into play as

— each adult exercises responsiveness towards the other/s, leading to an increase in trust (goodness-of-fit) for all;

-    each adult exerts some input or control over the diversity of opportunities (variation) offered by the situation, creating mutual control—that is, the greatest degree of autonomy compatible with the autonomy of others;
-    each adult practises involvement with the other/s in terms of talking and thinking, leading to the enhancement of initiative and further replication of ideas.

These are the processes of democracy. Just as interdependence and collaboration are the outcomes of meeting the fundamental human needs of an adult/child or an adult/adult dyad, so a major outcome of fulfilling the fundamental needs of large numbers of people around the globe is participatory democracy.

In a democracy, the interchange of ideas with members of other social groups, essential if inclusive decisions are to be made and the society held together, is ultimately dependent on citizens' feeling of goodness-of-fit, of being reasonably at ease within the larger society. Behm (2003, p 63) has drawn attention to the absence of this *fit* within societies that produce terrorism, societies whose philosophy has been described by a spokesperson: 'Between you and us there will be forever a ravine of hate' (Four Corners, 2002). Behm writes:

> The fact is that Islamic terrorist groups do not simply express ideological hatred of the US and 'Western values', but rather reflect the massive social, political and economic discontinuities that engender alienation and hopelessness—particularly among youth . . . Show the alienated groups that there is more to life than martyrdom.

Economist Thurow (1996, p. 276) also draws out the wider political implications of fit, calling for 'an understanding that free markets require a supportive physical, social, mental, educational and organisational infrastructure. More important, they require some form of social glue if individuals are not to be constantly battling each other'. That social glue is a sense of trust.

When people are able to move on from achieving some sense of trust to exploring *variation*, meeting their second need, the need for autonomy—doing what they want socially and politically, consistent with other people being able to do what *they* want— this is a brief definition of democracy, as well as of freedom and justice. As Amartya Sen (2000) notes, famines do not occur in a democracy. Combined action through the ballot box lays a powerful base for equality.

Societies in which people of whatever kind or occupation are encouraged, rather than stifled, in attempting to meet the third need, the need to pursue ideas, are in fact democracies. The specifically human need (because of our brain potential) to exchange new ideas with one another and *replicate* them through language, through published experiment, through discussion, means that we do not have to kill ourselves trying out options that the environment will not reinforce. Satisfying the need to exchange ideas with others, as Karl Popper remarked (in Dennett, 1995, p. 375), 'permits our hypotheses to die in our stead'. Democracies will continue to benefit from such exchange, since, as noted earlier, 'expanded insights feed in to an enhanced goodness-of-fit with the environment, and the process begins again'.

It is as, and only as, this developmental sequence occurs on a widespread scale—trust engendering autonomy empowering initiative—that our global future as a species will be assured. For the outcomes of not meeting our developmental needs also extend throughout communities and globally: child and adult abuse of many kinds, for example bullying, exploitation, vindictiveness, cheating, crime, cruelty of various kinds, terrorism. Such behaviours are carried out by people who, instead of trust, exercise mistrust; instead of autonomy, aggression; instead of the exploration of new ideas, the imposition of ideas. In the long run, if too widespread, such behaviours threaten the survival of the species.

3.   HOW DO EDUCATORS HELP TO MEET OUR DEVELOPMENTAL NEEDS?

Often they don't. As noted at the end of the first section, 'Meeting the need for new ideas—the need that education is specifically concerned with—occurs as the needs for trust and autonomy are first met, and met in that order'. Because this developmental sequence is not as yet widely recognised in society, it is frequently not recognised in education. Educators often see initiative as the first, rather than the culminating, outcome to be achieved. Hill (2001, p. 76), for example writing of education for moral responsibility, calls for approaches to the learner which:

> carry the individual from the mere getting of knowledge to the achievement of critical autonomy, and from this to a critical loyalty to humane personal and communal values.

Observation and this chapter suggest, however, that the reverse process is what actually happens in life: that how one *feels* about oneself and other people (one's 'personal and communal values') determines the degree or otherwise of self-initiated *action* of which one is capable ('achievement of critical autonomy') and that such autonomous exploration in turn influences one's approach to *thinking* and the 'getting of knowledge', leading to an enhanced *feeling* of goodness-of-fit, and so on and on.

Where educators ignore trust and autonomy and go all out for initiative, they fail to help students to meet their first two fundamental needs. So children continue to sit in their seats attempting to absorb and regurgitate information. If educators in their own lives have built and drawn on trust and autonomy and allow these internal resources an opportunity to operate among their students, the learners can do well. Otherwise their learning (and future achievements, jobs, success in life) may well suffer. And the societies which encompass them will also suffer as the bases on which the accomplishment of great initiatives must rest are ignored or down-played and the initiatives remain pipe-dreams.

We see an example of this in our own study where, in the responses respondents have made in both Tiers 1 and 2, the internal resource of autonomy has been down-played. As noted earlier in the chapter, its importance was acknowledged in the Item 1 Tier 2 ratings, and thereafter many respondents largely ignored it. Looking back in Chapters 2 and 3 at the ratings that have been given, first, to 'highly desirable' world features, and, second, to the attributes necessary to achieve these, it can be seen that high priorities have been given to

- connectedness/mutual relationships and to a variety of other sensitivities, attitudes and values that reflect *feelings* of goodness-of-fit (trust);

– desirable *ideas* to be carried through (initiative), e.g. sustainablity of planet earth, diversity, supra-national entities, social justice.

But given these sensitive feelings, how would we *act* to bring about the ideas they stimulate? In our ratings, low priority has been given in Tier 1 to Participatory Democracy, and in Tier 2 to Action Competencies. As Campbell Baikaloff and Power (Chapter 3, p. 66) have has noted, 'it could be argued that each of the sensitivities, attitudes and values, too, has limited significance until translated into actions'. In neither Tier have respondents emphasised how feelings would be 'translated into actions' (autonomy) which might lead to the carrying through of new ideas.

Perhaps we should not be surprised at this result. In countries where participatory democracy exists, it is often taken for granted, with widespread ignorance of the immense struggle to get it. In places where it does not exist, there is no model to demonstrate its benefits. In either case, respondents have failed to rate its benefits highly. We ignore the means, but want the ends, sustainability of planet earth, social justice and so on.

In the last section of this chapter, I shall be retelling a true story, one of hundreds my students, internal and external, have told me in their teacher education course (Henry, 2000). In one course ('Working with Parents and Community') in one semester, the task of the students has been to practise collaborating with families and to evaluate that collaboration. So this is a story about how we can translate the kindly feelings many of us undoubtedly have towards one another into a situation that can continue because it can be replicated. In particular, this story is about that educationally down-played factor of autonomy, and about what happens when adults engaged in care and education exert *mutual* control over the diverse opportunities in our environment. The story models, on a local scale, some principles that can serve universally in educating global citizens.

4.   MEETING DEVELOPMENTAL NEEDS ACROSS CULTURAL BOUNDARIES

Jean Carden, the senior author of 'Across cultural boundaries in child care' (Carden and Henry, 1996) was group leader of the preschool group in a Brisbane child care centre where more than a third of the families using the centre were Mandarin speakers from China, Taiwan or Hong Kong. The remaining two-thirds were local Australians. The children in the Mandarin speaking and English speaking groups kept very much to themselves, the Mandarin speaking children participating very little in any of the activities going on in the centre.

Distressed by the lack of understanding or common activity among the children, Jean wondered what could be done. She decided to seek the views of the adults involved with the children: the parents and her own colleagues. A letter sent home to parents (translated for the Mandarin speakers by a visiting member of the Ethnic Childcare Development Unit) asked questions such as: What should our centre's goals be for your children? Would you like your child to mix with children from other countries at our Centre? How important do you think childhood is? The ECDU worker then translated the responses for Jean.

With her colleagues Jean held informal discussions, asking how they felt about the Mandarin speaking families.

Though only just over a quarter of both the Mandarin speaking and the Australian families responded to the letter they were sent, Jean took their comments seriously. She was impressed at how similar the two sets of comments were. All the respondents, from both cultures, said they wanted the centre to provide care and stimulation for the children. All wished their children to play with *all* children at the centre and to learn from their varied backgrounds. All complimented the centre staff on their courtesy and their professionalism. An Australian parent said how important it was to know the children were cared for safely while parents were working. A Mandarin speaker said that the care provided by the staff was like the fertilizer and water that would help to turn a young plant into a fine tree.

In her conversations with her colleagues, Jean at first received very different messages. While staff members sympathised with the difficulties newcomers must have in a country where they do not speak the language, and while they valued the visits of the ECDU worker who gave the Mandarin speaking parents some explanation of life in the centre, the staff also revealed that they felt resentment towards these parents. They felt that the newcomers were treating them as low-status babysitters.

When Jean read out to the staff the translated responses of the Mandarin speaking parents, resentment changed to enthusiasm. Staff realised that inability to communicate must have led to misunderstandings. They were not regarded as low-status babysitters! They were courteous professionals! They began to plan ways of making the newcomers, both children and parents, feel more at home.

Over the next weeks, these ways included the retaining, part-time, of a second ECDU worker who enabled much more communication between staff members and Mandarin speaking parents. The latter began to stay a little longer in the afternoons, watching their children play and (through the ECDU worker) starting to exchange remarks with Australian parents at drop-off and pick-up time. The Mandarin speakers responded to a request for materials from their own culture. In home corner Mandarin speaking and Australian children began to dress up in Chinese silks and 'eat' with rice bowls and chop sticks. In the library area, the ECDU worker and children from both cultures began to share illustrated story books in Mandarin as well as English. Taped Australian and Mandarin songs were played in free play periods, and Australian children attempted to join in the songs sung by the Mandarin speakers and the ECDU helper. In their increasing play together, it was noted that the older Mandarin speaking girls were playing 'mother' in a gentle, serious way to younger children in contrast with the Australian children's more rough and tumble games, but along with these continuing differences, Jean recorded that the English speaking children were giving more attention and respect to the Mandarin speaking children.

If we look back to Table 5.1 in which adult behaviours are set out that have been found to help children to meet their developmental needs, we can see examples of all these behaviours in the short description above of the changes that occurred in the centre. In the discussion below, the Hess behaviours are numbered in the order of their appearance in Table 5.1.

All the adults, beginning with the group leader, helped to promote *trust*, not only in the children who lacked it, the Mandarin speakers, but also in the Australian children for whom apparent cuckoos had appeared in their nest. All the respondents to Jean's letter demonstrated underlying warmth (1) and regard (2) for the children in wishing them to mix with one another and learn from one another. What Jean saw above all was that if warm relationships and high regard were to be demonstrated, this could only be done by improving communication—in this case through translation, enabling attentiveness and engagement (3). She enlisted the aid of not one but two ethnic helpers/translators who could help children (and adults) to understand each other. For the newcomers a feeling of goodness-of-fit, was affirmed, too, through the appearance in the centre of materials, books and music with which they were familiar. And because the reactions of significant others are important in influencing our emotions (social referencing, Berk, 1998), all the children must have felt more comfortable as they began to see their parents at pick-up time communicating with the parents of the other culture.

As the adults laid the conditions for the children to feel more trust, they were then able to help the children to build their *autonomy*. Staff members encouraged the children to begin forming new relationships with one another (4) while, at the same time, they ensured by words as well as actions (5) the preservation of the children's somewhat differing patterns of play. Staff tried to be consistent in these approaches (6). The upshot, the group leader noted, was a change in the children's behaviour towards greater attention and respect for one another.

The upshot of these staff behaviours was a dramatic increase in the children's *initiative* or ability to handle new ideas. The centre's greatly enriched setting was a beacon that invited them to cross the cultural divide. This crossing was itself an achievement (7), triggered by the translations of the Ethnic Child Development Unit helpers. Their conversation (8) and information (9), modelled by the other staff members, empowered the children to embark together on making new connections through storybooks, unusual dress-up clothes, cooking utensils and music shared by the two cultures (10).

Just as we can remember occasional happenings in our own early lives that have made lasting positive differences in the way we continue to think (in other words educative happenings), so such educative happenings can occur for children from their earliest moments in schools or child care. As in this example, it is when adults in these settings use behaviours that affirm trust sparking an increase in exploration leading to an expansion of ideas that children are helped to meet their fundamental developmental needs.

But none of this would have occurred for the children in this centre, but for the operation of precisely *the same behaviours among the adults towards one another*. Not only between the children but between the adults was there a chasm at the beginning of the story. Two chasms, indeed, one between staff and Mandarin speaking parents, the other between these parents and Australian parents. At the point where we leave the parents and staff, all these groups had established mutually supportive relationships and had enhanced their internal resources of trust, autonomy and initiative (Item 1, Tier 2), as one final episode from the story will make clear.

For the Australian children, a favourite place to play was the sandpit, magnet for learning through digging, channelling, hosing, filling, emptying, building, planning, talking while tea–partying with water, sand and utensils. The Mandarin speaking children had always kept away from the sandpit, despite the staff's attempts to introduce them to it. As the Mandarin speaking parents began to feel at ease in the centre, they would often sit for a few minutes on the side of the sandpit in the afternoons, conversing through the ECDU helpers with other parents and staff. There they revealed that they were distressed at the removal of their children's shoes and socks, a cultural difference accounting for their children's aversion to the sandpit. As the parents watched, the staff were able to point out to them how much fun and learning there was to be had in the sandpit, but that it was not possible in shoes and socks. Could the staff help the children to remove these and then replace them when they left the sandpit? The parents happily agreed, the staff's knowledge and flexibility were advanced and the children joined the group with pleasure. A win all round.

In this episode we see all the Hess behaviours (Table 5.1) occurring between the adults at the positive poles of the dimensions of responsiveness, control and involvement. *Responsiveness* had already been established, beginning with the *goodness-of-fit* affirmed by the positive feelings expressed in Jean's letter to the parents. The warmth (1) and regard (2) which the Mandarin speaking parents had demonstrated for the staff, and which had been reciprocated by the 'courteous professionals', had led to an increase in engagement/attentiveness (3), as we see in this episode as the adults, confirming their *trust* in one another, sat together round the sandpit. Here all these adults exercised *mutual control* of the issue which concerned the staff members: how the Mandarin speaking children could come to enjoy the sandpit. All embarked on self-initiated (*autonomous*) communication with one another. While educational staff often see it as their role to tell parents what they should do, in this instance staff members consistently (6) listened to the Mandarin speakers' independent (4) and culturally different voice concerning shoes and socks, while simultaneously offering the parents a perspective (5) on the learning they could see before their eyes that was taking place in the sandpit. From this mutual exploration of the *variety* of opportunities offered by the situation, a further *involvement* of parents and staff took place as a choice was achieved (7) that satisfied all parties—removal and later replacement of socks and shoes. All the adults extended their *initiative*, gaining new ideas from one another by exchanging views (8), passing on information (9) about cultural differences on the one hand and learning opportunities on the other, the solution allowing full use of the stimulating resources offered by the sandpit (10). Adults from both cultures could take all these ideas further, *replicating* them as they interacted at home and in the centre.

5.   CONCLUSION

What we are seeing in this story is democracy in educational action. The behaviours between adults and children and between adults and adults that we have identified in Jean's child-care centre are the two-way behaviours that characterise a democracy.

Moreover, when these behaviours are enacted among adults, at the positive poles of the dimensions of responsiveness, mutual control and involvement (Table 5.1), they are examples of the principles of natural selection identified by Darwin (1859, p. 127) and discussed in Section 1: goodness of fit, variation and replication. Responsiveness leading to trust is an example of goodness of fit. Mutual control leading to autonomy in action by several people is an example of the exploration of variation (in this story multicultural variation). And involvement among adults leading to initiative is an example of the passing on or replication of workable ideas, which allow the process to begin again. It is through the operation of these dimensions that our species evolves.

The second facet of the process of natural selection identified by Darwin is the interaction of the organism with its *immediate* environment. Not a universal environment, for, as Gould (1996, p. 139) has put it: 'Natural selection can only produce adaptation to immediately surrounding (and changing) environments'. Similarly, Bronfenbrenner (1994, p. 62) defines human development as what 'takes place through processes of progressively more complex, reciprocal interactions between a child (or human being of any age) and the persons, objects and symbols in its immediate environment'. In Jean's child-care centre, Jean and the children's immediate environment included all the adults with whom they were closely associated. These were the people with whom they took part in 'progressively more complex, reciprocal interactions', with the results we have seen. When educators become aware that parents, along with children, are part of their immediate environment and begin to interact with them as Jean did in her centre, working together, even briefly, on aims, methods and evaluation of projects concerning children's developmental needs, a transformation will occur in education, as we adults as well as children increase our own internal resources of trust, autonomy and initiative, helping to meet our own fundamental needs.

In this study, respondents have given a range of responses in the ratings. Some have set store by all three of our fundamental needs related to feeling, action and thought. Many others, however, have emphasised positive feelings and then moved directly to implementation of ideas, with little suggestion of intervening participatory action to try out what we are exploring. I believe such a sequence will not work in the real world where all three fundamental needs are of essential significance, and where only if all three are at least moderately fulfilled through reciprocal relationships will our species continue to exist. Acting as colonisers, imposing one-way directives, will ultimately destroy our species. We need a plan of action, one that is uplifting, but which also works on an everyday level to meet our developmental needs and provide resources that can bring about a global community.

The model set out in Table 5.1, based on the widespread observations of human groups underlying Hess's studies, is such a plan for action. It is ordinary because it works. It is also uplifting, and will become more widespread as it is reinforced. A student of mine, a practitioner, gave a copy of the model to the parents of the children in her class. One of them said to her: 'I've put that model up on the wall in my kitchen. Every night before I go to bed I say to myself, I've done all those things today. I wish somebody would compliment me sometime, but they never do'. The teacher told me she began to look at this mother and learn from her behaviour with her child. She also complimented her.

We could all put the model up on our wall. Parents, educators, community members, as we interact with one another we are all practitioners.

6.   REFERENCES

Amato, P. 1987. *Children in Australian Families: The Growth of Competence*. Sydney: Prentice-Hall.
Behm, A. 2003. Softly, softly fight the terrorists. *Australian Financial Review 20*, 63.
Berk, L. 1998. *Child Development* (4th ed.). Boston: Allyn & Bacon.

Bronfenbrenner, U. 1994. A new head start for Head Start. *New Horizons in Education, 91*, 57–70.

Carden, J. and Henry, M.B. 1996. Across cultural boundaries in child care. *Educating Young Children* 2(1): 11–13.

Crittenden, P.M. 1985. Social networks, quality of childrearing, and child development. *Child Development 56*, 1299–1313.

Darwin, C. 1859. *The Origin of Species by Means of Natural Selection*. London: Murray.

Dennett, D.C. 1995. *Darwin's Dangerous Idea: Evolution and the Meanings of Life*. London: Allen Lane, The Penguin Press.

Erikson, E.H. 1950. *Childhood and Society*. New York: Norton.

Four Corners, Australian Broadcasting Corporation, 28 November 2002.

Gould, S.J. 1996. *Life's Grandeur: The Spread of Excellence from Plato to Darwin*. London: Jonathon Cape.

Henry, M.B. 1996. *Young Children, Parents and Professionals: Enhancing the Links in Early Childhood*. London: Routledge.

Henry, M.B. 2000. Open doors, open minds: working with families and community. In Yelland N.J. (Ed.) *Promoting Meaningful Learning: Innovations in Educating Early Childhood Professionals*. Washington DC: National Association for the Education of Young Children, pp. 105–116.

Henry, M.B. 2004. Developmental needs and early childhood education: evolutionary, my dear Watson. *Early Child Development and Care*, 307.

Hess, R.D. 1969. Parental behavior and children's school achievement: implications for head start. In Grotberg E. (Ed.) *Critical Issues in Research Relating to Disadvantaged Children*. Princeton, NJ: Educational Testing Service.

Hess, R.D. 1971. Community involvement in day care. *Day Care: Resources for Decisions*. Washington, DC: US Office of Economic Opportunity.

Hill, B.V. 2001. Educating for moral responsibility. In Campbell J. (Ed.) *Creating Our Common Future: Educating for Unity in Diversity*. New York: UNESCO Publishing/Berghahn Books.

Lubeck, S. 1996. Deconstructing 'child development knowledge' and 'teacher preparation'. *Early Childhood Research Quarterly 11*, 147–167.

Magnusson, D. and Cairns, R.B. 1996. Developmental science: toward a unified framework. In Cairns R.B., Elder G.H. and Costello E.J. (Eds.) *Developmental Science*. Cambridge: Cambridge University Press.

Ochiltree, G. and Edgar, D. 1995. *Today's Child Care, Tomorrow's Children*. Melbourne: Australian Institute of Family Studies.

Pierrehumbert, B., Ramstein, T., Karmaniola, A., Miljkovitch, R., and Halfon, O. 2002. Quality of child care in the preschool years: a comparison of the influence of home care and day care characteristics on child outcome. *International Journal of Behavioral Development 26*(5), 385–396.

Schaefer, E.S. 1981. Development of adaptive behavior: conceptual models and family correlates. In Begab M., Garber H., and Haywood H.C. (Eds.) *Prevention of Retarded Development in Psychosocially Disadvantaged Children*. Baltimore: University Park Press.

Sen, A. 2000. A system that works best for all. *The Australian*, 10 January 2000.

Thurow, L. 1996. *The Future of Capitalism*. New York: Allen & Unwin.

Werner, J.S. and Lipsitt, L.P. 1981. The infancy of human sensory systems. In Gollin E. (Ed.), *Developmental Plasticity: Behavioural and Biological Aspects of Variations in Development*. New York: Academic Press.

Chapter 6

INTRODUCING 'THE RIGHT TO FOOD AND A SUSTAINABLE ENVIRONMENT' INTO A CURRICULUM

Abraham Blum

1. THE GLOBAL ASPECT

The basic human right to clean air, water, food and shelter is one of the most fundamental global issues. These necessities are not evenly distributed over the earth. While air pollution is primarily an outcome of unsustained industrialised development in the North, lack of sustenance and malnutrition is the curse of so many in the South, above all in Africa. Yet, there is no division of problems according to region. Burning of large areas of rain forest has brought serious air pollution also to countries in the South. After fires were deliberately set—for profit—to large areas of rainforest in Indonesia and Malaysia and raged out of control, huge clouds of smoke and haze choked many parts of Indonesia and Malaysia, South Thailand and even the Philippines, 1000 miles away.

On the other hand, the poverty and hunger problems in Africa, caused by a combination of environmental and social factors, are much affected by a colonial past and an ongoing problematic agrarian policy in the industrialised countries of the North. Thirty percent of the population suffer from undernourishment. According to the World Food Report, every 7 seconds, a child under 10 years dies, and every 4 minutes, someone looses eyesight, due to vitamin A deficiency. Thus, both these menaces to basic human rights—the hunger problem and air pollution—(and many others) should be seen in a global aspect and taught accordingly.

2. ENVIRONMENTAL EDUCATION (EE) AND EDUCATION FOR SUSTAINABLE DEVELOPMENT (ESD)

Environmental education is part of education towards a global community. *Environmental* Education grew out of the *Conservation* Education movement, lead by national park wardens, rangers and nature protection organisations. In Britain, the approach was wider, from the beginning. It included besides nature conservation also the conservation of the cultural heritage—the countryside and historical sites. It was at the 'Keele Conference on Education and the Countryside' of 1965 that the term *environmental education* was used for the first time. A Council for Environmental Education was set up as a platform, on which many disciplines and protagonists of particular points of view could meet.

J. Campbell et al. (eds.), Towards a Global Community, 95–107.

Rachel Carson's (1962) 'Silent Spring' was a real shocker. She dramatically showed what could happen, if Man's intervention in nature would remain uncontrolled. Her book triggered a heated debate in the press and in the US Congress. Educators and especially science teachers started to include environmental issues like the use of pesticides, the damage caused by pollutions and the like into their curriculum. Now it was no longer a question of nature conservation alone, but one of fighting against damages caused by humans to the global environment, at a scale never experienced in history. The issue became political, also among educational policy makers. The first Environmental Education Act was enacted in the USA in 1970, and other countries followed.

While the EE movement gained momentum, also many conservation educators joined in, including those who emphasised mainly the love of unspoiled nature. While the latter concentrated on environmental awareness and appreciation, the others gave first priority to cognitive objectives like understanding the technological problems connected with the pollutions and acquiring the skills to counteract the negative developments.

The International Union for the Conservation of Nature and Natural Resources (IUCN), the protagonist of conservation education, called in 1970 a conference on environmental education, which was held in Nevada. It ended with a remarkable definition of *environmental education*:

> Environmental education is the process of recognizing values and clarifying concepts, in order to develop skills and attitudes necessary to understand and appreciate the inter-relatedness among man, his culture and his biophysical surroundings. Environmental education also entails practice in decision-making and self-formulating of a code of behaviour about issues concerning environmental quality. (IUCN, 1970)

Especially after the Brundtland Report on Environment and Development (Our Common Future, 1988), in which for the first time the term '*Sustainable Development*' was used, the insight grew that the global problems were not restricted to conflicts between nature and economy, but also between the industrialised North and the disadvantaged South. The emphasis shifted from trying to repair specific damages, to the notion that suitable development planning was needed, in order to prevent as much as possible a repetition of the mistakes made in the past. This planned development must be sustainable from both the ecological, as well as from the socio-economic and cultural points of view. It must include, in addition to the ecological care for planet Earth, also the struggle for more equity, social justice, democracy and respect for different views, beliefs and ways of life. For EE, this meant focusing on the meaning of these concepts and add them to the already existing objectives. It became necessary to enable and empower future citizens to become competent in the skills necessary to insure a really sustainable development.

Thus, many EE groups adopted the new concept of Sustainable Development Education or *Education for a Sustainable Environment* (ESD). Some suggested the even more holistic term *Sustainable Education*. While *Agenda 21*, as adopted at the UN Conference on Environment and Development (1992) in Rio speaks generally about 'changing values and lifestyles (consumption, production, etc)', the Alternative

Treaty on Environmental Education, agreed by the parallel NGO Global Forum, proposes a 'holistic, systemic vision'. The alternatives in Rio demanded 'the abolition of development, structural adjustment and economic reform programs, which maintain the current growth model with its disastrous impact on the environment'. To some environmental educators any form of further development is *a priori* unsustainable.

As often when an idea becomes fashionable, also opponents decide to follow the rule 'join them, if you cannot beat them'. Thus, multinationals and industrialists who exploit cheap labour and destroy non-renewable resources have jumped on the bandwagon of sustainable development. This must not deter those who really believe that sustainable development is possible and necessary, to leave the field to impostors.

The efforts of some EE theorists to debate, if EE is part of ESD or if it is the other way round, are not really productive. Practitioners are more concerned about what they can achieve, balancing their own rationale with the readiness or reluctance of their community to change. Therefore, I shall use in this chapter the shorter term *environmental education*, as still the most common one, but include under environment the issues of sustainable development on a global basis. For environmental education in formal school systems, especially when these are geared to final examinations, I shall call *Environmental Studies.*

Before reviewing what we have learned from the implementation of some exemplary environmental education curriculum modules, I want to discuss the different options a nationally directed school system has, when it wants to introduce environmental education (or any other new subject) into its schools. Of course, much of environmental education occurs outside the formal school system, mainly what Lucas (1973) has typified as education '*in* the environment', while education '*about* the environment' is typical for what was done in many science classes. The new EE curricula strive for the highest degree in Lucas' taxonomy, namely education '*for* the environment'.

3.   HOW TO INTRODUCE ENVIRONMENTAL STUDIES INTO THE CURRICULUM

There are four major strategies how to introduce a new subject into formal school curricula. These are, in the case of Environmental Studies

1. Infusing Environmental Studies elements into a number of existing subjects.
2. Inserting Environmental Studies as a new subject into the school curriculum.
3. Changing an obsolete subject to become Environmental Studies.
4. Inserting Environmental Studies as constituents into a new subject area.

The main problem in curriculum change is overcrowding. Usually, more new chapters are added than old ones discarded. Furthermore, school systems tend to be resistant to major curriculum changes. Still, as conditions change and new opportunities arise, one or another of these four approaches can be used, while others become unfeasible. Much depends on the situation existing at the time of decision making, the readiness of the system to change, the educational level, at which environmental education (or another value based subject with global aspects) is to be integrated into the curriculum and if the new subject will be compulsory or an elective.

When trying to introduce EE into the curriculum of a school system, one of the first questions is: Should environmental education be integrated into all school subjects or treated as a separate area of competence and skills, which deserve a specific and fixed slot in the curriculum? In the first case, students learn that environmental quality is not just another topic that has to be mastered as part of a certain school subject, but something that always pops up again and has many aspects and implications. On the other hand, especially at a higher level of education, there is a need to bring the scattered and diffuse elements together, to foster a coherent body of knowledge, application, action and dedication.

Scattering environmental education over many subject areas is easier at a lower level of education, where the curriculum is not yet divided up into many subjects and most of them are taught by one teacher, or only a few. Thus, coordination is easier than in high schools. At the elementary level, dedicated teachers can handle the knowledge needed easier than at upper secondary (senior high school) level. There, students prepare themselves for a professional or vocational career that involves the need for deeper understanding of environmental problems. For this, a specialised teacher is needed.

3.1.   Environmental Studies in the Light of the Israeli School Reform

In the following sections, examples will show how the different strategies to introduce environmental education into a national curriculum were used in the case of the Israeli school system, with varying degrees of success. To understand these developments, one must see them against the background of the school and curriculum reform, which triggered among others also the introduction of environmental education. Although the reform was enacted in 1965, its implementation took some decades. The basic idea behind the school reform was to take the last 2 years from the 8-year elementary school and to form, together with 9th grade, a 3-year junior high school, followed by a 3-year senior high school. The double purpose of this reform was (1) to upgrade the academic level of the new junior high school, where only university graduates should teach, and (2) to bring students from different neighbourhood elementary schools (and therefore from different socio-economic levels) socially together, at least during three crucial years of adolescence, before they divide off again, according to further study trends and abilities.

In 1965, the Ministry of Education sent a team of eight experienced teachers from different disciplines to a special 1-year long training programme in curriculum development and evaluation, with the goal to set up, after their return, a national curriculum centre. Although at that time the new subject matter curricula in the natural and social sciences were developed in other centres, the delegation studied as a group at the University of Chicago, The idea was that the overall educational rationale to be developed should be above pure subject matter considerations. The first assignment to the group was to develop a set of overall educational goals, which then should be translated into coordinated, disciplinary objectives and corresponding learning activities, much in the line of Tyler's (1949) and Schwab's (1973) ideas.

This happened only partially. In reality, the educational establishment remained rather conservative. Subject matter inspectors and the respective university professors, who had a strong influence on matriculation exams, prevented some of the planned changes in the basic curriculum, which among others, had foreseen a joint science and technology curriculum, with an emphasis on environmental, social and cultural issues. This was too much of a change, in the 1970s, a time, in which also in other countries the move towards 'integrated science' was not very successful in secondary school systems leading up to matriculation exams.

3.2. Infusing Environmental Studies into a Number of Existing Subjects

An interdisciplinary team of curriculum experts and experienced teachers was set up to review all relevant subject curricula for elementary and junior high schools, in order to detect opportunities, where teachers could insert environmental education activities. Quite a number of environmental topics were found in the syllabi of History and Nature Studies in elementary schools, and Geography and Science in junior high schools. These topics were listed in a booklet, together with ideas what teachers could do to further environmental education. The booklets, which were sent to all schools, contained also suggestions how to organise the whole school as an environmental centre for their neighbourhood.

Although no data were collected, the general opinion is that schools and teachers, who had already earlier been involved in environmental activities, felt strengthened, but most teachers continued to adhere to the syllabus as it was, and followed the more or less regulated students texts, with which they were most familiar. Some excellent exceptions confirmed the rule, but as a whole, this attempt, which was not accompanied by in-service training of teachers and principals, did not bring the hoped for breakthrough for EE.

3.3. Inserting Environmental Studies as a New Subject into the Curriculum

Like in many other countries, the senior secondary school curriculum in Israel is under the heavy pressure of the matriculation examinations, which sum up the high school achievements after grade 12. Introducing a new subject into the overcrowded timetable is quite difficult. During a discussion in the Pedagogical Secretariat, the highest educational forum in the Ministry of Education, all its members were 'basically in favour of introducing environmental education into senior high schools', but the final decision was to offer only an elective course in grades 10–12.

The Environmental Studies syllabus was the first (and so far the last, in Israel) that was based on a research of what prospective students know and believe about environmental issues (Blum, 1984). A representative sample of over 2000 9th grade students answered a questionnaire on the perceived seriousness of various environmental problems. They rated socio-environmental problems like road accidents, violence and vandalism, which affect the quality of life, especially high. Students were asked to rate the seriousness of the problems both in the country, as a whole, and in their own location. The ranking of the problems was very similar for the country as a whole and for their closer environment, but the rating for the seriousness in the country was always higher than that for their own locality (where they had not experienced some of the problems). The reason for that phenomenon became clearer, when the sources of information, as reported by the students, were analysed. The main sources were first of all the media (TV, radio and the press), followed by studies in schools, and talks with parents and friends. In the US, Australia and England too, the media were mentioned as main source of information, followed by talks with relatives and friends. In these countries, school was named only as third source (Blum, 1987).

In contrast to the relatively high awareness of environmental problems, students' knowledge of facts, concepts and possible solutions was low—similar to that of students in the Anglo-Saxon countries mentioned. The discrepancy between the high awareness of environmental problems and the low knowledge level was attributed to the superficiality of media reports, which appeal often more to emotions than to cognition. It became clear that the senior secondary school curriculum must be based on basic knowledge and intellectual skills, among them the ability to analyse environmental problems in a systems approach, and to choose strategies leading to balanced solutions.

In the choice of content, the experience accrued in other countries could be used. Conservation of energy and the use of non-renewable resources were prominent, but the emphasis was put on three issues that were less treated in comparable curricula of other countries (State of Israel, 1992):

1. *Development of Technology*—the historical aspect. Its purpose is to let students understand why the concern over environmental quality has become so urgent in our time of accelerated, technological developments.

2. *Systems Approach*—the integrative aspect. This approach is based on the fact that any change in an environmental system affects also other components in the system, and that therefore a holistic view of the system is needed.

3. *Environmental Planning and Management*—the applied aspect. Citizens must be prepared to take a responsibility for the environmental quality in their locality and in the country as a whole. Students should learn how to use environmental laws and opportunities to defend the quality of their environment. For this reason, emphasis was put on group projects that should deal with a real environmental problem, which is felt in the area in which the students live. A school class would divide itself into small groups that investigate different aspects of the chosen problem. At various stages of the investigation, the groups would pool their findings and thoughts. Based on an in-depth study of this problem, the class as a whole should develop alternatives suggestions for practical solutions, which take in account different legitimate interests. According to its rationale, this part of the curriculum should receive more time than the others and would count for a large part of the final examination grade. External examiners were expected to talk with the different groups about the work each contributed, similar to the evaluation of the biotopes, in the Biology curriculum.

Environmental Studies were recently renamed Environmental Science, in order to try and give them the same status as the traditional science subjects. Environmental Studies are offered at two levels. At the 'ordinary' level, students study concepts and principles and acquire knowledge from various content areas. Then, they concentrate in the 'specialisation step' on one environmental issue. At the advanced level, students should also investigate a real environmental problem of concern to their own environment, as described above. However, the idea of a larger project, within which small teams would investigate specific angles of the overall problem, and then pool their finding with those of other teams, in order to come up with balanced suggestions how to solve the problem, was 'watered down' in the recently revised edition of the curriculum. Now, individuals or teams of two students study an 'ecotope', similar to the 'biotope' investigated by students in Biology—the main 'competitor' with environmental science, and the most popular elective subject. Unlike Biology, the Environmental Science inspectorate can subsidise environmental excursions. This is another attraction for principals to offer Environmental Studies. The number of students who elect Environmental Science is growing from year to year. In 2003, some 7500 students from 165 schools sat for the final examinations (Ministry of Education, 2003).

3.4. Changing an Obsolete Subject to Become Environmental Studies

Still from pre-statehood times, Israeli elementary schools featured a non-vocational school subject called Agriculture. It was based on the idea that the return to the Holy Land, after the long diaspora, during which Jews were not allowed to own or cultivate land, should be combined with a return to tilling the soil. During the war of independence, in the late 1940s, the need to grow enough food for a rapidly growing population of refugee immigrants, put vegetable production in the school garden into the foreground, much like Rural Studies in wartime Britain. In the meantime, Israel developed its industry, and agriculture became intensified, highly sophisticated and science based. At the time of the curriculum reform during the 1970s, the science planning team suggested that the subject 'Agriculture' should be integrated as 'applied science' into an integrated science curriculum. The Ministry of Education did not accept this proposal. Still, the new curriculum tended quite distinctly into the direction of field experiments and environmental education. Therefore its name was changed to 'Agriculture and Environmental Studies'.

However, mainly due to the conservative, but influential, inspectorate for Agriculture and many teachers, who were strong in practical agriculture, but had a weak background in the sciences and practically no training in social science issues, the curriculum had to remain with a clear agricultural tilt. Still, the planners in the Israeli Curriculum Centre could develop a major module on 'Fighting Hunger', which balanced food production with global, social and cultural development issues.

At that time, rural development in the newly emerging countries of Africa, Asia and Oceania was looked upon with much optimism, and Israeli experts were deeply involved in many agricultural development projects. This point of departure could be used to let students discover and understand the reasons why hunger was a world problem, what agronomical solutions might be feasible, but also what social and cultural issues had to be considered.

3.5. 'Fighting Hunger'

This module (teaching-learning package) consists of (1) a small introductory reader, (2) eleven 'challenge cards', (3) short readers with additional information, (4) a simulation game 'End to Hunger' and (5) a teacher's guide.

In the introductory reader, students learn to differentiate between undernourishment ('quantitative hunger') and unbalanced nutrition ('hidden or qualitative hunger'). They read contradictory statements by experts on the question 'how serious is the problem'? Two statisticians base their different views—one optimistic, the other pessimistic—on the same set of data. Who is right? The same happens with statements of various development experts. What makes them differ? What are the reasons for hunger? Students are asked to think how far our judgment is based on our own values and prejudices.

Then, students form groups and investigate a specific sub-topic with the help of a 'challenge card' and additional readers. They search for further information, discuss it and present their findings to the whole class. The sub-topics concern either the basic understanding of the hunger problem or one of the approaches to solve it. Typical issues are: what food do we need? Who is underfed, and who is overfed? What is the hunger situation in various parts of the world? How can the vicious circle of hunger → weakness → inability to help oneself → frustration → poverty → hunger be broken? How can plant varieties be improved, e.g. through selection and cross-breeding for heterosis? Should we cut forests to get arable land or leave them intact? Raising animals for food—yes or no? Are there still untapped food resources? How can international cooperation help?

The simulation game 'End to Hunger' serves as peak learning experience (Blum, 1975) in the discussion about the global aspects of the hunger problem. The aim of the game is to give students an idea and a feeling how ecological, social and techno-logical factors affect the ability of a developing nation to provide its population with sufficient food and upgrade its economy. Built-in are the messages that international cooperation and education are likely to improve the lot of a nation and of the world as a whole.

The 'Fight Hunger' module was part of the 'Agriculture and Environmental Studies' subject. The agricultural inspectorate implemented it in 8th grade. The curriculum development team, together with the trial teachers, served as trainers, both during an in-service course and afterwards, where teachers felt they needed help. Thus, there was a smooth transfer of responsibility for implementation from the module's development team to the regional agricultural inspectors. The teachers were happy with the new topic, which dealt with a global problem that was much discussed at the time. It gave new justification to their school subject that had become less relevant in an urbanised society. Thus, they could hope for an improved status. They also liked the curricular approach, which allowed much freedom in choosing among the different case studies, and they enjoyed the enthusiastic response from students, who liked the creative group work, encouraged by the challenge cards and especially the simulation game as final, peak learning experience. In quite a number of elementary schools, in which grade 8 was the last grade (before the school reform), showing parents the outcomes of their 'Fight Hunger' activities became a central piece in the end of school fair.

The main problem arose from the fact, that the 'Fight Hunger' module was part and parcel of the school subject 'Agriculture and Environmental Studies', which after a few years became obsolete in the newly created junior secondary schools. At the same time, many biology teachers, who followed the upcoming environmental education trend, used the game. However, since a school needed only one set of the game and could easily duplicate the balance sheets themselves, the sales of the games could not reach the minimum units demanded by the publisher, who had won the tender of the Ministry of Education for its school books.

3.6. Implementation Problems for Environmental Education in Schools

Exchanging specific items in a current subject matter curriculum of a school system is *relatively* easy, yet we still hear so often how the need to update a curriculum is delayed, and schools are accused of not keeping up to date with new research findings. The main difficulty is not *what to add*, but *what to delete*, in order not to overload the curriculum. The problem is aggravated, when one wants to introduce a new subject into the school system, and even more, when the new subject area deals with global issues that demand familiarity with subject matter areas, in which most teachers have not been trained.

Writing about the conditions needed to succeed with environmental education in schools, Walker (1997) mentions among others:

- Committed teachers with specific expertise in relation to the problem being investigated, or an outside 'expert';
- Preparedness to confront one's own values and the values held by others;
- A community-based environmental problem, solvable by school students, which becomes the focus of the curriculum, and a community committed to environmental education.

Let me comment on these points, taking in account the Israeli experience with the implementation of environmental education in state schools that follow a centrally (mostly nationally) developed curriculum, often coupled with national examinations.

No doubt: teachers are the key. Even when they are committed, getting into a new subject matter area, for which they were not trained, is for many a frightening experience. For others it is a challenge. The latter are the ideal teachers during the trial period of a new curriculum, and they can become excellent peer advisers in the second stage. However, both types of teachers need in-service training. An 'expert' (the quotation marks are Walker's) can help in a specific case, if he or she is locally available. An expert can add authenticity and give students the advantage of being close to a primary source of knowledge. However, such an expert cannot replace the need for teachers to be trained in the methodology and the contents of the new curriculum. Of course, the more committed a teacher is and the more he or she is ready to take up a new challenge, the easier is the re-training effort. Often, the main difficulty lies in some teachers' inability or reluctance to do themselves what they tell students to do, namely to continue life long learning. In-service training must be part of any meaningful curriculum reform.

When the curriculum change is planned for a whole school system, experts in global, environmental and developmental issues are needed, but mainly at the planning level, which would include the preparation of learning-teaching materials. At that level, their contribution has the widest effect (Blum, 1988).

Preparedness to confront one's own values and that of others is certainly an important precondition for teaching a curriculum with affective and moral objectives. Therefore the topic of value judging in a democracy, and especially in multicultural situations is of highest importance in teachers' pre- and in-service training. In our experience, the first teachers to adopt a new environmental education curriculum were more dedicated to the value issue, compared with those 'joining the bandwagon' later on, but the former were sometimes also the less tolerant towards ideological opponents.

'A community-based environmental problem, *solvable by school students*, which becomes the focus of the curriculum, and a community committed [to environmental education]' is an ideal precondition for environmental education, but it is often not feasible, and in the case of global issues even not desirable. This precondition may exist mainly in communities, which constituted themselves on a green basis, but it is less common in typical governmental school districts, where many other issues or traditional school subjects are more focal. True enough, environmental education must be locally relevant, but school students, especially younger ones, cannot *solve* most real, environmental problems. Children should be educated towards a positive environmental behaviour, be able and ready to take upon themselves to work for a better environment, learn to analyse environmental problems and search for possible solutions, but this not yet '*solving* a (real) environmental problem' Furthermore, when we want to educate towards global issues and values, we cannot concentrate on local environmental problems alone.

3.7.   Inserting Environmental Studies as a Block into a New Subject Area

In the beginning of the 1990s, the Israeli Ministry of Education set up a committee to suggest how science teaching could be made meaningful for the majority of high school students, who do not major in a scientific subject and actually study science courses only up to 9th grade (15 years of age). The committee, headed by Prof. Harari, came up with some revolutionary recommendations, which were adopted by the Ministry of Education. Among other points, the 'Harari Report' recommended that all students in senior high school (10th–12th school year), who do not choose one of the 'classical' science or technology subjects, should study a new subject called 'Science and Technology in Society' (STS) as compulsory subject. The idea was to prepare science and technology literate citizens who could take part in the democratic decision making process about public issues, the understanding of which demands that kind of literacy.

The commission also made it clear that the STS approach implies the choice of relevant topics, and that depth and discovery are more important than 'coverage'. Therefore, no mandatory syllabus was devised. Curriculum development teams were invited to prepare modules (teaching–learning packages), from which teachers could choose. The modules should leave room for the teacher to add or delete learning activities. Thus, not all students would study the same topics, but all would be introduced into the integrated approach, as described in the curriculum guidelines (Blum, 2001).

Instead of a final 'paper-and-pencil' examination, a '*portfolio*' of students' achievements during the whole period of their studies is compiled, and this serves as basis for the final evaluation (Ministry of Education, 2002). In the portfolio system, all pieces of work, which the student has handed in (projects, reports on investigations, written exams etc.), are considered. In future, the results of a national exam paper might become part of the grade, but will not replace it. This is done to insure that schools will be able to focus on local issues or problem areas they are especially interested in. Although the future of STS is still uncertain, it seems that in the case of STS examinations, the decentralised, portfolio based approach has a good chance to be implemented, because this time it is backed by the scientists in the Steering Committee, who fully understand the methodological importance of portfolio evaluation.

This new approach and the guidelines for STS opened a new and excellent opportunity to get environmental education elements into the senior high school curriculum. Thus, for instance, *Yahas* (the Hebrew acronym for 'Objective: Environmental Education'), an educational development project at the Hebrew University of Jerusalem, developed two curriculum modules—'As Air to Breathing' and 'Technological Advances and Environmental Quality'. These modules contain study materials for students and teachers, role play cards, a video film and computer exercises, which were tested and published for use in schools, mainly in the frame of the new STS subject. According to the Yahas approach, students should ask three basic questions, which relate to any environmental/development problem:

1. What factors created or aggravated the problem? (To answer the question, *scientific knowledge* has to be applied.)
2. What *technological* or other solutions exist that could help to solve the problem?
3. What are the optimal solutions from the point of view of *society*? (Its members often cherish different values and hold contradictory interests.)

Basing itself on the experience with earlier curriculum reforms, the STS Steering Committee decided that only teachers who underwent training in the new methodology and in the new topics, a sine qua non in curriculum reform, should be certified to teach the new subject. Unfortunately, the funds for teacher re-training are insufficient. Therefore, the implementation of the STS as *compulsory* subject is being postponed from year to year. In the meantime, teacher training continues on a slower scale. Nine experienced teachers serve as part-time advisors to new STS teachers. At in-service conferences, teachers hear lectures from scientists and get to know new modules, which were prepared on a very wide range of topics. So far, several thousand students have studied STS, and in 2001 over 1700 students from 41 schools have been examined at the matriculation level. (STS Inspectorate, 2002). The schools, based on the portfolio evaluation system, determined the grades. In this context, it is interesting to note that the most popular modules chosen by teachers and students are those on environmental problems (e.g. air pollution) and health (e.g. drug abuse).

4.   CONCLUSION

This chapter dealt with the introduction of environmental education curricula into national or regional school *systems*, and their implementation problems. It is easier to integrate global community education elements (e.g. environmental education or education towards sustainable development) into single schools, where both teachers and parents are 'green' and empathic towards the direction of the new curriculum. Such schools can serve as examples to others, and educational policy makers sometimes hope that these exemplary schools will actually serve as multipliers and trigger a wider response from other schools. However, the rest of the community often sees them as outsiders, whose conditions are too different to imitate.

Introducing global/environmental studies into a whole school system is much more of a challenge. The difference between the development of exemplary schools and planning for a wide adoption of a new curriculum is quite similar to the change occurring in development cooperation in the third world. Also there, the trend is to change from single *projects,* which were often conducted under optimal conditions that could not be re-created in other places, to *programmes,* which were planned to cover a whole area. Of course, also programmes are usually introduced in stages, but the planning is from its beginning for a wide impact. The same should be true for curriculum planning.

As the case studies show, there are different ways how environmental education can be introduced into a school system. Choosing the one with the best chances to succeed depends in each case on the constellation of forces at the time, when decisions are made. Any new subject, even if it is only a block in a wider unit, is competing with the existent curriculum, with which teachers are confident. It can also threaten vested interests, e.g. those of a subject matter inspectorate or influential partners in policy making, as in our case. The case of our national curriculum centre showed that such a central institution can be influential, to a certain degree, in the fostering of interdisciplinary approaches, but it had also negative repercussions, like creating anxiety among those inspectors and educational managers who felt deprived of some of their former 'prerogatives'.

In those cases, in which final examinations are controlled or influenced by academic institutions, the cooperation of influential scientists can be of great help. In the deliberation with the various stakeholders, it is important to be flexible with the 'labels' attached to the new curriculum units. In the case of Israel, *professional committees* served as platforms to iron out upcoming opposition to the implementation of new environmental curricula.

However, the most important challenge in the implementation of curriculum reform when global issues are at the core, is the re-training of teachers. Also in our case, undertrained teachers and even inspectors felt threatened by new environmental curricula and found excuses why not to implement them. On the other hand, where the new curricula were introduced step-by-step, with teacher in-service training and methodological support, implementation was more successful. The service of former trial teachers as supporters of their peers (without becoming 'little inspectors') proved itself to be one of the best strategies in the implementation.

It is of paramount importance to change also the examination system e.g. from paper-and-pencil exams to portfolio evaluation, if one wants to keep up the spirit of the new curricula, which are based on scientific and social skills training through creative group and project work, challenges to value systems, and understanding that different stakeholders have to cooperate on a common platform. This in itself is an endeavour that takes time and training.

The fact that many teachers preferred environmental and health modules over others in the 'Science and Technology in Society' (STS) curriculum shows that these global issues attract teachers and students (STS inspectorate, 2002). The STS approach, which brings social and cultural aspects to bear on science and technology issues, helped also to contribute through STS modules *Education towards Sustainable Development*—a major global need.

5.   REFERENCES

Blum, A. 1975. Peak learning experiences in the context of curriculum evaluation. *Studies in Educational Evaluation 1*, 55–58.
Blum, A. 1984. What do Israeli high school students know and believe about environmental issues? *Environmental Education and Information 3*, 338–348.

Blum, A. 1987. Students' knowledge and beliefs concerning environmental issues in four countries. *Journal of Environmental Education* 18(3), 7–13.

Blum, A. 1988. Think globally, act locally—plan (also) centrally. *Journal of Environmental Education* 19(2), 3–8.

Blum, A. 2001. Sustainable development and environmental balance as goals in science-technology-society education. In: *Proceedings of the 1st IOSTE Symposium in Southern Europe*, Paralimini, Cyprus: University of Cyprus.

Carson, R. 1962. *The Silent Spring*. Boston: Houghton Mifflin.

IUCN. 1970. *IUCN-UNESCO Joint International Education Conference*. Gland, Switzerland: IUCN.

Lucas, A.M. 1973. *Environment and Environmental Education—Conceptual Issues and Curriculum Implementation*. PhD dissertation, Ohio State University. (Diss. Abs. International 33, 6064-A)

Ministry of Education. 2002. *Circular of the STS Inspectorate* (Science and Technology in Society) (Hebrew). Publication Department, Ministry of Education.

Ministry of Education. 2003. *Results of Bagrut Examinations in Environmental Science* (Hebrew). Pedagogical Secretariat.

Our Common Future. 1988. Oxford: Oxford University Press.

Schwab, J.J. 1973. The practical 3: Translation into curriculum.*School Review 81*, 501–522.

State of Israel. 1992. *Environmental Studies—An elective Program for Senior High Schools*. Jerusalem: Ministry of Education and Culture Curriculum Centre.

STS Inspectorate. 2002. Personal communication.

Tyler, R. 1949. *Principles of Curriculum*. Chicago: University of Chicago Press.

United Nations Conference on Environment and Development. 1992. The Action Plan—Agenda 21.

Walker, K. 1997. Challenging critical theory in environmental education. *Environmental Education Research 3*(2),155–162.

Chapter 7

EDUCATING FOR CAPABILITY FOR INCLUSIVE WELL-BEING

Richard Bawden

In the short time that it will take you, the reader, to read to the bottom of this page, countless numbers of people across the world will die of starvation. A very high proportion of them will be infants and young children. Even as you read on, many millions of others will be suffering from such acute under-nutrition and/or malnutrition that they will soon fall victim to one fatal infectious disease or another. And even as I type the following words into the computer in front of me, an unforgivably large percentage of the total human population on earth is suffering the unbearable pain and disabling effects of acute hunger.

From a technical perspective, this is a very difficult situation to explain, and certainly, to justify. In this era of hi-tech scientific agriculture, of the transnational flow of goods and services and 'global free trade', and of the world wide web of available information, such circumstances seem both inexcusable and, technically at least, essentially preventable. From such a perspective, poverty and hunger are functions of scientific ignorance. Once people come to understand the nature of science, and learn about its application in modern agricultural technologies, then, so the argument goes, more food could be grown, economic production could flourish, poverty can be alleviated and hunger could be a thing of the past. This could even be true in those parts of the world where conditions of soil, climate and water, etc., are less than optimal for food production, where conditions, either temporarily or permanently do not allow particular people access to secure and sustainable sources of food in their own locale, then the issue simply becomes one of distribution from locations elsewhere, where food could be grown in surplus amounts. Either way the solution, from this perspective, comes down to better education in the sciences and technologies of food production and distribution.

At base, the issue of what we might call the agri-food system, is thus merely a matter of matching the physical needs for food on the one hand with the means to both produce and distribute it on the other. There is plenty of evidence to suggest that, for the foreseeable future at least, there is more than sufficient production and distribution capacities on the planet to supply food to every one of its six billion inhabitants on a sustainable basis.

With so many hundreds of millions of human beings suffering from food deprivation across the world, however—and with so many nations apparently unable to assure their citizens a secure and sustainable source of food—the situation is clearly much more complex than the technical picture alone would indicate: For if it were otherwise, the problem would not exist at all.

J. Campbell et al. (eds.), Towards a Global Community, 109–123.

Even the addition of an economic perspective to the technical one is sufficient to add weight to the argument that technical ways of doing things are not up to the task of either explaining the situation or providing more effective strategies for change: Matching effective demand with price-sensitive supply through 'the market mechanism' is not at all the same thing as matching actual needs with the physical product to meet those needs! But even the integration of the economic with the technical is still insufficient to explain the true complexity of the situation, or its failure—or most especially, to provide indicators to 'the way forward from here': For once again there would be no problem if market forces, in conjunction with technical expertise, were truly effective in assuring equitable and sustainable distribution of food universally across the globe. The situation is clearly much more complex than even these two perspectives combined allow, and the suspicion is that we are failing to deal with it because of the way the process of development has conventionally been conceptualised and pursued. Indeed, as Habermas among others has emphasised, the undue reliance on technical and economic perspectives in these modern times, has singularly distorted our ways of 'doing things in the world'. What is needed, he has long argued, is equal attention to a third dimension of the process of taking effective action in the world—a third perspective that focuses on 'emancipation' and the equitable interaction between human beings in their pursuit of consensual actions for the common good (Habermas, 1984). Roling and Woodhill (2001), in reinforcing the usefulness of the three distinctions between different ways of viewing the world, argue that the interactive perspective is especially essential because it brings people into negotiation with each other in circumstances that call for explicit attention to differing values, goals and interests as fundamental to the development of collective interests and common strategies for action.

If the modernization process itself is becoming problematic because of its paradigmatic limitations, as writers such as Ulrich Beck and others are strongly suggesting with their theories of 'reflexive modernisation' and the 'risk society' (Beck, Giddens and Lash, 1994), then our entire way of approaching the further development of complex matters such sustainable agri-food systems will be necessary at all levels of social organisation, from the global to local. This in turn will place a penetrating focus on our current institutions of governance and service and indeed our prevailing social norms and mores, which are all appearing less and less adequate to the task of supporting sustainable development in any sphere of human activity (Beck, 1992). As one writer has recently put it in the context of natural resource management: 'Our institutions and mechanisms of governance seem increasingly archaic; a global economic system that does not value natural capital; technical single discipline and inflexible government agencies; inappropriate property rights; and social norms that value immediate individual material wealth over ecological integrity and social equity' (Woodhill, 2002, p. 2). Woodhill is among those who, for instance, see 'social learning' as an alternative to the two classical strategies for governance: (a) the assumption of exclusive responsibility for making decisions on behalf of its citizens and (b) the belief that social change is best left to 'market forces' with minimal interventions by governments. The contrast is for us as humans to accept our responsibilities for learning our own ways forward collectively, and this in turn implies the need to escape our old ways of thinking and doing things, and to collectively embrace the new. It will become necessary for us to not only learn our way forward but also to learn how to learn our way forward: And the emphasis on 'we' and 'us' here rather than on 'them', is of profound significance, as of course is the emphasis on learning, and especially on collective or social learning.

All of this is of considerable importance to the institutions of education—in all senses of the phrase (from formal schooling organisations, through policy and governance institutions, to curricula and accepted pedagogical practices). The new goal must be inclusivity—the democratic pursuit of participative development strategies that focus on sustainable and equitable improvements in 'well-being' that are inclusive of everyone (and indeed of the rest of 'nature' too). For development to be truly inclusive, the techno-economic mindset of traditional development must be expanded to also include perspectives that can be labelled ethical and ecological—where the latter is interpreted as the full range of relationships between people and nature from scientific to spiritual.

A wide spectrum of human values lie at the heart of this matter—and the trouble with reliance on only the technical and the economic perspectives of development with respect to agri-food systems, is that this key point is lost. The value that is placed on the life and well-being of every individual on earth is cited as one of the key hallmarks of contemporary 'modern' civilization. This necessarily must translate into a set of rights that all human beings should be accorded by the nation state of which they are citizens. The 'flip side' of this of course, is a set of ethical responsibilities that every civilized nation-state must ensure that the rights of its citizens are respected, protected and most essentially, enabled.

To live ethically—to make decisions that are ethically defensible—is to act on what it is that we feel we ought to do, only after taking the interests and preferences of others, fully into account (Singer, 1995). And such accounts need to particularly focus on the future as a key perspective, in order to include the needs and interests and preferences of those yet born, as well as to indicate potential future consequences of intended present actions.

The foundations for our ethics lie in the values that we hold, and how these influence what it is that we both think and feel about what it is that we should do to reach a future that is both sustainable and defensible. Tradition has held that two different sets of value assumptions are involved in ethical perspectives. The first of these (neo-Kantian) embrace a seemingly innate sense of right and wrong that asserts the primary significance of duties and rights. The second set (consequential) emphasises rights and wrongs in terms of the goodness or badness of the consequences of their outcomes.

Among the most basic of these rights and responsibilities to the well-being of all of the world's citizenry, is to assure its secure and sustainable access to food. Reflections on much of our so-called technical progress, reveals that it has often been achieved in violation of either or both of these value positions. We, and our institutions alike, have proceeded with little care or due attention to our 'duties' and responsibilities to others—be they other humans or other species in nature. We have also introduced technologies that have had indisputably destructive impacts on both bio-physical and socio-cultural environments in which we are embedded.

To borrow a phrase from the philosopher Prozesky (1998) our focus should now turn to development for 'inclusive well-being'. Prozesky's focus has been on ethics in the context of the challenge of 'national transformation' of post-apartheid South

Africa. His call has been for 'nothing less than an ethical renaissance' with 'a new surge of moral power is now needed' to ensure a 'general renaissance' of that nation.

With respect to the matters of concern in this present chapter, the good news is that a 'general renaissance' is indeed in the air. There is mounting evidence, from a whole variety of sources both within and beyond the global agri-food system, of such a surge in 'moral power' that the whole paradigm underlying the conventional approaches to the alleviation of starvation etc. is undergoing a vital, if still gradual, transformation. A fresh worldview that does embrace the need to pursue forms of development that are focused on improvements in 'inclusive well-being' is clearly emerging in various educational institutions, and research organisations across the world, and even on some national and international policy and governance landscapes. And while it justifiably attracts a great deal of 'bad press' and negative feelings among many in its present form, a process of responsible globalisation can provide both a momentum for, and processes appropriate to, further paradigmatic transformations 'for the greater good of all'—people and nature.

Perhaps the first step is the acceptance of the complexity of issues like sustainable universal food security, and indeed of ways of knowing and acting that not only accommodate such complexity, but also appreciate their own complexity. We are as complex in our thinking and learning and knowing as the world is in which we are embedded!

1.   THE MATTER OF COMPLEXITY

Hunger and starvation and malnutrition are certainly all included in the catalogue of issues that are increasingly recognized as being more than a little complex. Rarely, if ever is hunger a simple case of the lack of enough food in the world. Indeed one of the most obscene paradoxes of modern life must surely be that even as so many people are dying for lack of food, others are gorging themselves sick on too much. Obesity is becoming a matter of serious concern to the health officials of an increasing number of nations, and this is as stark a commentary on global inequality as any, in a world where hunger remains of such a primary concern to the health officials of so many other nations. Most obscene of all perhaps is the all-too-common occurrence of both syndromes concomitant with each other in the same country.

Another tragic manifestation of inequality and of the failure of the world's 'agri-food system' to alleviate starvation for all time, is the fact that there are farmers in a number of countries across the world who are effectively paid *not* to cultivate crops on their productive lands, but to leave them fallow in the name of 'rational economics'!

Starvation can certainly be a result of famine, which in turn is so often a result of harvest failure through drought or flood or other natural disaster, or through poor husbandry practices or lack of input resources and/or support services. It is, however, also an outcome of poverty and of the lack of capability of individuals to meet the food needs of themselves and of members of their own families and communities, for a host of different reasons. I use the word *capability* here in the sense that Amyrta Sen has characterised it—combining competency to achieve some basic 'human functioning which he or she has reason to value' with 'freedom' to express such achievement or competency (Sen, 1992) Sen sees such 'functionings' as ranging from the most elementary ones, such as being well-nourished, avoiding escapable morbidity and premature mortality etc., to quite complex and sophisticated achievements such as having self-respect, being able to take part in the life of the community and so on. And this notion of capability is entirely consistent with the belief of the radical Brazilian educator and humanitarian Paulo Freire, that what any individual can do is very significantly qualified by what that individual is free to do within the society and culture that he or she lives (Freire, 1970). For Freire, there were two opposing dynamics within societies: (a) a *cultural action for domination*, in which individuals are regarded as objects for the benefit of a sectarian few and (b) a *cultural action for freedom* in which all individuals are regarded as subjects who are both critically conscious of the world about them, and able to change their own circumstances.

While starvation and poverty are not the same thing, they are often profoundly inter-related, and in a vital sense, and all too frequently both have their foundations in institutional inadequacies and failures yet sustained through a culture of dominance. Thus they can be the result of inappropriate or misguided government policies for instance, or of blatant corporate corruption, or endemic bureaucratic incompetence, or even of punitive sanctions. All too frequently they reflect differences in priorities (and the values that guide them), between the citizens of a state and those who are charged with (or who assume) the responsibilities of governance for that state. A depressing fact in this regard is the 'madness' that the President of the World Bank has recently been reported as describing the situation where the nations of the world are currently spending collectively 20 times more on defence (warfare?)—$1 trillion—than on development—$50 billion (Wolfensohn, 2004).

One of the huge advantages of an increasingly globalised world should be that where any one particular state cannot discharge its responsibilities for food security for whatever reason, an international organisation will assist in one manner or another. Such assistance would range from the actual physical supply of food—as short-term relief from situations where it is not otherwise available—through to the more abstract and longer term assistance with the development of national policies and strategies that focus on food security. In practice, the rhetoric is rarely matched by the reality. For all that has been achieved worldwide by national governments, non-government organisations (NGOs), trans-national corporations and international development agencies, over recent decades in particular, sustainable food security remains an elusive goal still in many parts of the world. Returning to the issue of institutional archaism part of the tragedy lies with the international organisations themselves, and the set of institutional values that are reflected in the policies and development strategies of key development agencies such as the World Bank and the International Monetary Fund (IMF). As Joseph Stiglitz, an erstwhile chief economist at the World Bank and recent Nobel Laureate in economics has recently articulated in his severe critique of the Bank and of the IMF, the time has come for profound changes in the practices of these institutions and in the values that they reflect: In stark contrast to views that all too often prevail within such institutions, 'development is not about helping a few people get rich . . . [it]. is about transforming societies, improving the lives of the poor, enabling everyone to have a chance at success and access to health care and education' (Stiglitz, 2002, p. 252): And to a safe, secure and sustainable source of food too.

Education is among the most significant foundations for such a focus on the transformation of the process of development. An emphasis on literacy and numeracy and on the development of other competencies essential for contemporary life certainly remains a crucial in the process of development. But education must also fully embrace matters of human rights and associated responsibilities to mankind and nature alike, and most crucially, be accessible to all strata of society. As Freire was among the first to recognize, such 'education' starts with an awakening of consciousness as the first steps in a process of empowerment. Empowerment in this sense does not mean the redistribution of power but 'the restoration to individuals of a sense of their own value and the strengths and their own capacity to handle life's problems' (Folgar and Bush, 1996, p. 2). In essence it relates to freedom to search for one's own identity and to express that in terms of needs and hopes and aspirations and values, and as these change through time and circumstances, then so too does identity. As Emmanuel Levinas (1998) has put it, the 'I' is engaged in a continual, dynamic process of 'recovering' its identity through all the events in life that may happen to it—although it is always influenced to some degree by each such event and is never the same again!

The suspicion must be that too little emphasis has traditionally been placed on forms of education that are adequate for, and appropriate to, the task at hand. As already suggested, the situation with respect to sustainable food security is typically a complex matter that involves complicated sets of inter-relationships between many different actors within nation states, as well as across international borders. It also involves complex inter-relationships between people and land and indeed 'nature at large'. It has social, economic, political, technological and ecological dimensions. It also has psychological, spiritual, ethical and aesthetic dimensions. Rarely however, have conventional development projects and the educational strategies that have both informed them and been derived from them, reflected an appreciation of such complexity: Rarely too, have teaching practices incorporated strategies that have allowed or encouraged students to learn how to deal with complex situations that involve heady mixtures of human values and emotions and spiritual expressions in addition to scientific and economic reasoning.

That said there are encouraging signs from many quarters across the globe that this situation is changing for the better. A profound appreciation does seem to be emerging that nothing less than a change in fundamental 'worldviews' or paradigms is essential to accommodate respect for complexity and the development of new strategies for learning how to deal with it (Wheatley, 1999). The challenge cannot be overestimated, for it is not just the matter of food security that is complex, but so too the matter of how we humans make sense of the world about us in order to take responsible actions in it.

Rather than using rather abstract and distant examples to illustrate this contention, I want to now turn to my own personal experiences as an agricultural scientist/educator/scholar practitioner in 'international development'. 'First know thyself' was one of the vital exhortations of Socrates, and this has always seemed to be a sensible and responsible place to start in the development process. I have no hesitation, but some considerable shame, in admitting here that during the early years of my career as an agricultural scientist, I was 'trapped' (albeit in ignorance) by my own belief in the superiority of a techno-scientific approach to the development of agri-food systems.

It took a profound and protracted experience 'in the field' in a development project with the United Nations in Latin America some three decades ago, to bring me face to face with the limitations of my own perspectives on development, and thus on my pedagogical practices. In addition to the effect that these experiences had on my consciousness of my own professional inadequacies as an essentially technocentric agricultural scientist, I was extremely fortunate to be in the same part of the world as Paulo Freire, from whose work I was to gain so much inspiration—and indeed conceptual clarity. Not the least of this influence has been on the significance that I now attribute to the process of experiential learning and the vitally important understanding of such learning as the transformation of personal (and especially shared) experience in the 'real world' into the knowledge of it that is then used as the basis for meaningful action in (and to) it. As David Kolb (1984) has so clearly argued in echoing the Freirian stance experience is the primary source of learning and development and experiential learning is thus a primary process of intra-generational adaptation of humans to the ever-changing world about them.

As indicated earlier in this chapter, Freire strongly believed in the emancipatory notion of treating people as 'knowing subjects' rather than as 'objects' or 'recipients' (Freire, 1970) as the foundational basis for assisting them to achieve a deepening awareness both of the socio-cultural reality that shapes their lives and of their capacity to transform that reality. His ethos of, and approach to, a 'pedagogy of the oppressed' was to not only speak to my own freedom from the oppression of a limiting worldview through a growing consciousness of circumstances around me, but came to deeply inform my own practices as both scientist and teacher: Perhaps better put, I should refer to my *praxis* in these activities, for he was also to emphasise the profound significance of praxis as the dynamic and inseparable inter-connectedness between practice and the theories that both informed it and are formed from it. My own consciousness was critically raised about issues associated with hunger and starvation and about the inadequacies of the technocentric worldview that I had tacitly embraced, in the face of the issues that I came to directly experience. So too did I then attempt to translate that increased state of level of critical consciousness to others.

Both were difficult journeys, for as many, including Freire, have pointed out, we human beings are very loathe to admit inadequacies in the way we construe the world about us, and extremely reluctant to change the way we deal with it—at least without some extreme provocation: And I was certainly no exception.

2.   GREEN REVOLUTIONS AND PERSONAL TRANSFORMATIONS

My own career in agricultural development started at a time that coincided with the early days of the so-called Green Revolution—the development and cultivation of high yielding grain crops that could be grown by any farmer provided that he or she knew the appropriate knowledge and skills of the new practices, and who had access to particular science-based technologies, as well as to fertile land, water for irrigation and money to pay for it all!

There is no doubt whatsoever that the well-being of many millions of people on earth has indeed been greatly improved by the 'techno-scientific modernisation' of agriculture as represented at its technological best by the Green Revolution. And one of the most impressive manifestations of this claim is the transformation of India from a nation that was constantly beset by problems of food insecurity as recently as a decade or so ago, to one which is now firmly food secure, with more than 1 year full supply of reserve grain in storage: Which is still not to imply, however, that there are no hungry people in India or Indians dying from starvation, for to emphasise yet once again, the situation is never simply one of needs and production—or even of effective demand and supply.

It could even be argued that the reason that the planet is now able to support a human population in excess of six billion (and rising) is in large part because there has been such a concomitant growth in the production of staple food grains!

Yet that said, the *vision glorious* of the Green Revolution has failed to fully deliver its benefits on a universal scale; starvation, hunger and poverty remain endemic in significantly large parts of the world. Furthermore, even where the benefits of such modernisation have been obvious, they have not come without severe social, ecological and economic costs. Most modern agricultural technologies have some disadvantages in addition to their obvious advantages. Their introduction and use has brought a host of consequences that, while unintended, often include severe ecological damage to the bio-physical environment, as well as harm to human communities. One has only to think about the accumulation of pesticides in soils, ground-water and indeed in food itself, for instance, or the eroding or salinizing after-effects of deforestation on soil, or the displacement of farm labourers through the mechanization of many farming practices, to accept the truth of this contention. The quest for the 'well-being' of some has led, all too frequently, to reductions in the 'well-being' of others and/or to the 'well-being' of nature itself: Shades of the risk society and reflexive modernization! Even in those countries where the high yielding high-tech agriculture has been (could be) established, many millions of people still starve and remain impoverished. The green revolution has, thus far at least, failed to prove that it can assure food security—or even that techno-economic approaches to development can alone lead to sustainable or even equitable agri-food systems.

It took a change of professional focus and, most significantly also of country, to provide me personally with an experiential trigger to question my technocentric perspective on development. Within days of arrival in Latin America to assume my UN field position in 'animal health' I was to become conscious, for the first time in my life, of the total range of ways by which people secure food to support themselves and their families. Well conversant with the techno-economic issues on the supply side of the agri-food equation, I was suddenly made conscious of the complexity of the need side! On any given day in my new surroundings, I could witness variations on all five basic ways through which we human beings gain our food—(a) gather it ourselves, (b) cultivate it ourselves, (c) buy it, (d) be given it by someone else or (e) steal it.

The gathering of food, I quickly discovered, was not confined to the forests and open grasslands or seas and rivers of popular perception, nor even to the 'commons' of rural villages, but also to the waste bins of suburban households and restaurants and the garbage dumps of cities and towns. These latter sources of food supply may have been surprisingly reliable and sustainable but they posed very significant risks to the health of the 'gatherers' and to those who benefited from what was gathered. And the same risks applied for those who relied upon 'gathering' fish in the huge delta that lies at the mouth of River Plate, for the same body of water that was home to the fish that the fishermen sought to catch, was also the 'sump' into which a number of very large industrial plants on the shores of the delta, dumped their polluting wastes.

I was also to quickly discover that while the country's economy depended very heavily on agricultural production, and the countryside was essentially an endless pampas or fertile prairie, the ownership of the land was vested in the hands of very few families—who often acted as absentee landlords. Agricultural cultivation was certainly one of the key sources of food in the country, but the number of folk who could actually access land to grow their own food, was proportionately very small indeed. Small patches of cultivated land were certainly apparent in the countryside, and scrappy garden plots dotted some of the peri-urban areas, but the supply of food from such restricted areas would do little to meet the needs of the many thousands of people who lived cheek by jowl jammed into the 'favella' slums of the capital—or even in the rural villages and small settlements that occasionally broke the monotony of the endless pampas. With poor soils, little water and virtually no other technical inputs, the marginal resource-poor farmers and gardeners got little productive return from their labours; a situation further exacerbated by all of the other hazards that farmers face the world over with respect to the vagaries of the climate, plagues of pests and pathogens, and a host of other 'natural perturbations'.

Like all of the rest of the families in our comfortable suburb, we did our shopping at the local fresh food markets and the supermarket. With inflation running at over 100% per month, however, one could hardly argue that these sources of purchased food were either secure or sustainable. There was certainly food available, but it was far from reliably accessible to the majority of the citizens who earned considerably less than the families in our suburb—if indeed they had jobs at all at a time when the official unemployment rate exceeded 25% of the working population.

Under such circumstances it was not all surprising that many citizens were forced to resort to asking those who could, to give them food, and rarely an hour would go by without someone (often a child) appealing for food at our front door. Meanwhile the high attendance rates at schools were in part explained by the fact that free lunches were served for all students in many such institutions; for many, this would be their sole meal of the day.

The most poignant sight of all perhaps, in this context of the quest for food, was the measures that many householders felt that they were forced to take to prevent the petty theft of food by those 'opportunists' who would risk all by running into houses, grabbing the first thing that they could find of value to sell for food, and escaping as they could.

The ultimate irony in all of this was that education was universal and compulsory at least for primary and part of secondary schooling in our host country at that time—as it had been for very many years. Clearly no simple connection or causal relationship existed between education and food security. The situation that I confronted and experienced in such an embodied, experiential manner in Latin America, was obviously complex and involved a host of social, economic, political and cultural influences and relationships for which I was ill-prepared through my formal 'training' as an agricultural scientist. In this manner, my Latin American sojourn exposed me to the need to really come to terms with the systemic complexities both of the 'big picture', with respect to the agri-food system of an entire nation, and of the process by which I personally came to learn about them.

In this manner, I came to view the serious issues that I was personally confronting 'in the field', not essentially as limitations in scientific knowledge *per se*, but as inadequacies in the prevailing paradigm of techno-scientific agricultural development itself that held that hunger was essentially a function of a lack of technical and scientific knowledge. The challenge that thus arose out of my new level of consciousness, and new appreciation of the complexity of human nature, was essentially how to translate my own sense of transformation into pedagogical practices through which I could encourage a similar sense of 'empowerment', and nurture similar *cultural actions for freedom* that I had enjoyed, with others.

While my Latin American experiences were focused essentially on research (Bawden, 1979) and not on education *per se,* they certainly proved foundational to key transformations that I have made over subsequent years in my *praxis* as an educator as well as a scholar/practitioner in systemic development.

As it has transpired, I seem to have come to embrace three particular beliefs that perhaps best characterise what I now do (and indeed best describe my identity as to who I think I am!). Naturally enough, these are dynamic in their expression, although they have remained remarkably consistent in their foundational form, over three decades or more. Somewhat surprisingly perhaps, they relate to three particular questions once posed by the 18th century philosopher Immanuel Kant as central to arguments that he was mounting in the context of reason (Kant 1788 tr Smith 1929): What can I know? What should I do? What can I hope?

The aim in the last section of this chapter is not to provide details of how my subsequent professional life has unfolded, for much of that has already been well-documented particularly with regard to experiences at Hawkesbury Agricultural College (Bawden, 1999). Rather what I intend to now do, in bringing this chapter to its end, is to further explore the three Kantian questions in relation to *education for capability for inclusive well-being* drawing essentially on reflections on my own experiences in educational reform (and especially on an unpublished essay entitled *A Systemic Perspective on the SACSA Essential Learnings: A word or two from Socrates and Kant*).

The basic idea is not to relate these ideas and experiences directly to the specific matter of educating for sustained and secure food supply, but to present a framework for the type of educational reform that can be regarded as essential to improve the latter, although it has its foundations in classical philosophical literature. The connection is essentially the personal associations that I have experienced in a working life devoted to educational reform for capabilities within the agri-food system during which I have had the freedom to explore the ideas and experiences of others, and use them to inform my practice.

But again I emphasise the significance of being personally embedded in the issues and being introduced to experiential ways of learning to make sense of what was happening with a new consciousness.

3.   THE KANTIAN QUESTIONS: EDUCATIONAL FOUNDATIONS FOR CAPABILITY

As Kant saw it, the whole point of reason was its practical use in establishing moral ends where happiness equates with virtue. When used solely for intellectual pursuits it leads to fallacies. Kant is important to the issues being explored here in relation to education for capability, in a number of ways that extend past his connection of reason with morality—although that is pretty profound in and of itself! At first reading, there is a strong temptation to read the three questions from a purely instrumental perspective, with an emphasis on content. Thus the focus becomes what can I **know**? What should I **do**? What can I **hope**? The answers that one seeks in response to the three questions posed in this manner, tend to emphasise quantity, and curricula based on such an interpretation will focus on 'lists' of knowledge and skills that someone (the teacher or the curriculum designer or the university admission's office) decides is important for students-as-objects in the relatively passive process of the acquisition of 'bodies of knowledge' and 'sets of skills'—and even the 'articulation of expectations'.

From this perspective, in the context of the alleviation of starvation and poverty etc, education will be presented as an antidote to ignorance in society of the agri-food system, and the curriculum will, as a consequence, focus on those scientific facts and economic principles that 'need to be taught' if people are to 'learn' how to become more 'food secure'. Farmers will become better at farming through such education, the argument goes. In similar vein, politicians and bureaucrats will become better at governance, citizens will become better at earning money to support the food needs of their dependents and so on. In this paradigm, supported as it will be by cultural actions of dominance and institutional dependency, people will also 'be taught' how to convert their new-found knowledge into practical skills that will give them new competencies for dealing with the instrumental challenges of the world. In terms of 'hope' the citizenry will learn only to expect the minimum that any change in their current status, will allow.

The technocentric worldview will continue to prevail, and the real tragedy will be that few will know that or the impacts of that. An instrumental curriculum does not provide the medium (nor does the culture of dominance encourage the search) for questions about the nature and respective characteristics of different worldviews.

How much more exciting it is to read the Kantian questions with the emphasis placed elsewhere. What **can** I know? This is a question that takes into the very world of worldviews, a question that demands an exploration of the nature of knowledge itself and of the limits of knowing, and of the nature of differences between different forms of knowledge and different ways of knowing. It is now an epistemological question, that brings into focus the significance of beliefs and assumptions not just about knowledge and knowing themselves, but also about the impact that such beliefs have on other assumptions as they relate for instance to the nature of nature itself, or to the value-laden nature of human nature.

The emphasis on **can** rather than **know**—on the processes of knowing rather than the content—also encourages profound questions about the nature of the knower, and this reinforces the earlier comments about the importance of 'identity' as a focus for 'empowerment'. Kant himself, for instance agued forcefully for the difficulty of separating the knower from the known and proposing that the knower is creative in the process of knowing in the pursuit of becoming what he referred to as a 'self' or 'ego'. He was also committed to the notion of an inseparable unity between mankind and nature—what Gregory Bateson very much later, would come to call *an ecology of mind* (Bateson, 1972).

Under conditions of Freirian *cultural action for freedom*, we are quick to appreciate that as change is a constant within both 'society' and 'nature', then our identity is continually emergent. We are therefore continually engaged in the process of becoming [even when it is conceived in terms of 'recovering'] because there are constant challenges to our identity and to such aspects as our autonomy, our dignity, our integrity and our vulnerability—four ethical principles which 'are not only guidelines for the right of the individual to self-determination, but also for the protection of life and the private sphere of the person' (Rendtorf and Kemp, 2000). And this brings us to the second re-interpretation of the second of Kant's three questions: what we **should** do? In contrast to the instrumental practicality flowing from the emphasis on 'doing', this shift encourages a shift to ethical matters, and what it is that we ought to be doing rather than merely what it is that we think that we can do.

Here then is the imperative for our institutions, including most notably those for education, to support conditions appropriate for the citizenry to learn to live the 'good life': A life based on respect for, and commitment to, 'the ideal of the highest good' and a well-being that is inclusive of all life on earth, including 'those who cannot speak for themselves'—our as yet unborn children as well as non-human life forms in nature.

The thinking that should characterise our institutions from this ethical perspective should encourage a new consciousness of the nature and quality of the whole gamut of relationships that each citizen has with other people as well as with the 'rest of nature'. It is through such thinking that people should come to recognize how inter-dependent they are, both with 'society in general', and with 'nature as a whole'. As citizens we should be 'empowered' (again in the Freirian sense) to learn to come to treat other people and the rest of 'nature' with the respect that they merit and indeed, in the way that we ourselves would like to be treated by them (and it). We should become conscious of what we have to do to nurture our inter-dependency with the world in which we live, and how to minimize doing anything that threatens such inter-dependency, both now and, especially, into the future. This is the essence of sustainability which in turn relies upon, just as it dictates the need for, new forms of governance in which the formal institutions of government are 'only one part of a governance system and where the key feature is self-governance through interdependent individuals, groups, organisations and institutions that operate at different levels of collectivity' (Allen, Kilvington and Horn 2002).

And these types of questions in turn, bring into sharp focus the distinction between hope as a catalogue of expectations and hope as a driver for better futures. [For] what **can** we hope? This is an ever-expanding dynamic. In developing our personal visions for our own 'hoped-for' futures we can, under the right conditions of freedom, learn to appreciate that hope is virtually infinite, and the source of motivation and disposition. This interpretation of Kant's third question assumes a powerful aesthetic. Kant himself was much taken by the notion of happiness as the central theme of living where 'happiness is the satisfaction of all of our desires, *extensively*, in respect of their manifoldness, *intensively*, in respect of their degree, and *protensively*, in respect of their duration' (Kant 1788 tr Smith 1929).

The point to be emphasised here is that we come to learn about ourselves essentially through our engagement with others and with 'nature': The search for self-identity is inextricably bound up with the search for the identity of 'the other': Change one and you change the other where any use of technology will greatly expand the potential scale of such change—in both positive and negative directions.

Through all of this critical questioning, we must also continually critique the very way we claim that we come to know about any of it. What we do in this life reflects what we know and how we know it and so knowing about knowing is certainly essential. In addition to concerns about the ethical and the aesthetic in the pursuit of our identity, we must include the epistemological. In developing our own identity we need to do all that we can to assure that the identity of others who are also in pursuit of the 'good life', is not threatened. This means that we have to assume a particular responsibility for the way that we come to know what might constitute such threats. We have to learn how to evaluate the value and belief positions that we assume and the impact that these might have on others about us.

Finally, we must learn to recognize that in a dynamic and democratic society we are constantly judged for the actions that we take by others, because, ultimately, in a responsible society, our actions have ethical implications. As Habermas (1996) has recently emphasised, every act, even just an utterance, has ethical implications, and so every act of communication is not just a matter of 'sending and receiving' messages, but of ethical action—and that of course includes this and any other piece of writing that might, one day, be read by others. This has enormous implications for the form of deliberative democracy that would seem to be the essential foundation for sustainable development.

4.   A FINAL COMMENTARY

As mentioned above, it is useful to think of learning fundamentally as a process of adaptation (or co-adaptation) through which we develop judgments about the actions that we then need to take in the world about us in order to better fit it (or fit it to fit us—or both at the same time). And as also argued earlier, the touchstone for such learning is the quest for our own identity and the identity of others (and other 'things in nature') with whom (and with which) we are inter-dependent. Such is the extent of our inter-dependency, that while our search for self-identity is by definition a function of each of us as individuals, learning is essentially a social process—we learn with and through others with whom we are connected in massively complex networks of inter-dependent 'agents'.

And it is such inter-dependencies that reinforce earlier comments about the role of collective, social learning. We learn with and from each other in order to judge which actions we should collectively take in any particular circumstance in which we are involved. This process involves two fundamentally different ways of making sense of what is happening in that circumstance, as the basis for our actions to change it (in some way or another). As a process it represents two quite different ways of knowing that can be labelled experiential (the transformation of experience into knowledge) and inspirational (the transformation of innate insight into meaning). With experiential learning, the aim is to immerse ourselves in concrete experiences, and to then make abstract, conceptual sense out of what we sense though such immersion. We then use such thoughts to generate plans for action as a prelude to finally taking those actions. These actions in turn create new circumstances for us that trigger the need for more learning; and so on. This process is typically portrayed as a 'cycle of learning' (Kolb, 1984)—albeit one which constantly turns back on itself as a sort of recursive flux.

Inspirational learning in contrast, asks us not to immerse ourselves in the 'real external world of the concrete' (the sensual) nor to 'conceptualise the abstract' (the conceptual), but to 'disengage' from 'reality' and seek 'internal insight' through some form of meditation or contemplation (the spiritual) (Bawden, 2000). Both experiential and inspirational learning are important sources of knowledge (and thus meaningful action) and each complements the other profoundly. Both can also be complemented by propositional knowledge (theories as described by others) and practical knowledge (practices as demonstrated by others).

In addition to being able to learn about what we might refer to as the 'matter to hand'—the worldly circumstance that we are currently encountering—we can also learn about the process of learning itself (meta-learning) as well as about the particular perspective that we are bringing to bear on to both our learning and our meta-learning. This third level of learning we can call epistemic-learning and extend its compass to also include learning about the nature of normative values and assumptions on their influences on the processes of both learning and judgment.

In essence then, based on theories of 'cognitive processing' (Kitchener, 1983), we can (a) learn, (b) learn how to learn and (c) learn about the perspectives (worldviews) through which we learn—our prevailing 'windows on the world' as represented by our collective beliefs and assumptions. And we can do all of these from a position of critique—of being critical at each of these three 'levels' of learning, about 'our conduct in it' as well as about implications of interactions between them. The same might also be true about inspirational processes, although the logic is more difficult to establish for a domain in which conceptualisation is deliberately eschewed!

While such a systemic model of learning is far removed from the frameworks that currently prevail within development agencies and national education systems alike, there are many signs that its basic logic and its key elements are appearing in an increasingly wide variety of institutions concerned specifically with sustainable and secure agri-food systems.

In the face of what has seemed to be such intractable issues to date, we can but hope for such a trend to continue, as a further manifestation of the wisdom of Immanuel Kant, and the concerns for 'inclusive well-being' that his work has informed.

5.   ACKNOWLEDGMENTS

I want to particularly acknowledge Margot Foster from the South Australian Department of Education and Children's Services for encouraging me to articulate the significance of Kant's three questions to education for inclusive well-being, Martin Prozesky of the University of Kwa-Zulu Natal for introducing me to the construct and context of 'inclusive well-being' in the first place, and Harold Mattner, a doctoral candidate at the University of Western Sydney, for reminding me of the debt that I owe to Paulo Freire and of the significance of Freirian thought to educational reforms in which we have both participated.

6.   REFERENCES

Allen, W., Kilvington, M. and Horn, C. 2002. *Using Participatory and Learning-Based Approaches for Environmental Management and Help Achieve Constructive Behaviour Change.* Landcare Research Contract Report LC0102/057 prepared for the New Zealand Ministry for the Environment.

Bateson, G. 1972. *Steps to an Ecology of Mind.* Toronto: Chandler Publishing Co.

Bawden, R.J. 1979. A perspective for parasite management. *Agriculture and Environment* 4, 43–55.

Bawden, R.J. 1999. A cautionary tale: the Hawkesbury experience. In: van der Bor W., Peter Holen, Arjen E.J. Wals and Leal Filho W. (Eds.) *Integrating Concepts of Sustainability in Education for Agriculture and Rural Development* (Chapter 20). Frankfurt am Rhein: Peter Lang.

Bawden, R.J. 2000. Valuing the epistemic in the search for betterment: The nature and role of critical learning systems. *Cybernetics and Human Knowing* 7, 5–25.

Beck, U. 1992. *Risk Society: Towards a new modernity.* London: Sage.

Beck, U., Giddens, A. and Lash, S. 1994. *Reflexive Modernization: Politics, Tradition and Aesthetics in the Modern Social Order.* Cambridge, MA: Polity Press.

Folgar, J.P. and Bush, R.A.B. 1996. Transformative mediation and third party intervention: ten hallmarks of a transformational approach to practice. *Mediation Quarterly* 113, 263–278.

Freire, P. 1970. *Cultural Action for Freedom.* Cambridge, MA: Harvard Educational Review.

Habermas, J. 1984. *The Theory of Communicative Action*: Volume One—*Reason and the Rationalisation of Society.* Cambridge, MA: Polity Press.

Habermas, J. 1996. *Between Facts and Norms.* Cambridge, MA: Massachusetts Institute of Technology Press.

Kant, I. 1788. *Critique of Pure Reason.* tr N.K. Smith (1929). London: Macmillan and Co.

Kitchener, K. 1983. Cognition, meta-cognition, and epistemic cognition: a three level model of cognitive processing. *Human Development* 26, 222–232.

Kolb, D.A. 1984. *Experiential Learning: Experience as the Source of Learning and Development.* Englewood Cliffs, New Jersey: Prentice Hall.

Levinas, E. 1998. *Totality and Infinity.* tr. Alphonso Lingis (1998). Pittsburgh: Duquesne University Press.

Prozesky, M. 1998. *The Quest for Inclusive Well-being: Groundwork for an ethical renaissance.* Inaugural professorial lecture, University of Natal, Pietermaritzberg, South Africa.

Rendtorf, J.D. and Kemp, P. 2000. *Basic Ethical Principles: In European Bioethics and Biolaw.* Report to the European Commission of the BIOMED ll Project.

Roling, N. and Woodhill, A.J. 2001. *From Paradigms to Practice: Foundations, Principles and Elements for Water, Food and Environment.* Background Document for National and Basin Dialogue Design Workshop, Bonn December, December 2001. Dialogue for Water, Food and Environment Secretariat, Colombo.

Sen, A. 1992. *Inequality Examined.* Cambridge, MA: Harvard University Press.

Singer, P. 1995. *How are we to live: Ethics in an Age of Self-interest.* Melbourne: Mandarin.

Stiglitz, J.E. 2002. *Globalization and its Discontents.* New York: W.W. Norton and Company.

Wheatley, M.J. 1999. *Leadership and the New Science: Discovering Order in a Chaotic World.* San Fransisco: Berrett-Koehler.

Wolfensohn, J. 2004. Arms spending mad. *The Sun Herald*, 15 February 2004. Sydney

Woodhill, A.J. 2002. *Dialogue and transboundary water resources management: towards a framework for facilitating social learning.* In: Timmerman J. and Langaas S. (Eds.) *Environmental Information in European Transboundary Water Management* (Chapter 4).London: IWA Publishing.

Chapter 8

A SOCIAL JUSTICE STUDY: BRAZIL

Diva Lopes da Silveira

This paper discusses the question of social justice in a global world, focussing on Brazil. Though largely debated, this question has not yet been properly answered (Kelsen, 2001, p. 1). Trying to contribute to this debate, this paper raises a general thesis: social justice involves a *chaotic–solidaristic* integration (da Silveira, 2002) between the discourse towards the egalitarian rights and duties and its practical sustainability by ethics and democracy.

1. WHAT SOCIAL JUSTICE IS NOT

Latest scientific and technological advances should increase life quality. However, only a few benefit from them, as illustrated below (Kliksberg, 2001, p. 20–28).

Nearly 828 million people suffer from chronicle hunger, 2 billion from nutritional deficiencies and 1.3 billion from health services inaccessibility. Also, 7 million people die annually from diseases, such as tuberculosis, malaria and diarrhoea, which could be cured at low costs.

Besides, while 4.5 billion people earn less than 2 dollars daily, the 20% richest ones profit 82% and 68% from exportation and foreign investments, respectively. Their annual contribution of only 1% would guarantee primary education to all children of the world. Instead, external aid to developing countries decreased in 1997 from 0.7% to 0.2 % of the PIB.

In Latin America, democracy has improved, but out of 500 million people, 130 million still suffer from potable water shortage, 41% from bad nutrition and 160 million from health services inaccessibility. The infantile mortality rate per each 1000 children is 86.3 in Haiti; in Bolivia it is 75.1; in Nicaragua, 52.3 and in Guatemala, 48.5. In Brazil, the rate is 57.7. Annually, 2250 childbirth occur without any assistance, being infantile and maternal mortality rates five times higher than in developing countries.

No wonder Latin America has been internationally defined as the world's most inequitable region: while 5% of the richest people have 25% of the PIB, 30% of the poorest ones have only 7.6%.

2. SOCIAL JUSTICE DEFINED

Social justice raises many questions. Kelsen (2001, p. 1–7) argues that 'justice is that happiness warranted by a given social order'. But, what is happiness? A fair social order would guarantee happiness in an objective–collective sense, says Kelsen. But,

J. Campbell et al. (eds.), Towards a Global Community, 125–138.

Benthan (cited by Kelsen, op. cit., p. 3) argues that a just social order is impossible, even when it seeks both individual and collective happiness.

Maslow's (1954) notions of 'lower order' (objective) 'needs' (e.g. food, housing, education) and 'higher order' (subjective) 'needs' (e.g. self-esteem, self-realisation) may defy those theses.

Maslow holds that when a 'lower order need' is satisfied, a 'higher order' one emerges. For instance, being well employed may drive one to fulfil his dream of becoming a pianist. Would it be ethical to separate these needs, mainly by class, race or other categories?

If not, one may rephrase the theses above by adding some amendments: a just social order would guarantee individual and collective happiness on a sustainable basis, through a *chaotic–solidaristic integration* (da Silveira, 2002) between conflicting *social needs, economic demands* and *political priorities* (de Britto, 1991, p. 35–38). 'Sustainability' here involves a '... fundamental ethical (and democratic) questioning' (Bartholo, 2002, p. 6) and action towards the present and our *preferred futures*. 'Chaotic–solidaristic integration' would involve harmonic principles and actions, without ignoring possible contradictions involved in the process. Social justice would involve then 'imperfect hypothetical imperatives, such as desires, negotiations and reciprocity' (Gould, 1993, p. 49).

Such an integration requires objective (e.g. public policies) and subjective approaches. The latter includes appropriate attitudes and behaviours from each individual (see Chapter 3): for instance, high priority to ethical principles, love for others, responsibility, autonomy, solidarity and creation; conflict resolutions based on negotiation and reciprocity rather than on domination; and a profound concern with Nature and its sustainability. Also, a high priority to "the excluded, the minorities and the 'leftovers', those who do not buy nor sell, or are not missed" (Alves, 1995, p. 20–22).

3.   SOCIAL JUSTICE IN BRAZIL

This analysis of social justice focuses on recent literature, including daily newspapers of Brazil, the Latin America's largest country: 171 million people distributed among 27 states and 5507 municipalities. It argues that social justice involves both discourse and practice. In fact, Brazil is not poor of ideas, knowledge, solidarity, competence and responsibility—the 1988 Constitution is but an example, though the effective implementation of some of its determinations is still problematic.

4.   BRAZILIAN PROGRAMMES OF SOCIAL JUSTICE

The social justice programmes below focus on poverty, work, healthy, housing, agrarian reform, environment, indigenous population and education.

4.1.   Poverty

Brazil's poor population is 57 million, though to the actual Government the number is 50 million (Folha de São Paulo (Folha), 9th November 2002, p. A1). This number excludes the 'neo-poor', i.e. those with higher education or high school, but unemployed (Folha, 9th May 2003, p. A9). Half of the Brazilian workers perform a journey of 40–48 hours, but their income has decreased 10.1% since 1996 (Folha, 1st May 2003, p. B6).

Approximately 1.7 billion dollars should be invested in programmes to combat poverty. As the actual Federal Government has already paid nearly 7.7 billion dollars of interests to the FMI, very little has been invested in social programmes as yet. Nevertheless, the main governmental social programmes are:

- Basic Food Basket (17 dollars monthly), reaching 1000 thousand municipalities;
- School-Basket (5–15 dollars monthly) to families with children enrolled at school, reaching 10.7 million poor children;
- PETI (Programme for the Eradication of Infantile Work), (8–15 dollars, monthly), involving 810 million children;
- Youngster Programme (22 dollars monthly) to youngsters aged 15–17;
- Gas-Support (5 dollars, once every 2 months), reaching 8.5 million families;
- Nourishment-Basket (5–15 dollars monthly), reaching families with children up to 6 years and pregnancy.

To participate, poor families must register themselves into the Federal Government File of Social Programmes (Federal Decree, 24th July 2001), proving that their monthly income does not satisfy their 'lower order needs' (mainly food, transportation and clothes). Up to November 2002, only 52% of the families were registered, due to the excessive bureaucracy in some municipalities (Folha, 9th November 2002, p. A1).

4.1.1. Zero Hunger

This Programme, inaugurated in 30th January 2003, is co-ordinated by the Extraordinary Ministry of Food Security and Fight against Hunger (MESA) and the National Food Security Council (CONSEA). It intends to eradicate hunger and illiteracy, create jobs and workers' co-operatives, make agrarian reform and expand both the micro-credit access and skills training courses (Osava, 2003).

Municipal councils are responsible for the needed family's identification, donation distribution, people's education and deviations/waste avoidance. The Programme has attracted 27 million dollars from NESTLÉ; 11 million dollars from the United Nations Organisation for Agriculture and Food and the 'Zero Hunger' Support Association, which aggregates national and international entrepreneurs.

It began in Guaribas (Piauí, Northeast). A debit card allows 500 families to draw 17 dollars monthly from a state-owned bank (O Globo, 29th June 2003, p. 13). Where there are no banks, coupons are used.

But criticisms have emerged. For instance, the beneficiaries should use the money to buy other things than food only, as established; the Government's concern with food distribution is greater than with people's healthy (Jornal do Brasil (JB), 25th May 2003, p. A3); and poverty and inequality are not clearly associated in the programme (Carvalho, 2003, p. 13).

In fact, the beneficiaries receive monthly the Food-Basket, the School-Basket, the PETI and the Gas-Support, according to their needs. But, in Guaribas, the money received lasts, not rarely, 10 days only, and the nourishment is mainly beans and rice. Health and other basic needs, therefore, tend to become lower priorities.

4.2.   Work

The Brazilian unemployment average rate was 11.7% in 2002. In 2003 it is 12.8%. In 1997, unemployment of youngsters aged 15–17 was 13.8%. In 2002, it was 17%. In 1997 and 2002, it was, respectively, 10.9% and 14.7% for those aged 18–24. However, for older people (50–59), the increase was lower: 2.2%, in 1997, and 3.2%, in 2002. Importantly, in 2002, the number of workers with high school and higher education increased to 27% and 13.7%, respectively (Folha, 18th November 2002, p. B1; O Globo, 27th June 2003).

4.2.1.   PETI (Programme for Eradication of Infantile Work)

The 1988 Constitution prohibits youngsters aged below 14 to work. In fact, infantile work has decreased from 19.6% to 12.7%, between 1992 and 2001. Studying has been the only occupation of 87% of children (5–9 years) and youngsters (16–17 years). But, 5.5 million children are still working (JB, 13th June 2003, p. A4); 9.8% of them neither work nor study, and those who study and work, are in disadvantage at school.

Hence, the importance of PETI is evident, as it distributes 8.5–14 dollars to each poor child, who stops working in humiliating or inappropriate activities. But, from January to April 2003, this Programme spent only 10.76% of its total budget (84 million dollars). If this situation persists, the Programme shall be at risk (Folha, 2nd June 2003, p. C4).

In addition, part of the PETI's budget (85.5 million dollars) shall return to the National Treasury: until 2002, various families registered in the PETI had not drawn the benefit. Erroneous distribution of magnetic cards, small number of Bank agencies responsible for the Fund distribution and the beneficiaries' inability to use such cards, have been responsible for that.

As to the children's sexual exploration, in 1997 there were 2349 denouncers. The Federal Government is creating more 2500 titular councils (the actual number is 3009), and activating both the 'Call to Report' violence, and the Federal Policy.

The Government is also attentive to violence, such as the 'employment' of kids by drug traffickers, who pay them 35–1000 dollars per week to sell drugs in the streets. (Folha, 14th January 2003, p. C1).

4.2.2.   First-Job Programme

Launched last June, this Programme encourages the enterprises to hire poor youngsters, aged 16–24, who have low education and are looking for their first job. Micro/small, and macro firms, shall receive nearly 70 and 35 dollars, respectively, to complement the youngsters' monthly salary of 80 dollars. The dismissal of old employees ('substitution effect') is forbidden. The firms involved receive a Social Responsibility Certificate. The first goal is to create 260 thousand jobs in 12 months, though the initial Governmental expectation was 500 thousands jobs (Folha, 3rd July, 2003, p. A8).

The youngsters' professional preparation is also contemplated. In Mato Grosso State, whose juvenile unemployment rate is 17.1%, there are 500 vacancies for an industrial training course offered by the Senai. More than 5000 thousand youngsters are already enrolled. The course lasts 2 months, and grants free transportation, didactic material, uniform and food. The candidates selection considers their family income (up to three minimum salaries) and their educational level (preference is given to high school), (Folha, 4th June 2003, p. B1).

4.2.3. Youngsters Business

As part of the 'First Job', youngsters aged 18–24 can borrow, according to specified conditions, nearly 67 thousand dollars from the Workers Support Fund to initiate their own business. The payment can be made until 7 years after the loan. Five thousand projects may profit from this Programme.

4.2.4. Communitarian Work

The Federal Government, through various non-governmental organisations, plans to grant until 2004, 50 dollars monthly, during 6 months, to 50 thousand poor youngsters who want to develop communitarian work as their part time job. They must be enrolled in training courses to be selected. The Programme total budget is approximately 30.2 million dollars.

4.2.5. Kids' Talents

Poor youngsters aged 16–17 from Rio de Janeiro can take professional courses at the Estácio de Sá University. Among other activities, they learn how to calibrate tires at gas stations near the University and information retrieval, and study Rio de Janeiro's historical sites. The BR Distributor, the Estácio de Sá University and the Minor Crusade Institution sponsor them. They receive 35 dollars monthly, and job recommendations. Highly considered by the market, this Programme is taken as a Bank of Talents.

4.3. Health

Federal Government is investing approximately 180 million dollars to create Hospital Unities and ambulatories in large municipalities. They shall prevent day-to-day diseases, following-up the family's health. The Programmes shall begin in 2004 (Folha, 23rd April 2003, p. C3), but some are already in progress, as the Salvador Ambulatory Unit (Bahia, Northeast). It freely attends women, and gives lectures about familial planning, and contraceptive methods.

4.3.1. Mental Disturbance Research

Carried out by both USP and London University since 1999, this research involves children aged 7–14. Its findings have given relevant information about domestic violence, depression, hyper activity, nourishment disjunction and aggressiveness.

4.3.2.   Doctors Without Frontiers

It is an international non-governmental organisation aimed at producing and democratising the access to medicaments against neglected diseases, such as tuberculosis, leishmaniosis and malaria. Its budget for the next 12 years is 250 million dollars. The Fiocruz is one of its members (JB, 8th December 2002, p. A6).

4.3.3.   Humane Environment at Hospitals

The 'Alive Library', the 'Carmin' and the 'Happiness' Doctors' are some of the projects developed in public hospitals to treat young patients. The former, developed in 26 public hospitals of São Paulo, has already reached 70 million children. The patient–physician relationship is intermediated through reading. The latter, in 12 years of action in Rio de Janeiro and São Paulo, has improved 300 million kids' humour through entertaining activities. The 'Carmin project', in São Paulo, argues that, at the hospitals people discover their potentialities. Accordingly, it teaches painting, photography, design and art history to the kids at the UTI or common ward (Folha, 31st March 2003, p. C4).

4.3.4.   Free Distribution of Aids' Cocktail in Check

About 9.4 thousands new cases of Aids have emerged in 2002 among adolescents aged 13–19. Girls aged 13–19 represent 2.9% of these cases. Men are still the majority attacked by Aids: 257.7 thousand.

Brazilian patients are developing resistance to Aids' medicaments, it has been argued. An American research, however, declared that the Brazilian resistance index is 6.6%, while in other countries (e.g. Germany, France and USA), it is higher than 10%. Nevertheless, the free distribution of the Aids' cocktail is under surveillance (JB, 14th May 2003, p. A4).

4.3.5.   Maternal Mortality

Reaching 67%, it is caused mainly by mothers' high pressure, which could be avoided, if pregnancy had special care. The Federal Government hopes to reduce this index to 25% until 2007.

4.3.6.   Projects for Handicapped People

Unfortunately, some type of deficiency affects 14% of Brazilians. The Brazilian Decree No. 8213/1991 determines the enterprises to hire them according to their number of employees. For instance, 2% from 100–200 hundred employees and 5% from 1000 thousand employees. More than 100 macro enterprises are involved in the 'Citizen Project', whose employees are trained to help their handicapped colleagues. In addition, the Governmental 'Eye in the Eye' Project shall grant glasses to 3 million visual handicapped children from public primary schools. The Programme's budget is 54 million dollars.

4.4. Housing

Brazil faces a residence deficit of 6.6 million units, being 24% of them situated in metropolitan regions. Most of them belong to families earning three minimum salaries per month (O Globo, 22nd May 2003, p. 3). The main reasons for this are the country's economic instability, and the middle classes' difficulty to obtain a loan correspondent to 50% or 70% of the total value of the house they want to buy.

In Rio de Janeiro, two projects to correct such a deficit are under discussion: (a) to restore the city centre, mainly its historical sites, as well as its unoccupied buildings and (b) to build districts, with all basic sanitary conditions in the city's Northern urban areas. Together, both projects would reach 100 thousand people. Financial resources would come from the Union General Budget.

Another project is the Residential Leasing Programme with a budget of 1 billion dollars. It has attended 21,041 families earning monthly six minimum salaries (approximately 480 dollars).

As to the rural areas, the Government has established a partnership with the MST to build, still in 2003, 1200 thousand residences priced, on the average, 3000 thousand dollars each. Approximately 110 million dollars shall come from Incra and the Union General Budget.

4.5. Agrarian Reform

As the Agrarian Reform, though established by the Art. 184 of the 1988 Constitution, has not involved all rural workers yet, the MST has systematically occupied lands it takes as non-productive. This has caused conflicts resolved by Law.

Until June 2003, 2534 families have been settled in rural areas, constituting about 4.2% of 60 thousand families, the initial actual Government's expectation. But the budget was reduced to 83 million dollars, a third of what was initially estimated (O Globo, 29th June 2003, p. 12). This has led the MST to mobilise 140 thousand people to camp near the roads while demanding rural unoccupied lands. Such pressure is accelerating, but not neglecting *flexible negotiations*, to solve the impasse.

4.6. Environment

Brazil has the world's largest areas of tropical forests, biodiversity and fresh water. But, their non-sustainable usage in the last 10 decades has been devastating (Thomas, 2003).

Only 7% of the original Atlantic Forest is left. More than 15% of the Amazon Forest has been destroyed, and 50% of their biomass has been altered. Also, the cattle-raising has burned 17 thousand kilometres of land in Amazon. Yet, 10% of the 20 million of Brazilians who live continue unemployed, and the resulting environmental impact has reduced the resources of other activities in the region, such as fishing and rubber extraction. Trying to correct these and other impacts, the government has implemented public policies, such as helping 10 million victims of drought in Northeast.

4.6.1. *Water for Life, Water for All—(O Globo, 2nd June 2003, p. 22)*

Fifteen percent of the world fresh water is in Brazil, but part of is located far from large populations. In the Amazons State with its large rivers, live only 12% of the Brazilian population, while in North East, South East and South, where approximately 70% of the population live, there are only 16% of water resources.

The World Foundation for Nature is launching the 'Water for life, Water for all', a Programme to be developed in 4 years through four courses of action:
*   societal mobilisation towards the Planet shortage of water;
*   socio-environmental research;
*   formulation and implementation of water resource management models and
*   a large debate about water public policies.

It hopes to guarantee a sustainable administration of the issues involved. To these ends, the Programme has already been granted approximately 1.700 million dollars.

4.7. *Indigenous Population*

In Brazil, there are no more than 380 thousand indigenous. Yet, they suffer from crucial problems, four of them are briefly described below.

First, indigenous living near the frontier with Colombia have been subjected to criminal actions from the narco-traffic and the Farc (Colombia Armed Revolutionary Forces), such as recruiting and kidnapping. The Federal Police Cobra Operation and the Frontier Special Platoon act in the region since 2000. Also, they collect data about the indigenous' identification, number, age, gender, marriage and educational qualification. A difficulty is that, afraid of revenge from those criminal organisations, the indigenous tend to omit information about the absent ones (Folha, 18th May 2003, p. A12).

Second, some tribes from Roraima (North) claim for their lands' possession since the 1970s. Though their lands have been demarcated in 1998, their ratification is still pending (Folha, 21st May 2003, p. 9).

Third, from 2001 to 2003, there were 56 deaths of children below 5 years of age, mostly due to malnutrition. The infantile mortality rate is 62.7 per thousand childbirth in 58 indigenous villages. But, the actual Government has invested about 1700 million dollars in their agriculture, animal creation, among other activities. Basic food baskets are also at their disposal (Folha, 21st April 2003, p. A2).

Finally, about 20 thousand indigenous from Amazon are lacking medical care due to the shortage of Federal Government funds. They are suffering from digestive parasitosis, an implication of potable water inaccessibility. Ninety-five deaths have been registered in 2002. Awareness of the situation led the Government to repass funds for the construction of artesian wells, among other services (Folha, 6th June 2003, p. A11).

4.8. *Education*

4.8.1. *Literacy*

Brazil has 11 million illiterates: 21% in Northeast; 9.2% in North; 8.1% in Centre-West; 5.7% in Southeast and 5.2% in South (O Globo, 15th June 2003, p. 34).

In 33% of the cities (from 1796 Municipalities, mostly in North and Northeast), 90% are 'functionally illiterate', i.e. they have not concluded the first 4 years of study, or can read and write a few words only (O Globo, 5th June 2003, p. 10).

In Guaribas, the 'Zero Hunger's' pilot city, 92% are 'functionally illiterate' and 55% of the children aged 10–14 do not read nor write. Jordão (Acre State), the city with the third lowest human development and income indexes, has the country's highest illiteracy percentage: 60.7% (O Globo, 4th June 2003, p. 12).

Differently, in São Paulo (South) and Rio de Janeiro (Southeast), illiteracy reaches 383 and 119 thousand people, respectively, representing 5% of the total population of both cities.

Besides regional differences, gender, age and race have distinguished illiteracy in 2001. Between men (10.7%) and women (9.6%), the difference was small. It increased when the age group was considered: 13% (15–24) and 18% (25–34). But, for black and white people, the difference was greater: 5.7% and 15.4%, respectively.

MEC-UNESCO partnership. The MEC-UNESCO and the Brazilian Extraordinary Secretary of Illiteracy Eradication shall invest, respectively, 200 thousand dollars, and nearly 91 million dollars in literacy programmes. They expect to reach 20 million adults, and youngsters aged above 15 (Folha, 20th May 2003, p. C3).

Literate Brazil. This Programme shall teach, first, a hundred thousand illiterates from Brasilia (Brazil's capital). University students are being trained for this purpose. It shall be extended to more 200 thousands illiterates who live nearby the capital (JB, 22nd May 2003, p. A21).

Literacy for rural workers. Nearly 200 thousands rural workers are illiterate (Noblat, 2003), as well as several of the MST's members (Movement of Rural Workers without Land). To eradicate rural workers' illiteracy, a partnership was created in June 2003 between the MEC and the National Association for Agricultural Co-operation, a non-governmental organisation, which represents the MST. Accordingly, 1500 thousands literate rural workers shall be trained to teach their illiterate comrades.

Literate maré. This Programme teaches illiterate or 'functional illiterate' people, aged 16–29, who live in a slum called 'Maré' (Rio de Janeiro). Under the Unibank, Roberto Marinho Foundation and the Viva Rio Movement partnership, 299 people are attending telecourses to conclude primary school. The assumption is that education free people from violence. Hence, the investment on people who dropped out school and became either 'street kids', or unemployed. Similarly, the 'Petrópolis Community Programme', organised by the Viva Rio Movement, which has already attended 60 thousand poor people (O Globo, 22nd March 2003, p. 17; O Globo, 20th October 2002, p. 32).

Talents timely initiation (TTI) programme. Some talents cannot be fully accomplished late in life. In fact, middle classes' and elite's children in Brazil (and other countries) tend to develop their talents in a proper age. But, what about the poor children's talents? The TTI is an opportunity for poor children to develop their talents, and have a job in the future. Its inclusion in educational programmes, as a regular and free procedure, could be accomplished through public policies which articulate: (a) partnerships among education, market place, society, artistic organisations and government, providing the poor children financial and technical conditions to fully develop their identified talents—for instance, studying piano from the first to the last year of the process and (b) an agreed-upon contract for the TTI Programme's beneficiary, when properly employed, to repay in kind or money the benefits received, so to help others in similar conditions. In practice, it is a long and perhaps never finished process, whose implementation 'would be more effective and democratic, the earlier it starts, and the longer it lasts' (da Silveira, 2000, p. 54). This Programme is still under discussion by a few professionals of education, but given the will, it could be implemented in Brazil and other countries as well.

4.8.2.   Primary Education

It lasts 8 years as part time journey, involving children from 7 years of age. The MEC plans to extend it to 9 years full-time journey, including children aged 6. This tries to reduce educational differences between low and middle classes—in general, children from the latter attend full-time kindergarten and pré-school.

The minimum income law. Since 1997, this Law grants 5–15 dollars monthly to poor families, provided that they enrol their children at school.

Applied to Federal District's primary schools, this Law showed a decrease of dropping out, learning failure, 'street kids' and infantile work. Also, the improvement of children's and parents' motivation towards the future, and women's revalorisation (Wertheim, 2003). This Law, therefore drives poor people to pursue their 'lower' and 'higher order needs'. Though its implementation still demands attention, it has been recommended by the UNESCO, as a strategy to combat violence and people's learning difficulties.

Thrush project for handicapped people. Despite their high relative representation (approximately 14% of the Brazilian population), only 0.065% (105) of handicapped people have taken entrance exams for higher education. Nearly 39% of the permanent handicapped children between 7 and 14 years do not attend school (Nicoletti, 2003, p. 4). Brazilian Educational Institutions are, in general, not properly equipped to assist handicapped people, but consciousness about it is expanding in the country.

The 'Thrush Project' illustrates this point. From October 2003 onwards, a Sailing Vessel-School shall teach basic notions and sociological analysis of sea survival to handicapped students older than 18 years. It will depart from Portugal, going through Amazon, United States and Europe, stopping in Brazil after 14 months of study. The crew includes a physician, a university teacher and students of cinema from the Federal Fluminense University.

4.8.3. High School Education

Lasting 3 years, it attends youngsters aged 16–19. In 2002, 8.71 million pupils were enrolled, being 4.25 million in evening classes. But, there are still about 5 million youngsters out of high school, or still attending primary schools.

In 2004, the MEC intends to expand high school's duration to 4 years, and, gradually, make it obligatory to all. Thus, the number of teachers shall increase, as well as the School-Baskets for pupils taking evening classes (Folha, 13th June 2003, p. C1).

Free transference from public to private school. The Government of Rio de Janeiro is offering, for the next 3 years, 10 thousands free vacancies in private high schools to pupils who finished public primary schools. This is so due to the lack of vacancies in the latter.

Criticisms, however, have already emerged: public schools should be built, instead; cultural, educational, social and economic differences exist between the transferred and non-transferred pupils, and between teaching methodologies used by each institution type. Nevertheless, the Programme motivates poor and low middle class pupils to continue their studies, which otherwise would impossible.

4.8.4. Higher Education

As public universities tend to concentrate 60% of the richest students (O Globo, 13th June 2003, p. 29), the MEC is requesting the ex-students a contribution, proportional to their salaries: 2% from annual salaries of 10–17 thousand dollars and 3% from above. If approved by the Congress, approximately 7 billion dollars shall be collected annually. This money shall improve the university's vacancies, the university teachers' salary and teaching-research activities.

The quota system for Black People. Not rarely, black population is excluded from higher education. In 2000, out of 4056 freshmen from the Rio de Janeiro Federal University (Southeast), 76.8% were white, and 20.3%, black/mestizo; and out of 3499 freshmen from the Paraná Federal University (South), 86.5% were white and 8.8%, black/mestizo. At the University of Brasilia (Centre-West), out of 528 freshmen, 63.7% white and 35.3% were black/mestizos. But at the Maranhão Federal University (Northeast), the difference was smaller: out of 907 freshmen, 47% were white and 42.8% were black/mestizos (Folha, 22nd February 2003, p. C4).

Within this context, it was approved, in 2001 'the quota system', offering vacancies in public universities to black/mestizos candidates. The index for each university has not been clearly defined yet. To be selected, they have to pass the entrance examination, like the other ones, and prove their monthly income. Some universities of Rio de Janeiro used this system for the first time, in 2003, not without difficulties resolved by Law. The debate is all over Brazil, without clear definition as yet.

All these programmes show ethical and democratic responsibility towards social justice. Some have less than 6 months of existence, others are still waiting for implementation, and a few professionals of education have only briefly discussed the TTI. But, despite their conflicts and their potentialities, government and society are trying to put their discourse of equality into practice. Hence, the importance of awareness of social justice as a *chaotic–solidaristic* integration between the discourse and practice, whose sustainability requires ethical and democratic principles.

5.   CONCLUSION

Though this study could not deepen the issue of social justice, it is hoped that it emphasised relevant questions. Some of them are: the citizens right to satisfy both their 'lower' and 'higher order needs'; their egalitarian access to education, including the children's talents development; their rights and duties towards work, health, housing, the environment, societal togetherness, solidarity and responsibility.

Finally, five main indicators of social justice may be suggested:
- Egalitarian (re)education towards both the principles of *indivisible humanity* and our *preferred futures,* and against the *trivialisation of injustice* (Déjours, 2001);
- A vision and practice of *justice as a social category* (Kelsen, op. cit, p. 4);
- A *solidaristic–chaotic integration* between 'lower–higher order needs', demands and priorities;
- A participatory decision-making process involving 'relevant others' (e.g. the government, the society, the productive sector, among others);
- The effective implementation of agreed-upon public policies.

Whether these and other *solidaristic–chaotic* propositions shall be implemented with success or not shall depend upon each one of us.

6.   REFERENCES

Alves, E.F. 1995. Incluídos, excluídos e sobrantes. *Em Foco* 1, 20–22.

Bartholo, R., Ribeiro, H. and Bittencourt, J.N. 2002. *Ética e Sustentabilidade*. Rio de Janeiro: E. Papers.

Campbell, J., Baikaloff, N. and Power, C. 2001.*Towards a Global Community: Educating For Tomorrow's World*, Synopsis 1 Paper.

Carvalho, J.M. 2003. História julgará Lula pelo combate à pobreza. *O Globo* (newspaper), p. 13.

da Silveira, D.L. 2000. Educação Igualitária, mestiça e sustentável: um espaço para a Iniciação Oportuna de Talentos (IOT). *Revista Científica* 1(4), 51–59.

da Silveira, D.L. 2002. Educação Ambiental e Conceitos Caóticos. In: Pedrini, A. (Org.) *Educação Ambiental: Reflexões e Práticas Contemporâneas* (5th ed.). Vozes: Petrópolis, Rio de Janeiro, pp. 188–259.

de Britto, L.N. 1991.*Educação no Brasil e na América Latina—questões relevantes e polêmicas*, Vol. 2. São Paulo: T.A. Queiroz.

Decreto Federal no. 3.877. Institui Programas Sociais do Governo Federal. 24th July 2001.

Déjours, C. 2001. *A Banalização da Injustiça Social* [Souffrance en France: La banalisation de l' injustice sociale] (4th ed.). (Trans. by Monjardim L.A.). Rio de Janeiro: Editora FGV.

Folha de São Paulo (Folha) (newspaper). 2002. Lista não contempla 18,7 milhões de pobres. *Folha*, 9th November 2002, p. A1. Source: Economic Applied Research Institute, IPEA.

Folha de São Paulo (Folha) (newspaper). 2002. Trabalhador está mais velho e escolarizado. *Folha*, 18th November 2002, p. B1. Source: IBGE.

Folha de São Paulo (Folha) (newspaper). 2003. Tráfico paga até 12 mil de salário a garotos. *Flora*, Quotidian, 14th January 2003, p. C1. Source: DCS/Ensue/Forces.

Folha de São Paulo (Folha) (newspaper). 2003. UFBa revela perfil racial do ensino superior. *Flora*, Cotidiano, 22nd February 2003, p. C4. Source: IBGE.

Folha de São Paulo (Folha) (newspaper). 2003. Grupos humanizam ambiente hospitar. *Folha*, Cotidiano, 31st March 2003, p. C4.

Folha de São Paulo (Folha) (newspaper). 2003. FUNASA aponta crianças índias com desnutrição grave. *Folha*, O País/Política, 21st April 2003, p. A2. Source: IBGE.

Folha de São Paulo (Folha) (newspaper). 2003. União anuncia verba para ampliar o Programa Saúde da Family. *Folha*, 23rd April 2003, Cotidiano, p. C3.

Folha de São Paulo (Folha) (newspaper). 2003. Brasileiro perde 10% da renda desde 96. *Folha*, Dinheiro, 1st May 2003, p. B6. Source: IBGE.

Folha de São Paulo (Folha) (newspaper). 2003. Exclusão. *Folha*, Brasil, 9th May 2003, p. A9.

Folha de São Paulo (Folha) (newspaper). 2003. PF apura sumiço de jovens índios na fronteira. *Folha*, 18th May 2003, p. A12.

Folha de São Paulo (Folha) (newspaper). 2003. MEC e UNESCO assinam acordo para investimentos em alfabetização no Brasil. *Folha*, 20th May 2003, p. C3.

Folha de São Paulo (Folha) (newspaper). 2003. Governo admite rever demarcação de reserva. *Folha*, O País, 21st May 2003, p. 9.

Folha de São Paulo (Folha) (newspaper). 2003. Redução de gastos afeta setor social. *Folha*, Cotidiano, 2nd June 2003, p. C4.

Folha de São Paulo (Folha) (newspaper). Curso gratuito atrai 5.500 pessoas em MT. 2003. *Folha*, 4th June 2003, p. B1.

Folha de São Paulo (Folha) (newspaper). 2003. Índios ficam sem atendimento médico. *Folha*, Brasil, 6th June 2003, p. A11. Source: FUNASA.

Folha de São Paulo (Folha) (newspaper). 2003. Ensino Médio será obrigatório, anuncia MEC. *Folha*, Cotidiano, 13th June 2003, p. C1.

Folha de São Paulo (Folha) (newspaper). 2003. Lula lança 1o. Emprego com menos verba. *Folha*, Brasil, 3rd July 2003, p. A8.

Gould, S.J. 1993. *Dedo Mindinho e seus Vizinhos* [Eight Little Piggies, Reflections in Natural Science] (Trans. by Flaksman S.). São Paulo: Companhia das Letras.

Jornal do Brasil (JB) (newspaper). 2002. As doenças esquecidas. JB, O País, 8th December 2002, p. A6.

Jornal do Brasil (JB) (newspaper). 2003. Casos de Aids entre adolescentes preocupam. JB, 14th May 2003, p. A4.

Jornal do Brasil (JB) (newspaper). 2003. MEC tem ajuda para alfabetizar. JB, O Pais/Politica, 22nd May 2003, p. A21.

Jornal do Brasil (JB) (newspaper). 2003. ONU: fome e sede São alarmantes no país. JB, O País/Política, 25th May 2003, p. A3.

Jornal do Brasil (JB) (newspaper). 2003. Trabalho infantil recua. JB, O País/Política, 13th June 2003, p. A4. Sources: IBGE, PNAD, 2001.

Kelsen, H. 2001. *O que é Justice?* [What is Justice?] (3rd ed.). (Trans. by Borges L.C.) São Paulo: Martins Fontes.

Kliksberg, B. 2001. *A Justiça Social—uma visão judaíca*. São Paulo: Maayanot.

Maslow, A.H. 1954.*Motivation and Personality*. New York: Harper & Row.

Nicoletti, A. 2003. Deficientes são menos de 1% dos inscritos nos grandes vestibulares do país. Fovest. *Folha*, 3rd July 2003, p. 4–5. Source: 2002 Census.

Noblat, A. 2003. MEC e MST firmam convênio. JB, O Pais/Polìtica, Rio de Janeiro, 1st June 2003, p. A2.

O Globo (newspaper). 2002. Petrópolis tenta levar jovens de volta à escola. *O Globo*, 20th October, 2002, p. 34.

O Globo (newspaper). 2003. Projeto leva ensino a jovens carentes. *O Globo*, 22nd March 2003, p. 17.

O Globo (newspaper). 2003. Onde mora o brasileiro? *O Globo*, Projetos de Marketing, 22nd May 2003, p. 3.

O Globo (newspaper). 2003. Metade dos analfabetos do Brasil está em apenas 10% dos municípios. *O Globo*, O País, 4th June 2003, p. 12.

O Globo (newspaper). 2003. Só em 19 cidades alunos estudam oito anos. *O Globo*, O País, 5th June, p. 10. Source: Illiteracy Map, Inep/MEC.

O Globo (newspaper). 2003. Universidade Pública concentra mais ricos. *O Globo*, Economia, 13th June 2003, p. 29.

O Globo (newspaper). 2003. São Paulo, Minas e Bahia têm hoje mais de três milhões de analfabetos. *O Globo*, Economia, 15th June 2003, p. 34. Source: PNAD, 2001.

O Globo (newspaper). 2003. Desemprego sobre para 12,8%. Renda cai 14,7%.*O Globo*, Economia, 27th June 2003, p. 23. Source: IBGE.

O Globo (newspaper). 2003. Seis meses do Governo LULA. 29th June 2003, p. 13.
Osava, M. 2003. *Lula Launches War on Hunger—Both Causes and Effects*. Available at:
    http://www.globalpolicy.org/socecon/develop/2003/0130zerohunger.htm-10k, accessed on 11th
    June 2003.
Thomas, V. 2003. O meio ambiente e o progresso social. *Folha de São Paulo*, Opinião, 17th June 2003,
    p. A3.
Werthein, J. 2003.*Pobreza e Educação: Rompendo o Círculo Vicioso*. Available at:
    http://www.unesco.org.br/noticiais/artigos/artigowq.as, accessed on 1st June 2003.

Chapter 9

EDUCATING FOR CARING AND HUMANE CONNECTIONS

Judy Lawley

WAIRUA
'Nanny, what is Wairua'? The child asked, eyes wide:
Wairua, my moko, is what gives us life.
Handed down to us from a time past.
At the moment of your beginning,
You shared with me the Wairua of our tupuna,
For I am your link with the past,
And you are my link with the future.

The aroha of the whanau has Wairua,
And their words, their laughter, their tears.
The Marae, tangi, waiata and Whakapapa
Have a Wairua that strengthens us, gives us pride.

So too the sunrise and sunset.
The soft summer rain, the raging storm,
The song of the birds in the trees,
The waves on the beach,
The mist rising from the bush,
The moonlight on the water,
And the embracing darkness of the night.

To sit quietly in the wharenui or the urupa
And feel the presence of your tupuna is to feel Wairua.
Your arms about my neck, your breath on my cheek,
Fills me with a special Wairua,
For there is a Wairua in all things that give meaning to life,
To love, to the future.

So, moko, open your mind,
Let your heart love,
Your eyes see,
Your ears hear,
And your hands feel.
Give of yourself, my moko,

J. Campbell et al. (eds.), Towards a Global Community, 139–155.

For in giving, you receive,
And the Wairua grows.

Anonymous

1.   INTRODUCTION—THE GLOBAL WHANAU/FAMILY

This poem about a New Zealand Maori grandmother is offered here in the hope that readers will find it an appropriate and satisfying expression of love, care, giving and spirituality. If this is so, then it represents a small sharing between the various cultures of the author and readers around the globe.

New Zealand Maori culture draws deeply on a sense of spirit (wairua) and, perhaps above all else that is important to the human spirit, recognises that life flows from generation to generation and that the spirits of those who have gone before (whakapapa) live on to guide not only the moko (grandchildren), but all members of the whanau (family). The whanau may be as large as we wish it to be—the wider the network of kinship and trust, the greater the whanau. This short essay on caring is about the dream of the global 'whanau'.

> Caring for each other must be the major interest and characteristic of people. People must live in awareness that we share in one big family, and damage in one part is felt by the other parts of the family . . . People must live in cooperation with each other regardless of their political values and orientation, and religion. (Response by a New Zealand participant in this study)

2.   THE DEFINITIONS AND CONNECTIONS OF CARING

There are six closely linked terms to be aware of in a discussion of caring. These are caring, service, empathy, compassion, connectedness and love.

There is also a seventh term that stands apart from and in apposition to these six. Acknowledgement of this term enhances our understanding of the meaning of caring. It is indifference. Indifference is the most insidious cause of dehumanisation because it eludes identification or naming. Anything that helps oppose indifference is a highly desirable feature of a global future. This opposition is not merely a change of attitude, but entails a critical engagement with and interrogation of the choices and aspirations that shape our lives as individuals, and also the lives we lead through our ever-widening circle of relationships within families and our various communities of connection. *The worst crime of all is indifference*, as said by the English playwright George Bernard Shaw.

Love is not discussed here in detail, as that would require a very large book all of its own. But the stance here is borrowed from 'A Short Treatise on the Great Virtues, the Uses of Philosophy in Everyday Life', by Andre Comte-Sponville (2001, p. 288)—2 years on the French best seller list and so far translated into 24 languages.

> There are three types or three degrees to love: want (eros), joy (philia), and charity (agape). . . . And compassion? It may well be the principal content of charity, its truest affect, indeed its real name.

> In any case, compassion is what charity is called in the Buddhist East, in this respect more lucid and realistic ... than the Christian West. (Comte-Sponville, 2001, p. 288)

Hence we find that compassion is more pertinent to a discussion on love than caring, and this is nicely summed up by Comte-Sponville like this: 'Love and do what you wish, or be compassionate and do what you must' (Comte-Sponville, 2001, p. 117).

Maughn Gregory talks about caring in close connection with empathy:

> The process of caring is the same for strangers and for intimates: we keep ourselves aware of when and how we interact with them; we seek to understand them as far as is practical, we attempt to empathise with what they must need or want from our interaction, and we act to fulfil that need or want, unless we decide that doing so would violate our own conscience. As Nell Noddings describes: When we struggle toward the reality of the other ... we also have aroused in us the feeling, 'I must do something'. When we see the other's reality as a possibility for us, we must act to eliminate the intolerable, to reduce the pain, to fill the need, to actualise the dream. 'When I am in this sort of relationship with another, when the other's reality becomes a real possibility for me, I care'. (Noddings, 1984 in Gregory, 2000, p. 66)

The Learning to Be UNESCO-APNIEVE Sourcebook for teachers and others, 2002, presents this definition of compassion from Cherie Carter Scott (2000, p. 67).

> Compassion is a human quality essential for pro-social, altruistic behaviour where one showing compassion suffers on account of other's suffering. This is different from one's own suffering. Compassion is the act of opening your heart, lowering your barriers to emotions and approaching to connect with others. This is the emotional glue that keeps you rooted in the universality of human experience, as it connects you to your essence and to those around you.

The 'Love and Compassion' chapter in *Learning to Be* goes on to say:

> His Holiness, the Dalai Lama of Tibet affirms Compassion as 'Karuna', concern and connectivity.... broadly speaking compassion has been stated to be manifested as altruistic behaviour, pro-social behaviour, and pro-environmental behaviour. (UNESCO-APNIEVE, 2002, p. 67)

Professor Lloyd Geering pleads for compassion and connection on a global scale:

> We do not live by bread alone but by the love, compassion and good-will which we can show to one another ... in the world to come we humans find we are dependent wholly on our inner resources, yet not

so much individually as collectively. The challenges which lie ahead cannot be overcome by any one person or group working on their own but only by the human species working as a whole...unless we humans are strongly motivated to become a global society, we are likely in the imminent future to suffer horrendous catastrophes which will be of our own making. The realisation of the global society will require from the whole of humanity creative thinking, self-sacrificing endeavour of the highest order, and all the mutual goodwill of which we are capable. (Geering, 1999, p. 162)

Empathy is an inherent part of compassion. This tightest of connections is succinctly and perfectly expressed in the Buddhist terms *doku and bakku. Doku* is the empathetic ability to feel the suffering of another. *Doku* becomes *bakku* when it naturally leads to action that eliminates the cause of the suffering. So *bakku is doku* in action. This surely is the absolute essence of caring—unless values are turned into action then all attention to caring is for nothing. At the 1998 UNESCO summit on values education in New Zealand former Governor General, Sir Paul Reeves gave a clear message to teachers, parents and all adults that values are only meaningful in action. He stated: 'We must not ask children to do what we do not do ourselves. History has been built around the gap between what we say and what we do'.

In the introductory poem Nanny tells her moko: 'Give of yourself, my moko, for in giving, you receive, and the wairua grows'. More than anything else, including empathy, compassion or love, caring is about giving, serving and connecting to others. These three are soul mates. The ability to care depends on the healthy development of human and humane connections that lead to *values in action* as best practiced in service and giving. This is a two-way street. Just as the only true expressions of caring and feeling connected to others are the actions of giving and serving, so too, as people have opportunities to give and serve, they learn to care. This is simply the old human development principle that actions do not always follow feelings, very often actions lead to changes or developments in feelings and in core life values.

Herein lies the nub of teaching caring—whether that is in schools, in families, in community groups or at work. It is all about giving children (and adults too!) opportunities to practice caring by connecting with and helping others.

Mahatma Gandhi expressed it thus:

> Watch your thoughts, they become your actions
> Watch your actions, they become your habits
> Watch your habits they become your values.

In case the 'me' generation needs further convincing of the benefits of caring, new research in this area should be helpful to them. Here is one such research outcome.

Between 1970 and 1999 the average American family received a 16% increase in income (inflation adjusted). However, the percentage of people who described themselves as 'very happy' fell from 36% to 29%. Drawing from the academic field of 'happiness economics' the March 2003 lead article, 'How to Live a Rich Life', in *Fast Company* magazine, reported that what is now being discovered is that beyond a certain level of economic wealth, happiness is more about relationships than more money. The article reported:

> Our lifestyles are packed with stuff, but we lead emptier lives. We're consuming more but enjoying it less... more people in the world know the meaning of Gucci and Lexus than know the meaning of life. Hence the latest trend: spending less and living better.

Robert Putnam (2000) suggested that there are substantial health and happiness benefits from building social capital and encourages investing more time in relationships and social activity, particularly by giving service and caring to others. So it appears there is something in caring and serving for everyone. Even the 'less than altruistic or compassionate' can be appealed to on the basis that they will be healthier and happier the more they care for others.

That the message of care and service is universal does not need further elaboration. Just one brief quote will highlight this universality. The Buddhist leader, Daisaku Ikeda of Japan stated: 'Human brilliance derives from the light of altruistic action. People are truly human only when they endeavour to dedicate their lives for their friends'. From: 'Legacy of Peace' An exhibition of inspirations from Mahatma Gandhi, Martin Luther King and Daisaku Ikeda, touring six western and eastern countries in 2003.

3.   CARING AND THE INTERNATIONAL SCHOOL CURRICULUM

Material in this chapter is predominantly drawn from the author's experience of values education in New Zealand schools over the last 5 years. Having said that, it must be hastily added that, in preparing, testing and introducing a model for values education in schools, ideas and teaching materials were gathered from New Zealand, USA, Australia, Canada, India, England, Scotland, Hawaii and other countries. Many of those resources are listed in the appendix to this chapter. They reflect the global and universal nature of values education as a whole and illustrate that the value of caring is as 'international' in definition and application as any of the other universal values. The 200 or so values are considered common to all major cultures and religions of the world. There is, of course, a myriad of differences in the ways people of different places and cultures care and connect with one another. But the wonderful thing about a global approach to strengthening these values in young people and their teachers is the discovery that there are so many similarities, not only in the core values held by people of all cultures and religions of the world, but also in the constructive (and destructive) ways they are practiced in daily life.

New Zealand is an agricultural economy, reliant on dairy farming. Craig Norgate, is the Chief Executive of the country's largest business, a conglomerate representing most of the dairy industry. He recently stated in an interview that what was most wrong with New Zealand was 'lack of service'. Such reactions to the 'me' generation of the latter part of the 20th Century are common. The cry to think beyond 'me' and to lead our lives for 'the common good' is hopefully growing, and it would be good to think that this present global education study is playing a part in a steady movement towards the day we wake up to find values and priorities have moved from a 'me' focus to 'we'. People will have got the message that survival of the human species, from the personal to the global, is going to depend on caring and connecting with others at many different degrees of closeness and distance.

As suggested by Geering above, we obviously will need the steady movement towards a virtuous world of individuals that pool their collective wisdom across the globe to pick up some serious speed wobble. We need to reach a 'tipping point' soon. At a White House press conference in June 2000, Bill Clinton explained that social change reaches a 'tipping point' when 'people kind of get it'. He was referring to the magic moment when ideas, trends and social behaviours cross a threshold, tip and spread like wildfire—the concept put forward by Gladwell (2000) in his sensational book 'The Tipping Point: How Little Things Can Make a Big Difference'.

The tipping point concept is important to the understanding that practicing and teaching caring and connectedness in schools can make a difference to the future of the world. Indeed it may well be our greatest hope for finding a way forward that will make any difference at all. There are two pathways to reach the 'tipping point' via the international school curriculum, one to do with schools as a critically important 'communication point' for spreading the message, the second to do with the place of skills learning or action competence, for caring.

Firstly, it is not only true that caring schools help to develop caring young people that grow up to be caring adults, but that they can exert a significant influence on the cities and nations they serve and, through international networks, on the world. Our greatest hope for the future lies in schools that learn, in schools that lead. Where better can creative thinking take place and where better can international networks be formed. In 'The Global Classroom' (1999), Townsend and Otero suggest that teachers can take children in the classroom beyond the knowledge of what is happening around the world and how they are connected to other countries, to deeper understandings of international issues. Students, they say, need contact with global agencies such as Wildlife Fund, Amnesty International and UNICEF.

> Students need to learn that they can change things that they see as being unjust, but that it takes planning and support to do so. The old community education adage of 'Think Globally and Act Locally' has now been replaced by 'Think and Act both Locally and Globally' and we should encourage our students to think and act at both levels. (Townsend and Otero, 1999, p. 186)

Unfortunately travel on this first path is not happening at a great speed. The numbers of schools that place noticeable emphasis on the development of 'caring people' as a key school goal remains, probably in most countries, a small percentage of total school numbers. Willing teachers and school leaders struggle to find time in their over-packed knowledge dominated subject areas to teach about values of caring, compassion and empathy and to build classrooms and school climates where everyone belongs and feels connected. The policy makers repeatedly make statements like: 'there is no room in the school curriculum for values education as an "add-on", it must be embedded into the subjects we already teach'. (Hon. Trevor Mallard, Minister of Education—speech to UNESCO, NZ National Values Summit, October 2002). Furthermore, it is nigh impossible for most secondary schools and many primary schools to enable teachers to receive the training needed for them to fully develop caring and cooperative learning environments. The following statement shows that New Zealand is clearly not alone in this difficulty.

> We are profoundly disappointed that worthy declarations and even formal communications have in most countries not made a real impact on curricula, on teacher training, on classroom practice and on resource materials. On the eve of the 21st century we remain too often locked into outdated categories and attitudes. (Participant Statement: UNESCO Peace Conference, Geneva, 1999.)

Despite this reality check there are good things happening in schools, so let us move back to a more hopeful position and consider the second pathway to the 'tipping point'. This second pathway, building action competence, is about moving knowledge and understanding to action. It is about the 'tip' over the edge it takes to make that crucial move. An optimistic view that could be taken of the potential for the human race across the planet to become a more caring and connected global whanau or family is that 'action competence' is the means of travel, the path and the light at the end of the tunnel all rolled into one. The glaring omission here may appear to be the motivation for people to take action that shows real caring and connectedness. Motivation is a very complex aspect of human nature far beyond the scope of this short discussion. Nevertheless, we have the view presented above that experience or action leads to a change in feelings and therefore core values. Following on from this it is logical to conclude that changes in feelings and values lead to further action and so the cycle can, in an ideal world with all factors being favourable, continue. Further, there are the well-researched writings of Alfie Kohn, who suggests that it is intrinsic in human nature to care, that there is nothing about human nature that makes selfishness inevitable. He disagrees with the worldview that lies behind the attitude of many teachers to their students, the view that generally describes 'human nature' in negative terms and assumes that generous and responsible behaviour must be forced down throats of children who would otherwise be inclined to care only about themselves. Kohn states:

> A review of several hundred studies has convinced me that this cynicism is not realism. Human beings are not only selfish and self-centred, but also decent, able to feel—and prepared to try to relieve—the pain of others. I believe that it is as 'natural' to help as it is to hurt, that concern for the well-being of others often cannot be reduced to self-interest, that social structures predicated on human selfishness have no claim to inevitability—or even prudence. (Kohn, 1990, p. 12)

Kohn's writings are well supported by the success enjoyed by schools that offer opportunities for students to build their 'caring' skills and to experience the satisfactions of giving, serving and feeling connected to others both close and far from their immediate field of intimacy. It is basic education theory that school experiences have a profound influence on the development of character, further it has been shown that this influence is sufficiently strong to provide positive support for a child who may be subject to negative and 'character destroying' influences in other environments—such as at home.

Kohn's view of the inherently 'responsible and caring' nature of children is supported by the programmes that guide and resource schools and teachers for the planned and deliberate teaching of the universal values—including of course caring and service. The Virtues Project, described below, is one such programme. The author is confident that no whole school strategy or classroom curriculum that sets out to promote caring would not be based on the premise that a teacher's task is to bring out the ability of every child to 'be good' and 'do good'. A note must be inserted here about the word 'teaching' in relation to values. It is often heard in values education debates that 'values are not taught', they are 'caught'. This view has some usefulness as a reminder that that 'we do not ask young people to do what we do not do ourselves' and programmes such as The Virtues Project place appropriate emphasis on the teacher's own personal development in relation to the universal values. However, it is inaccurate and unfair to denigrate the word 'teach' by suggesting values cannot be taught. This view appears to be confusing 'teaching' with 'telling', and is therefore erroneous in today's world of wide-ranging education methods where teaching is about 'supporting to learn'.

4.   WHAT SCHOOLS ARE DOING

There was discussion above about the potential of schools to lead global change in caring and connecting. And there was a caution that we may be moving too slowly to reach the 'tipping point' where the whole of our world as we know it 'gets the message'. Nevertheless, there is a movement in schools that some education writers have been bold enough to caption 'the quiet revolution'. It may be slow and sometimes it is difficult to be positive, especially when: 'The world our kids are going to live in is changing four times faster than our schools'. (Dryden and Voss, 1999, p. 6)

In working with hundreds of New Zealand schools the author has never found disagreement that schools must operate from an explicit and passionate values base of respect and care. And there is no argument with the evidence that teaching children to care and using teaching methods that incorporate cooperative learning significantly enhances their thinking and skills development.

What remains to consider now is just how 'the quiet revolution' actually takes place within the individual school. First and foremost it is about leadership. Once again, within the limits of this discussion, we can only lightly touch on this major concept. But there is no need for a full treatise on school leadership in order to simply accept that it if there is a strong will in the school leadership, particularly embodied in the school principal, to create or reform a school as a caring learning community, then it will happen.

If leadership is weak it will take place only in ad hoc ways in classrooms where individual teachers may have courage and wisdom. But the effectiveness of that teaching will be somewhat, but fortunately not completely, undermined, if they are not operating within a whole school culture that reflects those same values. The importance of the school leadership for schools that care is well documented—refer for example, Ryan and Bohlin, Deal and Peterson or Sergiovanni in the Resources at the end of the chapter.

In 2001, the New Zealand Ministry of Education requested a full evaluation study of Living Values a values education project for schools that began in 1999. This study also reported that the school leader was a crucial factor in the varying degrees of success enjoyed by the 20 schools that piloted the project. Unless school leaders organise the time, take the initiative and provide strong moral and resource support to their teachers, teaching for values such as caring will remain haphazard.

4.1. The Living Values Project

A school that takes on the Living Values approach to values education works through four stages:

- Consultation through the whole school community using The Living Values School Survey Kit (2000).
- Setting action plans for integrated values education throughout the school— usually for a year, often with term 'sub-plans', using The Living Values Action Kit (2002).
- Implementation of the plans.
- Review of progress, celebration and new plans.
A Living Values school takes care of the three C's
- **Core** values—an explicit set of core living values recognised by everyone in the school community.
- School **Culture**—the school wairua (spirit) lays the foundation of a values-based learning community and puts the core values into practice.
- The learning **Curriculum**—clearly specified values education topics and pro- grammes and enhanced exploration of the values aspects of all curriculum areas.

The Living Values model uses a four-part framework for values education re- sources and programmes that accepts 'care' and 'respect' as so much the heart of values education that the framework of self, others, society and the natural environ- ment finds itself written in three ways:

Values about self	Respect for self	Care for self
Values about others	Respect for others	Care for others
Values about society	Respect for society	Care for society
Values about the environment	Respect for the environment	Care for the environment

This framework is widely used in New Zealand, Australia, UK and possibly other countries. For instance it is the basis of this statement provided by Edwards in Chapter 1:

> Care, care of self, of others, of society and of the earth, lies at the heart of learning to live meaningfully, purposefully and coop- eratively amidst the change and uncertainty (young people) will increasingly encounter.

4.2. School Values Statements

Schools that carry out the Living Values survey according to the guidelines provided are 'buying in' to basic principles that start them on a sound path towards becoming a caring learning community. The survey methodology rests on the principle that school leadership may accept special responsibilities of organising, managing, initiating and encouraging. But caring, compassion, empathy, service and connecting are individual qualities of character and as such cannot be achieved purely through leadership or a 'top down' only approach. Put another way, these qualities rely on teaching principles that empower individuals towards self-responsibility for these qualities. The survey models this principle by asking schools not to give the questionnaires to students, staff or parents until they are happy with a consensual agreement from staff members. Some school communities are able to involve parents and students in this decision-making, but 'leadership' principles in the opinion of the author, allow the compromise position that staff 'buy-in' is sufficient to get moving. For many schools consultation with parents and students is not well developed, and the survey may be an early step towards improvement.

The survey tells all school members what the true values of the school are—in desire as well as in practice. Survey results always bring surprises, particularly around lack of knowledge of the school values. On a more positive note these was consistency from the 2000 people in the 1999 pilot study about the values they wanted taught at school. For the purposes of the survey that was developed for schools from the pilot study the responses were grouped into eight categories, most of them relating closely to caring and service:

• Self-respect, self-esteem and self-care.
• Kindness, caring, consideration, empathy, understanding.
• Respect for elders and authority.
• Respect and tolerance for all people regardless of differences
• Friendship/relationship qualities: fairness, trust, cooperation.
• Sense of community spirit and service to others.
• Honesty and integrity.
• Leadership characteristics such as responsibility, reliability and courage.

It must be remembered that many schools start this work from a point that is challenging to say the least. The survey may, for example, 'open some cans of worms'—such as identifying bullying among students as well as teachers, showing that quiet and well-behaved students were being ignored, that only academic achievement and sports were substantially rewarded or that values stated by the school principal weren't modelled by her or other staff in practice.

Following the school survey, nearly always the first action a school takes is to establish, with consultation across the school, a set of core values that will become well known to the whole school community and will be the foundation of a more caring learning environment. The statements below show how statements vary widely. This is as it should be—for a values statement should truly reflect the special and unique culture of a school.

The Middleton Grange 7 C's (A co-educational school, years 1–13, a special character Christian school)
Compassion, Courage, Cheerfulness, Courtesy, Co-operation, Common Sense, Commitment

The Rutherford Way (Co-educational state school, years 9–13)
Respect, Understanding, Tolerance, Honesty, Excellence, Responsibility, Fair play, Opportunities, Reliability, Discipline (self)

Kadimah College (A co-educational Jewish school that accepts all religions—
years 1–13)

Identity—respect for the individual, tolerance for diversity and commitment
to community

Middot—encouraging good deeds exemplified by compassion, kindness and
empathy

Learning—fostering a culture which promotes knowledge, fulfilment and
creativity

T'Fillah—prayer, beliefs and spirituality

For successful values education development a school needs a values lead team
that includes the school principal. The lead team takes responsibility for the writing
and implementation of the action plans. These plans include

- Key objectives or areas of focus.
- Activities to achieve those objectives.
- Performance indicators.
- Who is responsible for each objective/tasks.
- Timelines.

4.2.1.   Otari School

Otari School is a state school for years 1–6 that enrols children in three separate
units—Maori immersion, Montessori and Mainstream. The following summary
shows that key initiatives in the first year of values education development had a
strong focus on staff training. The school's values statement is based on the four-part
values education framework referred to above, a practice quite common in New
Zealand schools. The Otari values statement here also includes the explanation that
follows each value—also a common practice. The explanations are not included when
the values are printed on school material—such as letterhead, notebooks, newsletters,
rulers.

Values statement.

Self-acceptance and self-respect. To ensure that children have the right to be
themselves, able to develop their own potential, physical, emotional, aesthetic,
spiritual, intellectual, moral and social. To have a sense of personal meaning
and identity.

Respect and concern for others and their rights. Sensitivity and concern for the
well-being of other people and respect for life and property.

Social responsibility. Commitment to exploring and promoting the common
good. Includes the encouragement of each person to participate in democratic
processes—value diversity of cultural expression.

Environmental responsibility. Appreciating the interdependence of all elements
of the environment encourages respect and concern for natural heritage.

Values education initiatives.

- Training, all teachers, in the NZ Health curriculum (note: the 1999 NZ Health
curriculum for school places new emphasis on values and holistic—mind, body
and spirit—education).

- Training for all teachers and training available for parents in The Virtues Project.
- Development of environmental education scheme.
- Purchase of resource material on world religions and social issues (Note: the school board decided to stop Christian Bible lessons in favour of teaching children about the major religions of the world).
- Homework centre for underachieving students.
- Curriculum plans in all core teaching subjects include work in all four areas of the values statement.
- Teacher training in Glasser Quality School model.
- Teacher training in Philosophy for Children.

4.3.   Teaching Values, Teaching Caring—School Programmes

It may appear that a values statement is an example of a 'top down' enforcement approach to making children more 'good and caring'. Unfortunately, it is quite common to find schools 'teaching' their core values through little else besides principals' newsletters, assembly speeches and classroom daily notices. Such a 'preaching' approach is much criticised and rightly so. It fails, on its own, to understand the basics of how children learn and the importance of modelling and practical experience to gain real autonomy and maturity in caring. It can, however, be defended on the basis that it is useful for children to gain 'straight-up' knowledge of what the caring group of values looks like. Quotes, songs, poems, descriptions of the values are all useful, but not if that is the sum total of a school values programme. These methods should be nothing more than a starting-point to lay a foundation during the year or two it may take for teacher development initiatives such as those of Otari School above.

There is no substitute for good teacher training based on proven programmes such as The Virtues Project, LVEP (the UNESCO supported Living Values Educational Program, which is not the same as the New Zealand Living Values project of similar name), or Philosophy for Children.

It is essential that, as a school sets up action plans (step 2 of the Living Values model), programmes and strategies are included that give students opportunities for becoming more closely connected with their school and wider 'family'. One of the best programmes to achieve a sense of connection to the world beyond the school gate is Service Learning.

Service Learning has gained wide acceptance in United States secondary schools, offering opportunities for students to combine the more basic skills such as literacy and numeracy with project management and other life skills. Character is developed as students feel empowered by their success in making a difference to their community, and realise the benefits of serving and caring. Service learning is a particularly good strategy for putting into practice the value of 'care for society'—it takes young people beyond their immediate circle of family, friends and school and begins their journey into the wider word of local, national and global citizenship.

Two other excellent school programmes recommended by Living Values, programmes that balance the 'top down' approach of direct 'preaching' about values, are The Virtues Project and Philosophy for Children. These two are singled out here for mention because they both provide training opportunities for teachers and have been successfully taken up by New Zealand schools. But both programmes have originated in other countries, Canada and USA, respectively, and both are used in schools across the globe.

Philosophy for Children is essential for good values education because, more than any other programme, it offers teachers increased ability to enable children to think, analyse and to grow their confidence for understanding their own values and the values of others. By learning to discuss philosophical questions and the experience of feeling valued and connected to others through the 'community of inquiry' classroom context within which Philosophy for Children is taught, children grow in self-esteem and consequently in their ability to give and care for others. Teachers report outstanding results in terms of creating caring classrooms and more successful learning in other curriculum areas.

4.4.   The Caring Classroom

As pointed out above, the nub of values education, of teaching children to care, is to provide opportunities for 'doing it', to develop 'action competence'. The primary setting for providing caring experiences is the classroom. Hence, much values education resource material focuses on how to create caring classrooms.

In caring classrooms students accept ownership and responsibility for what happens there and they are able to respond to the question 'how do we want our classroom to be'? Being part of a classroom that shares responsibility for what happens there, rather than the old 'teacher makes the decision' provides children with rich experience for answering two core questions in life: 'how do I want to be in this world'? and 'how do I want this world to be'? In caring classrooms children learn about caring through their experiences of satisfying connections—they feel a strong sense of belonging, thus meeting a basic need that is well documented in mental health research. Refer to *Mind Matters* in the appendix.

5.   CONCLUSION

This discussion has put forward arguments for moving personal and shared values towards more caring and connections between people throughout the global community. By proposing that schools are probably better placed than anywhere else in the communities we know to lead 'the values revolution' the discussion has looked briefly at ways schools can do this and already are doing it.

It may seem the movement is so slow to reach 'the tipping point' that we may despair of seeing a time where caring and connectedness dominate materialism and competitiveness. Traditions are built over many generations, they take many generations to change. The present global trend for sustainability will not achieve any significant success without core values of caring and connectedness—global efforts like this one will all draw together over time to give greater strength to the power of caring.

We believe significant change has the best chance through the efforts of our schools. Schools that make sure children belong and feel connected, have the will and the skills to care, work on two levels of growth and development. They

- create a whole school culture of care and respect which develops feelings of identity and belonging that stretches beyond the school gate to include families and other members of the wider community in which the school exists;
- develop caring classrooms that incorporate cooperative teaching methods and opportunities for discussing and living universal values such as caring.

There are resources below that give practical strategies for both levels. This is a short selection of materials that are known to be popular with schools in New Zealand. But, they are relevant and useful for schools throughout the world. A much more comprehensive resource list can be found in The Living Values Action Kit, included in the Resource list.

6.   REFERENCES

Comte-Sponville, A. 2001. *A Small Treatise on the Great Virtues—The Use of Philosophy in Everyday Life*. Holt/Metropolitan. (Reprinted, 2003, by Vintage, Random House, London, UK.).

Dryden, G. and Voss, J. 1999. *The Learning Revolution, The Learning Web*. New Zealand: Wellington.

Geering, L. 1999. *The World to Come: From Christian Past to Global Futures*. Santa Rosa, CA: Polebridge Press.

Gladwell, M. 2000 *The Tipping Point: How Little Things Can Make a Big Difference*. New York: Little Brown.

Kohn, A. 1990. The brighter side of human nature: altruism and empathy in everyday life. *Basic Books*, Pegasus Group. U.S.A.

Gregory, M. 2000. Care as a goal of democratic education. *The Journal of Moral Education* 29(4), 446–461.

Putnam, R.D. 2000. *Bowling Alone: Collapse and Revival of American Community*. New York: Simon & Schuster.

Townsend, H. and Otero, G. 1999. *The Global Classroom*. Sydney, Australia: Brown.

UNESCO-APNIEVE. 2002. Cherie Carter Scott in *Learning to Be* (p. 67).

UNESCO Peace Conference. 1999. A Participant Statement. Geneva.

7.   RESOURCES

7.1.   *The Living Values Project*

The Living Values Survey Kit, 2000,
The Living Values Action Kit, 2002
www.living-values.org.nz
Email: jlawley@iconz.co.nz

7.2.   *Universal Values*

Character Education, Heidel and Lyman-Mersereau, 2000. Four books for years 1–5 and 6–12. Each book covers around nine universal values, with stories and activities from learning and understanding to 'embracing' the value.

Living Values: An Educational Program, Diane Tillman and Pilar Quera Colomina, With Activities from Educators Around the World, 2000, Health Communications, Inc. There are activities books for ages 3–7, 8–14, young adults, refugee children and an Educator Training Guide. Refer to Living Values in Part Two. www.living-values.net.

Sathya Sai Education in Human Values, Carole Alderman, 1995. Activities based on the Sathya Sai Human Values programme—Five universal values: Right conduct, peace, truth, love and non-violence. Lesson plans for primary school classrooms.

The Virtues Project Educators Guide, Linda Kavelin Popov, 2000. Simple ways to create a culture of character. A very comprehensive guide of stories, quotes, activities and more. Refer to The Virtues Project in Part Two. www.virtuesproject.com.

7.3. Mental Health

MindMatters—A Mental Health Promotion Resource for Secondary Schools, 2000, Commonwealth of Australia.

7.4. Philosophy for Children

Creative and Critical Thinking—Strategies for Classroom Inquiry, Susan Wilkes. Examples of small modules with different topics and for different ages, mostly for Primary level.

Discovery, Elfie, Kio and Gus, Pixie and Harry Stottlemeier. IAPC (Institute for the Advancement of Philosophy for Children) Matthew Lipman and Ann Sharp. Stimulus novels and extensive teachers' manuals. Primary and Intermediate levels.

Philosophy with Kids 1–3, de Haan, MacColl and McCutcheon. For 5- to 7-year-olds. Discussion plans, exercises and games to promote philosophical inquiry using picture books. Published by Longman.

Strategies for Successful Schooling, Lynne Hinton, 2000. Education Horizons, Vol. 6, No. 2. The implementation of Philosophy for Children across a whole school is outlined.

Teaching for Better Thinking—the Classroom Community of Inquiry, Laurance Splitter and Ann Sharp. Not a resource book, but a new classic on P4C.

Thinking Stories 1–3, Philip Cam. Stories and teaching manuals—for 10- to 12-year-olds. Published by Hale and Iremonger.

7.5. Service and Citizenship

Democratic Schools, Michael Apple and James Beane (Eds.), 1999. Stories of four US schools that use democratic and critical education practices as guides to their entire curriculum and are organised around a deep concern for social justice. The schools are academically successful and socially critical at the same time.

Discovering Democracy, A programme for Australian schools. www.detya.gov. au/schools.publications/discovering_democracy.pdf.

Freedom—Towards Human Rights and Social Justice, Bruce Stevenson and Maeve Stevenson, 1999, Longman, New Zealand. A practical classroom resource for secondary schools.

Skills for Action—Developing Personal and Social Responsibility Through Service, Lions-Quest International Quest Life Skills, New Zealand, Inc., 1995. Full programme at all levels.

Values Education—Developing Self-Esteem and Citizenship, 1999, Prim-Ed. www.prim-ed.com.

7.6.   Global Education

Creating Our Common Future, Educating for Unity in Diversity, Jack Campbell (Ed.), 2001, UNESCO Publishing/Berghahn Books.

Globalisation of Education—and the Wo International Centre at Punahou School in Honolulu Hawaii, 2001. This mission of the International Centre is to 'support and initiate programs that promote appreciation of cultural diversity and global responsibility for Punahou and the community at large'. (Available from the author of this chapter)

The Association for Supervision and Curriculum Development, US, www.ascd.org—Global Education Professional Development Online Course.

The Council for Global Education www.globaleducation.org—a forum for international cooperation for the social, intellectual and moral development of children.

The Global Classroom, Activities to Engage Students in Third Millennium Schools, Tony Townsend and George Otero, 1999, Hawker Brownlow Education.

The Way to Do is to Be, 1999, Oxfam Publication, Seoul Conference, Universal Values and Community Approaches.

Visions of a Better World, 1993—A United Nations Peace Messenger Publication, Global Cooperation House, London.

An opportunity to support a 'slum school' in Nairobi. www.pips.at/huruma/ Also refer UNICEF and other sites in Chapter 9, Values Education Online.

Teaching and Learning for a Sustainable Future, UNESCO Internet Programme.

7.7.   Whole School and Professional Development

Building an Ethical School, Robert J. Starrat, 1994, The Falmer Press, London. Practical, wise and with an extensive bibliography.

Building Character in Schools, Ryan, K. and Bohlin, K. 1999, Jossey-Bass.

How Our Schools Can Teach Respect and Responsibility, Lickona, T., 1991, Bantam Books, New York.

Learning: The Treasure Within, Delors, J., 1998, UNESCO Publishing/The Australian National Commission for UNESCO. Free from UNESCO in NZ.

Moral Leadership, Getting to the Heart of School Improvement, Sergiovanni, T.J., 1992, Jossey-Bass.

Redesigning Education A Guide for Developing Human Greatness, Stoddard, L., 1993, Hawker Brownlow Education.

Rethinking Leadership, Sergiovanni, T.J., 2000, Jossey-Bass.

Schools that Learn, Senge, P., 2000. A fifth discipline field book for educators, parents and everyone who cares about education. Doubleday, New York. 600 pages of knowledge and strategies.

Shaping School Culture, the Heart of Leadership, Deal, T. and Peterson, K., 1999, Jossey-Bass, San Francisco.

The Courage to Teach, Parker J. Palmer, 1998, Jossey-Bass, San Francisco.

What's Worth Fighting for Out There? Hargreaves, A. and Fullan, M. 1998, Teachers College Press, New York. Third of a trilogy—What's Worth Fighting for in the Principalship? and What's Worth Fighting For in Your School?

7.8.   *General Topics—Character Building, Classroom and Whole School Strategies, More on Thinking About Values*

Character Education—Books 1–4, John Heidel and Marion Lyman-Mersereau, 2000, Hawker Brownlow Education, Australia. Two books for years 1–6 and two for years 7–13. A complete plan for engaging a school community in character development. School-wide, monthly focus on a universal value and strategies to incorporate character education.

Class Discussion—A Powerful Classroom Strategy, Margaret Dempster and David Raff, 1992, Hawker Brownlow Education, Australia. Provides a structured approach for class meetings and discussions based on Glasser's philosophy of schools without failure.

Creating a Caring Classroom, Steve Horne, 1997, Scholastic Inc., US. Ideas for creating a peaceful, respectful learning environment that is alive with discovery.

Creating a Values-Based Literature Program, Centre for Learning, 1999, US. A summary of 284 titles in the Novel/Drama series that gives full discussion/learning plans for each title and lists the ethical values found in each piece of literature.

Cultural Futures, NZ Futures Trust, UNESCO/NZ Futures Trust, 2000, New Zealand. A kit of three folders to develop young people's future thinking and raise public awareness.

Esteem Builders, Dr. Michel Borba. A self-esteem curriculum from the USA for improving student achievement, behaviour and school climate.

Inclusive Schools in Action: Making Differences Ordinary, Nancy Waldron and James McLeskey. Strategies and ideas for respecting differences and for inclusive practices in schools.

Quality Circle Time, Jenny Mosley, 1996, LDA, UK. www.jennymosley.demon. co.uk

The Anti-Bullying Handbook, Keith Sullivan, 2000, Oxford Unversity Press, New Zealand

The Soul of Education: Helping Students Find Connection, Compassion and Character at School, Rachel Kessler, 2000, ASCD, US. Curriculum modules. A living values choice from the large range of ASCD (US) resources online at www.ascd.org.

The Values Book—Teaching 16 Basic Values to Children, Tamera Bryant and Pam Schiller, 1998, Gryphon House Inc., US. Easy activities and projects to learn values and build character.

Chapter 10

EDUCATING FOR CONFLICT RESOLUTION AND PEACE

David Woolman

Conflict and conflict resolution have always been a natural part of the human experience; however, the systematic study of the processes by which conflict is resolved has only developed over the last 60 years. The goal of this scholarship is to establish a reliable knowledge base that may serve as a means for improving human relations. If education is understood to be a preparation for life, it seems appropriate to find space in the curriculum for learning about the causes and effects of conflict and the means by which conflict can be transformed into a positive force in human development. Even though the curriculum of most schools is already at or over capacity, there are still many strategies for integrating lessons about conflict resolution into the existing course of study.

This transnational research project identified instruction in the practical skills of conflict resolution as one of the critical needs in educating for tomorrow's world. The study found a consensus favouring the preparation of youth with competence in conflict resolution through peaceful means such as collaboration, dialogue, mediation and negotiation. Furthermore, it was deemed important that students understand how to apply these skills in diverse social and political situations where conflict had become an issue demanding attention. This chapter will provide teachers with a brief introduction covering core concepts in the knowledge base about conflict and conflict resolution, ideas that link education with conflict resolution, the rationale for such instruction and patterns for curriculum integration. This will be followed by a review of selected programmes, some practical applications and a list of resources for teachers.

1. CONFLICT: BASIC THEORY

Human conflicts of many degrees of complexity and intensity are found between and within individuals, groups and countries around the world. Social conflict typically arises when two or more parties pursue objectives that are incompatible; in the ensuing struggle either side hopes to achieve its goal and vanquish the claims of the opposition. In the case of individuals, a person may be attracted to two or more mutually exclusive activities. The potential for conflict increases with social complexity, wider participation and rapid cultural change. Activation of conflict depends on one or both party's perception that its goals are being blocked or compromised by the other; this perception may reflect an accurate view of reality, or it may be no more than a by-product of anxiety and fear.

J. Campbell et al. (eds.), Towards a Global Community, 157–177.

Different types of conflict are distinguished in the literature. Cultural diversity causes wide variations in the degree and forms of conflict expression; these may range from passive rituals to verbal exchange or physical aggression. Morton Deutsch (1973) identified six types of conflict, based on a measure of proximity to reality (pp. 11–15). For example, the 'true conflict' is one that is seen objectively by both parties and is difficult to resolve without cooperation and compromise. On the other hand, a 'contingent conflict' occurs where there are conditions that can be easily rearranged, but neither party recognises this fact. Another case is the 'displaced conflict' in which the active or manifest conflict is the by-product of a deeper, underlying conflict. By contrast, the 'misattributed conflict' involves a clash between the wrong parties over the wrong issue; this type of conflict often occurs in cases of social domination when controlling groups use internal conflict to divide the subject population. Deutsch concludes his typology with 'latent conflict', a situation where conflict should exist but is repressed, displaced or misattributed; last, but by no means least, is 'false conflict' which has no basis in reality and is caused by misperception.

Another perspective on conflict is offered in the work of Kurt Lewin (1935), who established the need to consider the role of multiple interdependent factors in explaining the real-life setting of inter-group conflict (pp. 80–94, 122–125). For Lewin, individual behaviour is determined by a field of psychological forces that are shaped by the positive and negative attributes of goals in any given situation. Conflict results when the forces associated with different goals have equal strength. He identified three types of conflict; the first, in which two goals are positive and equally attractive, is called 'approach–approach'; the second, where one goal has both positive and negative outcomes is labelled 'approach–avoidance'; the third, with two goals both being negative, is typed as 'avoidance–avoidance'. An important aspect of Lewin's classification of conflict is the emphasis on the role of perceived outcomes as a motivation for conflict resolution.

Lewis A. Coser (1956) draws a distinction between realistic and non-realistic conflict (pp. 48–55). Realistic conflicts involve concrete goals, anticipation of gain and means that are geared to attainment of the desired outcome. On the other hand, non-realistic conflict involves the expression of aggressive impulses without any functional objective other than the venting of anger or frustration. Another variation of conflict occurs in the case of competition; the contest between two parties may be latent or active, however, once active, they may engage in two modes of conflict. Kenneth Boulding (1957) describes these options as either a 'conflict set' with each actor striving to gain at the other's expense, *or* a 'trading set' with potential manipulation of ends and means that benefit each party (pp. 111–121). Deutsch (1973) likewise differentiates between destructive and constructive conflict (pp. 351–359). Destructive disputes, being driven by bias, misperception and social pressure to achieve victory, often escalate and expand beyond the original causes and resist resolution. Constructive conflicts, by contrast, facilitate social change through a process of problem solving with mutual gains. In the first case, everyone loses; in the second, the outcome is usually win–win.

Conflicts have a multitude of causes. Some struggles involve different values, religious beliefs, economic priorities, political ideology and principles of conduct. Conflicts may centre on the problem of limited or scarce resources, such as land, minerals, money, property, time and water. Discontent arising from poverty and the quest for human dignity is another source of conflict motivated by the denial of human rights and basic needs like participation, freedom, health, nutrition, education and security.

Theory on the origins of conflict has been divided for many years by competing ideas about human nature. Those who regard humankind as innately aggressive, corrupt and dangerous perceive conflict as natural. In this case, individuals or groups seek power and dominance over others using any means, including violence, to achieve this goal. The alternative perspective is known as 'relative deprivation theory'; this thesis denies that humans are inherently aggressive and maintains that conflict is caused by contingent social conditions, such as corruption, exploitation, poverty or scarcity of resources. The growing complexity of society tends to multiply inequality and differential rewards that fuel conflict (Webb, 1986, pp. 169–174). Nonetheless, it is evident that not all social discontent leads to conflict; consequently, it is also necessary to account for the process of motivation in conflict production. Culture and particular circumstances are mediating variables that influence the linkage between deprivation and conflict. Revisionists stress the malleable and adaptable nature of humans and maintain that conflict behaviour actually reflects both inherent and contingent factors.

Another strand of theory in anthropology and sociology views conflict as a functional process for maintaining group association and solidarity, social structure and leadership. In this perspective, conflict is caused by the problem of discord in-group organisation and may become a means for transforming divergence into a new consensus. Georg Simmel (1955), one of the first scholars to analyse conflict, observed that 'a certain amount of discord, inner divergence and outer controversy, is organically tied up with the very elements that ultimately hold the group together' (pp. 17–18). Max Weber (1949), another founder of sociology, held that 'conflict cannot be excluded from social life' (pp. 26–27). The effects of conflict vary according to the rigidity of social structure; in open, pluralistic groups, conflict can resolve tensions, restore stability and improve social integration. On the other hand, in closed, tightly structured groups, conflict may be repressed and eventually produce so much stress that the social structure may be changed. The potential for conflict to produce disruption and violence increases whenever the groups involved are poorly integrated into society and whenever the conflict attacks the general consensus of the society. In this respect, conflict may become a means by which in-groups differentiate themselves from out-groups.

Competing perspectives on the effect of conflict are found in the field of psychology. Sigmund Freud's claim that civilisation results from a conflict between individual biological drives and demands for social conformity has been contested by others, such as Erich Fromm, who discount the dominant role of conflict in human development. In Freud's view, this conflict produces anxiety in individuals; on the one hand, this might lead to a repression of desire and neurosis, on the other hand, an individual may sublimate desire by channelling energy into some new creative activity. Repression and neuroses are unresolved conflicts that are implicated as a cause of many forms of social pathology. Carl Jung, by contrast, defined this lack of resolution as the individual's failure to achieve self-realisation. The relationship between unresolved individual conflicts and antisocial activity has many impacts on civil order and stability.

Conflict is also regarded as a potential positive force in-group dynamics. For example, conflict can motivate new concerns, relieve stagnation and empower personal as well as social change. Louis Kriesberg (1982) claims that conflicts are 'essential . . . in changes pertaining to the reallocation of power and rules about how collective decisions are made' (p. 313). Conflict provides a forum to discuss problems and explore solutions; as such it becomes a means for the group to revitalise its norms and adjust to new conditions. In this context, Coser (1968) describes the social utility of conflict: 'Conflict prevents the ossification of social systems by exerting pressures for innovation and creativity; it prevents habitual accommodations from freezing into rigid moulds and hence progressively impoverishing the ability to react creatively to novel circumstances' (p. 235). A conflict that permits open disclosure of competing claims may contribute to resolution of tensions and restoration of stable integration within a group; conversely, conflict may enable individuals or groups to strengthen their identity and gain more effectiveness in a bargaining situation (Coser, 1956, pp. 39–48, 154–155; Deutsch, 1973, pp. 8–10).

Unfortunately, it is also true that conflict may result in negative outcomes that block resolution of underlying issues and cause so much destruction that the revival of antagonism in future is virtually assured. For example, genocidal attacks, war and other violent encounters may reinforce retribution based on historical memory. Cycles of violence, once initiated, become difficult to arrest. In some cases, however, this effect can be mitigated through settlements based on fair compensation, justice, reconstruction and terms of reconciliation.

2.   CONFLICT RESOLUTION: CORE CONCEPTS

All conflicts have a finite time span, nonetheless, the duration and outcomes may vary greatly. Some conflicts are left to run their own course, whereas others may be subject to intervention by third parties with an interest in the outcome. The end of a conflict may or may not resolve the underlying issues at stake; often the end of one conflict lays the foundation for the emergence of a new conflict. However, conflict resolution that neutralises the causes of the quarrel and enables disputants to resume constructive relations is a highly valued goal.

Theory does not agree on either the possibility or means for conflict resolution. Kriesberg (1982), for example, holds that conflicts are often multiple, cyclical and interlocking: 'A particular struggle may end and the objective conflict remains or is changed only a little . . . the outcome may be . . . a new conflict, while many other struggles between the adversaries continue' (p. 319). He envisions conflict process as a spiral, with seven sequential stages: these begin with the basis, or causal framework, followed by the emergence, initiation, escalation, de-escalation, termination and outcome of the conflict. Each stage can impact other stages, and sequence reversals are also possible due to feedback and anticipation. For example, events during the termination phase might cause fear of the outcome that translates into a renewal of escalation. Kriesberg (1982), however, views conflict as a dynamic and malleable process; he notes that 'escalation is not inevitable and endless . . . the processes that result in escalation are dependent on certain conditions, other conditions would halt or reverse the movement toward escalation' (p. 319).

Coercion, persuasion and reward are the principal strategies used to pursue goals in a conflict. Disputes usually terminate in one or the other of three possible outcomes. A win–lose result means one side benefits at the expense of the other; the lose–lose ending consists of mutual damage or a compromise with each side giving up some major goals; finally, the win–win option involves joint problem solving that satisfies the interests of each side. The latter outcome is most desirable as a positive resolution of conflict; as such, it is often viewed as the standard of success in efforts to arbitrate, mediate or negotiate an end to conflict.

Two opposing viewpoints on ending conflict are held by the proponents of inherent or contingent theories of human nature. Those who see conflict and violence as innate human traits claim that these tendencies can be controlled but never eliminated. They believe that violent conflict can only be contained by coercive power embodied in alliances, diplomacy, military intervention, treaties or balance-of-power arrangements. On the other hand, those who regard conflict and violence as the result of intolerable environmental conditions believe that conflict and violence are not inevitable and can be prevented or resolved by changing the objectionable factors in the environmenAlternatives to the control of conflict by coercive power and hierarchical decision-making emerged in the 1960s in the field of industrial relations. Here it was discovered that productivity increased when labour and management established a climate of cooperation in decision-making, interaction and problem solving (Burton, 1986, pp. 174–179). A similar paradigm shift in international relations was pioneered at the London-based Centre for the Analysis of Conflict. In this case, an alternative to the traditional reliance on conciliation, litigation, mediation and negotiation was tested and found viable. In this new departure, conflicting parties engaged in open dialogue to reveal all their goals and objectives and received knowledge from experts about the process of conflict resolution; instead of bargaining from fixed positions, each side was free to modify its position and priorities until a final agreement for settlement was achieved. Mutual awareness and understanding was proven effective in reducing the intensity of conflict and facilitating the movement toward resolution of the issues.

Our understanding of the criteria essential for conflict resolution has continued to develop. The importance of distinguishing human interests that are negotiable, like terms of trade and roles in partnerships, from human needs that are non-negotiable, such as values, cultural identity and human rights, is now recognised. Needs theory stresses the importance of avoiding 'zero-sum' outcomes that would cause deprivation and sow seeds of future conflict. Win–win outcomes in conflicts over non-negotiable needs, while difficult to achieve by negotiation, may nonetheless be nurtured through problem solving.

The means by which a conflict is settled can become a cause for future conflict when non-negotiable needs are denied or underlying deep issues are ignored. A democratic process with transparency and full participation is regarded as essential to conflict resolution. John Burton (1986) defines this as a process 'in which bargaining of needs against interests can be avoided, and in which the parties concerned can define needs and interests and cost the consequences of preserving interests at the expense of needs ... to enable parties to move from point A to point B, conscious of the outcomes ... ' (p. 179).

There are many different approaches to conflict resolution. Each country maintains a justice system based on the rule of law that adjudicates internal conflicts; international law is, as yet, an imperfect system due to the inviolability of state sovereignty. Moreover, legal systems are subject to political corruption and influence that impairs their credibility as agencies of conflict resolution. The fact that most court decisions reflect the 'win–lose' paradigm further compromises their agency in resolving conflict. Many conflicts are resolved through intervention by social service agencies, public commissions, ministries and other government offices and institutions.

International conflict today is of great concern because of the dangers of nuclear war and mass destruction by biological and chemical weapons. Nevertheless, war has cast its dark shadow upon human history since the beginning of civilisation. One study of the last 3500 years of history found that wars were being fought in all but 270 years of that time span. Several strategies are employed to try to prevent conflicts from erupting into violence. In the 'good offices' approach, a third party tries to restore communication and negotiation between the disputants but has no power of decision in the interaction. Conciliation or mediation, by contrast, empowers the third party to convey suggestions about how the conflict might be resolved. A third party helps disputants identify and confront issues, facilitates their mutual understanding, establishes norms for interactions, maintains standards of respect and persuasion in communication, suggests the types of solution that are possible and builds acceptance for the agreement by emphasizing the benefits of resolution. Fact-finding by international commissions can be used to support this process when agreed to by the countries involved; prolonged inquiry may also permit a cooling of tensions and forestall war. States in conflict may also opt to submit their case to arbitration, however, they retain the right not to comply with the award if they regard it to be unjust or in error. Nonetheless, in the 19th century, compulsory arbitration was employed in 238 cases of international conflict resolution. Another option in inter-state conflict is for one state to unilaterally initiate de-escalation as a means of reducing tension so that a gradual and reciprocal process toward resolution can begin.

The field of peace research, which is concerned with the ways and means to achieve non-violent conflict resolution, identifies three basic approaches to conflict. First, a 'negative peace' is established when peacekeeping forces intervene to stop the fighting, separate warring parties and maintain a cease-fire through observation; however, the issues causing the crisis remain unresolved at this stage. This strategy may be complemented by peacemaking, which strives to resolve the conflict through bargaining, diplomacy, negotiation and mediation. A third approach, peacebuilding, aims to reduce social discontent and prevent war by creating conditions that foster 'positive peace'; this entails development projects that improve economic opportunity, education, health, housing, living standards and political participation. Other essential steps in peacebuilding include provisions to assure equality of opportunity, human rights, security and social justice.

Another type of conflict reduction occurs through the creation of institutions for political integration. Whenever groups are excluded from political participation, conflict has the potential of evolving into revolution against the established order. On the other hand, inclusive democratic societies that distribute benefits widely are less prone to violent conflict. Compacts, contracts and constitutions establish a relationship between divergent parties that is based upon common agreement about the principles that govern social and political life. The durability of such arrangements typically depends on the degree to which internal conflicts are resolved and each group's self-interests are satisfied within the compact.

The psychology of conflict resolution is quite varied because of the diversity of situations. In the type of conflict identified by Freud, the most effective resolution is through sublimation, in which the individual channels the energy produced by unmet libidinal drives into constructive and creative activity. Empowerment and self-realisation are other examples of this dynamic resolution of conflict. Paulo Freire's proposal for 'conscientization' as a means of awakening the latent potential of impoverished people exemplifies a similar process applied to social development. In the type of conflicts identified by Lewin, the means of resolution are also varied. A confrontation between two positive goals is usually resolved by the choice of one or the other goal. Conversely, the case of approach–avoidance is more problematic; vacillation is usual and resolution may be elusive because the person cannot overcome the repulsion and may try to prevaricate or avoid the situation. Avoidance–avoidance conflicts entail even greater resistance that may result in incapacity or complete withdrawal from the situation; conflict resolution in this case is the most difficult to achieve.

Some important insights on conflict resolution have come from the field of social psychology. Deutsch, for example, regards the development of productive conflict toward a win–win outcome as comparable to the stages of creative thinking. In this analogy, a problem is first recognised but efforts to solve it by conventional means fail; this frustration results in withdrawal, during which the problem is perceived in a new way. The experience generates new insights that lead to a resolution of the conflict. In cases of interpersonal or inter-group conflict, this process is facilitated by cooperation between the parties, open communication, mutual trust, recognition of the other's legitimacy, adherence to rules, experience with negotiation, flexibility, a capacity for imagination and commitment to the resolution process as a key to a better future.

3.   EDUCATION FOR CONFLICT RESOLUTION

The turbulent history of the 20th Century provided the context for the first efforts to integrate the study of peace and conflict resolution into formal education. This century saw unprecedented levels of violence, with two devastating world wars, a multitude of bloody civil, ethnic and inter-state conflicts, worldwide expansion of nationalism and the invention and proliferation of weapons of mass destruction. These threatening conditions inspired some scholars to engage in the systematic study of conflict resolution and to initiate the new field of peace research. Another positive step in this century was the first historical efforts by nations to create a world organisation dedicated to seeking peace and the prevention of war. One by-product of these developments was a recognition that the mission of education should include the preparation of students for effective national and world citizenship by encouraging critical thinking, problem solving, international understanding and a commitment to conflict resolution as a means to achieving world peace.

Following the First Hague Convention on world peace in 1899, groups of educators in Europe and the United States initiated a movement to teach peace and international understanding in schools. This effort challenged the prevailing ethnic intolerance and national conflict that had caused recurrent wars in Europe. The establishment of the International Bureau of Education in 1926 sought to promote tolerance and intercultural understanding as a means to counteract international conflict and tensions. This movement continued after 1945 through many United Nations programmes; most notable today is the UNESCO Associated Schools Project that strives to foster awareness of world issues, human rights, disarmament, problem solving and the need for understanding cultural diversity.

Systematic study of conflict and conflict resolution began in the late 1950s with the founding of the Centre for Research on Conflict Resolution at the University of Michigan and the International Peace Research Association (IPRA) in Oslo, Norway. In the 1960s, integration of conflict resolution with education continued. The World Order Models Project (WOMP) developed problem-based curricula focused on economic welfare, environmental restoration, minority political participation, social justice and war prevention as a means for conflict resolution. Methods of study in WOMP reflected the process for transcending conflict. The steps included diagnosis of the problem, prognosis, development and evaluation of alternatives, visualisation of 'preferred worlds', and the planning of realistic means for progress toward this future goal. The World Association for Schools as an Instrument of Peace was organised in 1967 in Geneva to provide in-service education to K-12 teachers on teaching human rights and peace. Another group, the International Association of Educators for World Peace, founded in 1969, has spread to 50 countries with its advocacy of education for conflict resolution and human rights.

The 1970s brought a further growth in the professional organisation of education for conflict resolution and peace. In the United States, the Consortium on Peace Research, Education and Development (COPRED) formed the Peace Education Network to foster education on non-violent conflict resolution and social justice. In Europe, IPRA established a Peace Education Commission which produced a handbook and initiated courses for translating research into action on conflict issues. Paulo Freire's idea of a 'dialogic pedagogy' that connected literacy with social needs assessment to empower people oppressed by poverty was influential. Standards of education for international understanding, cooperation and peace were adopted by the United Nations in 1974; this mandate resulted in numerous publications, including handbooks and guides on teaching about conflict and peace. The 1978 UNESCO Conference on Teaching Human Rights developed guidelines for curriculum development, teaching methods and instructional material. Many schools introduced units on human relations training.

The persistence of nuclear proliferation and the Cold War in the 1980s motivated the development of disarmament education in Europe, where most countries stood on the frontier dividing two nuclear superpowers. UNESCO sponsored a World Congress on Disarmament Education in 1980 and issued a teacher's handbook with suggestions for curriculum integration. Teaching about the arms race and nuclear disarmament spread around the globe as this movement gained support in Australia, Europe, Japan, New Zealand and the United States. In the United States the 1980s saw the introduction of programmes to counteract school violence by teaching conflict resolution, peer mediation and peacemaking. Another initiative in this decade was the effort by International Textbook Research to identify and reduce prejudice in school textbooks.

In some developing nations, education within communities has aimed to promote social change that resolves conflict. In India, for example, Gandhi's methods of non-violent resistance and self-reliance have been used to reveal injustice, combat exploitation, restore human dignity and instil self-respect. In Latin America, community literacy programmes have empowered people to identify the causes of their underdevelopment and explore alternatives.

The closing years of the 20th Century brought new initiatives in education for peace and conflict resolution. Fifty years of Cold War conflict ended with the collapse of the Soviet Union; however, new conflicts have multiplied with resurgent nationalism, nuclear proliferation, economic competition, environmental crises, terrorism, genocide, racism, gender inequality, ethnic and religious intolerance and rising youth violence. In the context of these manifold problems, schools have responded with new programmes of study to build competency and understanding in environmental education, world problems, multicultural education, conflict resolution, peacemaking, and social living skills. The rationale for conflict resolution education remains consistent with that of the past. Education should provide students with an awareness of the social and political issues that cause world conflict and equip them with the skills of critical thinking, rational judgment and social living skills needed for constructive citizenship.

4.   CONFLICT RESOLUTION IN CURRICULUM

The treatment of conflict resolution in curriculum should reflect the natural presence of conflict in all levels of human experience. Individual students with internal conflicts that interfere with learning may be helped by counselling, psychological intervention or reading in which they encounter therapeutic stories. Interpersonal and inter-group conflict within a school can be addressed by programmes that teach the skills of conflict management, negotiation or mediation. Social and political conflicts within a society should be critically explored through problem-based units in civics, history, literature or social studies. Likewise, the study of international relations and the dynamics of conflicts that result in war or peace is integral to curriculum about current affairs, political science and world history.

The challenge of teaching about conflicts and their resolution has produced a diversity of thematic approaches; in many cases, education is linked with advocacy that promotes the goal of conflict resolution. Some of the more familiar programmes have focused on teaching conflict resolution skills, nuclear disarmament, environmental preservation, international understanding, multicultural education, respect for human rights and the achievement of peace through world order. Within each of these movements, there is also a diversity of approaches. Robert Aspeslagh (1986), for example, distinguishes six major themes within the field of peace education: abolition of prejudice, conflict resolution, control of human aggression, non-violence, participation in political action for social change and promotion of world citizenship and government (pp. 187–188).

Methodology varies greatly in these curricula, however, emphasis on active learning and student participation is widespread. Some learning vehicles include active engagement, cooperative activities, dramatisation, games, group discussion and projects, interactive technology, intercultural associations, puppetry, role-playing and simulation. Specific behavioural outcomes are implicit in most curricula that focus on conflict resolution. Most of this learning depends on acquisition of skills in reasoning and human relations. In the former, this involves critical thinking, decision-making, evaluation of evidence, objective analysis, problem solving and understanding cause and effect relationships. In the case of human relations training, the focus is on cultivation of skills for active listening, brainstorming alternatives, communicating effectively, controlling emotions, evaluating perceptions, managing anger, respecting diverse perspectives, understanding other cultures and working towards consensus.

Another critical variable in effective education for conflict resolution involves the organisation of pedagogical relationships within the school. Authoritarian schools, which limit student participation, demand obedience, suppress conflict and emphasize only rigid standards of performance, are not conducive to the kind of democratic education that facilitates learning how to resolve conflict. A better social climate for this instruction can be achieved when the school becomes a community in which teachers are trusted and interact freely with students in solving problems; students, likewise, will gain positive reinforcement through participation and adoption of responsibility. Reduction of competition and emphasis on cooperative learning further enhances the opportunity for skill-building in conflict resolution.

Curriculum integration is the most common strategy for accommodating the need to add new content to the school's programme of study. In practice, this means that units, lessons or learning activity packages are inserted into existing courses. This may be articulated across all subjects. For example:

- In art, students can study how visual expression relates to social conflict.
- In health, they may be taught ways to control anger and emotions.
- In language arts, reading and writing provide many windows to view conflict, and speech students can build skills of effective communication.
- In math, the training and problem solving is transferable to analysis of variables involved in solving problems resulting from conflict.
- Music appreciation can be a means for the study of social conflict as expressed in song.
- In physical education, students can experience the process and outcome of competitive versus cooperative sports.
- Science affords many opportunities to study the control of conflict and cooperative relationships in biology, along with the many problems in environmental ecology.
- In social studies, conflicts of an economic, political, psychological and social nature may be addressed in many courses from different perspectives, such as democratic government, international relations, historical relativity, social justice and peacebuilding.

International understanding is a long-standing goal of educators interested in peace and conflict resolution. This is based on the belief that the potential for war and social conflict may be diminished by fostering awareness, direct association and respect between peoples of different cultures and nationalities. A collateral goal is to improve international relations and citizenship by building a solid foundation of knowledge about the world. The curriculum initiative known as global education has sought to achieve these objectives using the integration model. Many facets of global studies curricula are relevant to the study of conflict and its resolution. For example, Merryfield (2002) identifies the following strategies as components of global studies:

- Create multiple and long-term opportunities for cross-cultural experiences through class visits by international students, field trips, service learning, travel and global online interactive projects.
- Critically evaluate stereotypes and misperceptions about other cultures.
- Investigate the effects of unequal power relationships in the past and present with emphasis on the causes and consequences of injustice, oppression, poverty and racism.
- Study issues from multiple conflicting perspectives to achieve understanding of the effects that diverse values and interests have upon people's outlook (pp. 18–21).

Outcomes in global education include: awareness of global interdependence and the linkages between local, regional and worldwide issues; insights about cultural diversity and culture change at home and abroad; and understanding the causes, effects and possible solutions of one or more current world problems (Collins, Czarra and Smith, 1998, pp. 311–317).

Another strategy for conflict resolution education involves either the introduction of specific courses that teach this process as a social skill or training programmes that focus on preparing selected individuals to perform mediation or negotiation in a school setting. In many cases, the demand for this instruction arises because a climate of disruption is jeopardising the school's educational mission. The skills gained through this training are usually applied directly within the school to remediate the situation and restore a climate of peace that is conducive to learning.

5.   EXEMPLARY PROGRAMMES

The Programme for Young Negotiators (PYN), a product of the Harvard Negotiation Project, began in 1993 in Boston public schools, where it achieved notable success in reducing disciplinary problems and in improving student skill with interpersonal communication and conflict resolution. PYN was later adopted as a component of middle and high school curriculum in urban school districts across the United States and Canada. The basic principles for PYN were derived from the classic treatise on win–win negotiation, *Getting to Yes: Negotiating Agreement without Giving In*, by Fisher, Ury and Patton. PYN teaches a process of achieving goals through dispute resolution. In one assessment of PYN, Richard Bodine and Donna Crawford (1998) report that 'the perspective-taking skills and critical thinking skills taught in negotiation courses help students learn that in order to satisfy their own interests, they must empathise with the interests of others' (p. 63). The United States Departments of Education and Justice cite PYN as an outstanding programme for teaching conflict resolution and violence prevention.

The first phase of PYN implementation consists of intensive negotiation training for administrators, teachers and community youth service persons; this is followed

by a 10-week curriculum that covers key concepts and develops the skills that drive the process of negotiation. These include
- defining the dynamics of negotiation
- goal-setting
- collaborating for win–win outcomes
- understanding attitudes and perceptions
- practicing empathy
- developing and recognising interests and positions
- creating, evaluating and choosing options through brainstorming and bargaining
- dealing with angry persons through active listening
- helping each other
- practicing negotiation skills using cases based on reality

Interactive methods like games, role simulations, active discussion and writing exercises are used to make learning challenging and exciting.

After completion of the PYN negotiation course, learning is further reinforced by extension activities. These encompass
- Integration of negotiation ideas into the language arts, math, science and social studies curriculum.
- Formation of a student negotiators' club.
- Creation of special negotiation periods for students to work together on resolving conflicts.
- Proposals by students of new cases for study and role-play.
- Negotiation workshops for the community and parents.

Another option enables schools to expand the negotiation course into a whole-school programme. The PYN programme instils awareness that goals and interests are best achieved through collaboration rather than aggression and violence; most significantly, it provides training and practice in the skills of negotiation that increase students' capacity for constructive and effective social interaction.

Another approach to conflict resolution involves mediation by a third party to assist disputants who are unable to negotiate a settlement of their differences. The Community Boards Programme, initiated in San Francisco in 1976 to provide a mediation service for neighbourhood conflicts, extended its operation to school districts on a partnership basis in 1982. It first established the Conflict Managers Programme to train students to act as peer mediators in conflicts involving fellow students. Training varied from intensive workshops to longer courses. Peer mediation was widely adopted by many school districts across the United States, however, it was soon recognised that more comprehensive training was needed for the program to succeed. Community Boards, for example, decided to supplement its peer mediation project with a whole-school approach; curricula were developed to teach communications skills, problem solving and conflict resolution techniques to students, teachers, administrators and parents. Integration of conflict resolution activities into mainstream curriculum was also promoted. School programmes were then linked with other community efforts through partnerships. This arrangement resulted in: provision of school-trained mediators for neighbourhood service; a cross-referral system to coordinate school–community disputes; parent collaboration in cases where child mediation required support for behaviour modification and communication; and organisation of youth groups to promote the active participation of young people in mediation and resolution of community problems. The great strength of the Community Boards programme is the recognition of the need to build bridges between school and community agencies for a coordinated approach to the problem of youth conflict and violence (Amsler and Sadella, 1987).

More comprehensive approaches have introduced conflict resolution education at the classroom level with the intention of expanding this instruction into a whole-school programme. Some common elements of the classroom approach include integration of conflict resolution into curriculum, application of negotiation and mediation in daily school life, cooperative group learning and the study of content that generates controversy.

The Teaching Students to be Peacemakers programme (TSP), which originated in Minnesota in the 1960s, is a K-12 programme for teaching negotiation and mediation with emphasis on fostering constructive relationships between adversaries and building their capacity to achieve win–win agreements. The foundation for TSP is the establishment of a cooperative classroom community with less emphasis on competition and more cultivation of teamwork, effective communication and mutual support. Formal instruction in the process of conflict resolution is conducted throughout the year using daily or biweekly sessions of half-hour duration. All students receive sequential training that covers the nature of conflict, the rationale and effects of different resolution strategies, the process of problem solving negotiation and the procedures for mediation of disputes. The objective of TSP is to demonstrate the greater value of a conflict resolution that enables all parties to fulfil their needs while improving their relationship at the same time. This is what is known as a 'win–win' settlement. Implementation of TSP depends on intensive faculty training and teamwork.

In the negotiation component of TSP, students learn to communicate their needs and feelings in a reasoned way; to recognise and understand the other's perspective, needs and feelings; to develop creative options and plans to resolve the problem on the basis of mutual gain and to select the best resolution that will benefit both parties and strengthen their cooperative relationship. The mediation component provides students with an understanding of the role of a mediator in each stage of this conflict resolution process. This includes: first, the cessation of hostilities with separation of antagonists and institution of a cooling-off period; second, the agreement to commence mediation with an explanation of the process and concurrence on rules; third, helping disputants begin and sustain negotiation by guidance of the process and, fourth, finalising a settlement and securing a commitment from each party to honour the agreement.

Following this training, all students participate in a classroom-based peacemaker programme that enables them to apply and practice the skills of negotiation and mediation in real cases of interpersonal conflict. These skills are refined and reinforced continuously from grades 1–12 with new instruction and opportunities for practice. Learning is deepened through lessons based on conflicts in history, literature and science, using role-playing, problem solving and critical thinking.

The TSP programme was adopted by many schools in North America and has spread to Asia, Europe, the Middle East and South America. Studies of the program's effectiveness found that, after training, students could apply their knowledge of conflict resolution procedures both in and outside the school. Research also documented a gain in students' preference for win–win negotiation when confronted by the alternative win–lose choice. Another significant effect of TSP training was a 60% reduction in classroom disciplinary problems (Bodine and Crawford, 1998, pp. 81–85, 103–106; Johnson and Johnson, 1995, pp. 99–103). Perhaps the most important achievement of TSP is its empowerment of students to envision conflict as a positive opportunity for change and to take the initiative in negotiating their own conflicts without depending on adult intervention.

The Resolving Conflict Creatively Programme (RCCP) is a more comprehensive school-wide programme founded in 1985 as a joint effort of Educators for Social Responsibility and the New York City Board of Education to prevent youth violence, promote intercultural understanding and build a cooperative, caring environment in the school and community. RCCP spread to 60 New York schools and, since 1993, the programme has been adopted by school systems in eight other states.

RCCP has five components: preliminary teacher training, K-12 curriculum, peer mediation, administrative support training and parent involvement. Teachers are first given an intensive course that covers the basic ideas and skills of conflict resolution, emotional control, intercultural understanding and social interaction. Teachers practice methods like brainstorming, student-driven discussions, cooperative learning groups, interviewing and role-playing. RCCP mentors provide scheduled teacher support during every year of the project.

The K-12 curriculum strives to cultivate attitudes and behaviours that will counteract aggression and prevent violence as a response to conflict. Objectives include building awareness of different options for conflict resolution, developing the skills needed to carry out these options, encouraging intercultural respect, teaching resistance to prejudice and empowering students to take responsibility for creating a peaceful world. The core skills developed in this programme are: affirmation of feelings, recognition of bias, challenging prejudice, peacemaking, management of anger, fostering cooperation, communicating effectively, listening carefully, resolving conflicts, solving problems, imaging positive futures and appreciating all types of diversity. The course runs all year, with weekly sessions of 30 to 45 minutes and integration of concepts into academic subjects. Curricula are differentiated for the elementary, middle and high school levels.

After the first year, students and teachers collaborate in the selection of students for peer mediation duty. These individuals receive training in the mediation process. Thereafter, they wear special shirts and patrol the cafeteria, hallways and playground during recesses to intervene wherever needed to defuse incipient conflicts.

Training of administrators is essential for achieving a school-wide environment based on the principles of creative conflict resolution and intercultural understanding. Likewise, the involvement of parents in workshop activities that build awareness of the skills of conflict resolution and interpersonal relations is critical to the success of RCCP. Parents may spend many hours with children and can become key players in reinforcing RCCP principles in the home and community.

The RCCP programme has documented its effectiveness in violence prevention and enhancement of academic learning. For example, students who receive high levels of continuous RCCP training exhibited diminished 'hostile attributions, aggressive fantasies and aggressive problem solving'. In addition, it was found that these same children showed better math and reading scores on standardised achievement tests than those students who received low levels of RCCP training. One national assessment concluded, 'RCCP evaluation shows that by teaching children constructive cognitive strategies, violence prevention interventions can impact their subsequent behaviour' (Aber, Brown, and Henrich, 1999, pp. 9, 13).

Some other key findings impact on RCCP's implementation. On the one hand, the programme's success was dependent on teachers being behaviourally and psychologically committed to the RCCP approach. Abstract concepts like 'peace' and 'active listening' required creative methods and concrete practice to facilitate learning by younger students. Finally, very high-risk children required extended reinforcement; some strategies included pairing the children with positive peer leaders, parental outreach, community service activities and more intensive training.

6. PRACTICAL APPLICATIONS

Education that provides students with understanding, skills and experience in conflict resolution has many important present and future applications. Several programmes described above were designed as a response to immediate problems of disruptive behaviours and violence in schools. Conflict resolution education is, first and foremost, a means to create a peaceable school environment conducive to learning. However, as shown in the programmes, the effectiveness of school-based curricula also requires an extension of this education to the family and community where violence is often incubated or reinforced. In this context, the applications of conflict resolution training encompass a wide range of situations like marital counselling, domestic violence, reform of juvenile offenders, correctional rehabilitation of criminals, restorative justice and peace building in areas affected by ethnic or racial conflicts. Students who learn how to resolve conflict benefit by gaining essential skills for constructive social interaction and goal achievement.

Conflict resolution training may also strengthen the values and skills needed in the practice of effective citizenship. In a democratic society, individuals must balance self-interest and social responsibility; frequently, this requires conflict resolution skills. Moreover, citizens in a democracy choose political leaders and influence government policies through participation in voluntary organisations and interest-based campaigns. Citizens who are informed and skilled in the process of peaceful conflict resolution are more likely to demand government adherence to this process in the management of domestic and international relations. Likewise, students who are well-grounded in the theory and practice of conflict resolution are better prepared for understanding the dynamics of conflict in the world and the role of democratic, international institutions in building a more peaceful global society.

7. REFERENCES

Aber, J.L., Brown, J.L., and Henrich, C.C. 1999. *Teaching Conflict Resolution: An Effective School-Based Approach to Violence Prevention: Research Brief.* New York: Columbia University, National Centre for Children in Poverty.

Amsler, T. and Sadella, G. 1987. *The Community Board Program.* San Francisco, CA: The San Francisco Community Boards.

Aspeslagh, R. 1986. Peace education. In: Laszlo, E. and Youl Yoo, Y. (Eds.) *World Encyclopedia of Peace,* Vol. 2 (1st ed.). Oxford: Pergamon Press, pp. 182–190.

Bodine, R.J. and Crawford, D.K. 1998. *The Handbook of Conflict Resolution Education: A Guide to Building Quality Programs in Schools.* San Francisco, CA: Jossey-Bass.

Boulding, K.E. 1957. Organization and conflict. *Journal of Conflict Resolution 1*(2), 122–134.

Burton, J.W. 1986. History of conflict resolution. In: Laszlo, E. and Youl Yoo, Y. (Eds.) *World Encyclopedia of Peace,* Vol.1 (1st ed.). Oxford: Pergamon Press, pp. 174–179.

Collins, H.T., Czarra, F.R. and Smith, A.F. 1998. Guidelines for global and international studies education: challenges, culture, and connections. *Social Education 62*(5), 311–317.

Coser, L.A. 1956. *The Functions of Social Conflict.* Glencoe, IL: The Free Press.

Coser, L.A. 1968. Conflict: social aspects. In: Sills, D.L. (Ed.) International Encyclopedia of the Social Sciences, Vol.3. New York: MacMillan, pp. 232–236.

Deutsch, M. 1973. *The Resolution of Conflict: Constructive and Destructive Practices.* New Haven, CT: Yale University Press.

Johnson, D.W. and Johnson, R.T. 1995. *Reducing School Violence through Conflict Resolution.* Alexandria, VA: Association for Supervision and Curriculum Development.

Kriesberg, L. 1982. *Social Conflicts* (2nd ed.). Englewood Cliffs, NJ: Prentice Hall.

Lewin, K. 1935. *A Dynamic Theory of Personality: Selected Papers.* New York: McGraw Hill.

Merryfield, M.M. 2002. The difference a global educator can make. *Educational Leadership, 60*(2), 18–21.

Simmel, G. 1955. *Conflict: The Web of Group Affiliations.* Glencoe, IL: The Free Press.

Webb, K. 1986. Conflict: inherent and contingent theories. In: Laszlo, E. and Youl Yoo, Y. (Eds.) World Encyclopedia of Peace, Vol.1. Oxford: Pergamon Press.

Weber, M. 1949. *Max Weber on the Methodology of the Social Sciences.* Glencoe, IL: The Free Press.

8.   APPENDIX: RESOURCES FOR TEACHERS

8.1.   Articles and Books

Adams, S.K. and Wittmer, D.S. 2001. 'I had it first': teaching young children to solve problems peacefully. *Childhood Education 78*(1), 10–16.

Allan, J.K., Nairne, J. and Majcher, J. 1996. *Violence Prevention: A Group Discussion Approach.* Toronto, Ontario: Ontario Institute for Studies in Education.

*Australian Resource Kit: Conflict Resolution in Australia.*1988. North Hobart, Tasmania: Adult Education, Division of TAFE, Education Department.

Barnes-Robinson, L., Jeweler, S., and Zimmer, J. 1996. *We can Work It Out!: Problem Solving through Mediation, Elementary Edition.* Washington, D.C.: National Institute for Citizen Education in the Law, National Teens, Crime and the Community Programme.

Bastida, A., Cascon, P. and Grasa, R. 2001. *Educar en el conflicto: Cuadernos de pedagogía.* Madrid: Los Libros de la Catarata.

Beekman, S. and Holmes, J. 1993. *Battles, Hassles, Tantrums, and Tears: Strategies for Coping with Conflict and Making Peace at Home.* New York: Hearst Books.

Berman, S. and LaFarge, P. (Eds.). 1993. *Promising Practices in Teaching Social Responsibility.* Albany, New York: SUNY Press.

Best Practices of Non-violent Conflict Resolution In and Out of School: Some Examples. (2002). Paris: UNESCO.

Bickmore, K. 1993. Preparation for pluralism: curricular and extra-curricular practice with conflict resolution. *Theory into Practice 36*(1), 3–11.

Bodine, R.J. and Crawford, D.K. 1998. *The Handbook of Conflict Resolution Education: A Guide to Building Quality Programs in Schools.* San Francisco, California: Jossey Bass/National Institute for Dispute Resolution.

Bowen, L.S. and Gittier, J.B. 1991. *The Role of Formal Education in Conflict Resolution.* New York: Garland.

Brandoni, F. (Ed.). 1999. *Mediación escolar. Propuestos, reflexiones y experiencias.* Buenos Aires: Paidos.

Brunson, R., Conte, Z. and Masar, S. 2002. *The Art in Peacemaking: A Guide to Integrating Conflict Resolution Education into Youth Arts Programs.* Washington, D.C.: National Endowment for the Arts and U.S. Department of Justice, Office of Juvenile Justice and Delinquency Programme. Partnership for Conflict Resolution Education in the Arts.

Burgess, H. and Burgess, G.M. (Eds.). 1997. *Encyclopedia of Conflict Resolution.* Santa Barbara, California: ABC-CLIO.

Burton, J.W. 1996. *Conflict Resolution: Its Language and Processes.* Lanham, Maryland: Scarecrow press.

Canadian Resource Guide to Restorative Justice and Conflict Resolution Education Programs. 2001. Ottawa: Correctional Service of Canada.

Carlsson-Paige, N. and Levin, D.E. 1998. *Before Push comes to Shove: Building Conflict Resolution Skills with Children.* St. Paul, Minnesota: Redleaf Press.

Carruthers, W.L., Carruthers, B.J.B., and Day-Vines, N.L. 1996. Conflict resolution as curriculum: a definition, description, and process for integration in core curricula. *School Counselor 43*(5), 345–373.

Cascon Soriano, P. and Papadimitriou, G. 2000. *Resolución noviolenta de los conflictos.* Aguascalientes, Ags. Mexico: Perro Sin Mecate.

Cho, Y.S. (Ed.). 1999. *World Encyclopedia of Peace*, 8 Vols. (2nd ed.). Dobbs Ferry, New York: Oceana Publications.

Clarke, P.S. 2000. *A Culture of Peace: A Teaching on Alternatives to War and Violent Conflict.* Vancouver, British Columbia: CoDevelopment Canada.

Classroom Conflict Resolution Training for Grades 3–6. 1995. San Francisco, California: Community Board Programme.

Cohen, R. 1995. *Students Resolving Conflict: Peer Mediation in the Schools.* Glenview, IL: Scott Foresman.

Cohen, R. 1999. *School Mediator's Field Guide.* Watertown, MA: School Mediation Associates.

Conflict Managers Training Manual for Grades 3–6. 1995. San Francisco, CA: Community Board Programme.

Conflict Resolution in the Schools: A Manual for Educators. 1996. Washington, DC: National Institute for Dispute Resolution.

Conflict Resolution/Peace Education. 1996. Olney, MD: Association for Childhood Education International.

Cornelius, H. and Faire, S. 1995. *Tú ganas, yo gano. Corro resolver los conflictos creativamente y disfrutar con las soluciones.* Madrid: Ed. Gaia Ediciones.

Cowen, D., Palomares, S., and Schilling, D. 1992. *Teaching the Skills of Conflict Resolution.* Spring Valley, CA: Interchoice.

Crawford, D.K. and Bodine, R.J. 1996. *Conflict Resolution Education: A Guide to Implementing Programs in Schools, Youth-Serving Organizations and Community and Juvenile Justice Settings: Program Report.* Washington, DC: U.S. Department of Justice, Office of Justice Programmes, Office of Juvenile Justice and Delinquency Prevention and U.S. Department of Education, Department of Elementary and Secondary Education.

Curhan, J.R. 1996. *Life Negotiations: The PYN Curriculum for Middle Schools.* Cambridge, MA: Programme for Young Negotiators.

DeBeneditti, E.J. 1993. *Conflict, Resolution, and Diversity: A Manual of Participatory Activities.* Pittsburgh, PA: Edupress.

Deutsch, M. 2001. *Practitioner Assessment of Conflict Resolution Programs.* New York: Columbia University, Teachers College. ERIC Clearinghouse on Urban Education.

Deutsh, M. and Coleman, P.T. (Eds.). 2000. *Handbook of Conflict Resolution: Theory and Practice.* San Francisco, CA: Jossey-Bass.

Drew, N. 1987. *Learning the Skills of Peacemaking: An Activity Guide for Elementary Age Children on Communicating, Cooperating and Resolving Conflict.* Torrance, CA: Jalmar Press.

Dreyfuss, E. 1990. *Learning Ethics in School-Based Mediation Programs.* Chicago: American Bar Association, National Law-Related Resource Centre.

Evans, B. 2002. *You can't Come to My Birthday Party! Conflict Resolution with Young Children.* Ypsilanti, MI: High/Scope Educational Research Foundation.

Face to Face: Resolving Conflict without Giving In or Giving Up; Curriculum for Americorps and the Corporation for National Service. 1996. Washington, DC: Americorps National Service and National Association for Community Mediation.

Feuerverger, G. 2001. *Oasis of Dreams: Teaching and Learning Peace in a Jewish-Palestinian Village.* New York: Routledge.

Finch, S. 1998. *An Eye for an Eye Leaves Everyone Blind: Teaching Young Children to Settle Conflicts without Violence: A Handbook for Early Years Workers.* London: The National Early Years Network and Save the Children.

Fisher, R. and Ury, W. 1991. *Getting to Yes: Negotiating Agreement without Giving In.* New York: Penguin Books.

Fitzell, S.G. 1997. *Free the Children! Conflict Education for strong peaceful minds. Conflict resolution skills for Pre-K through Grade 12.* Gabriola Island, British Columbia: New Society Publishers.

Fostering Peace: A Comparison of Conflict Resolution Approaches for Students, Grades K-12. Grinnell, IW: Iowa Peace Institute.

Fountain, S. 1995. *Education for Development: A Teacher's Resource for Global Learning.* Portsmouth, New Hampshire: Heinemann.

Fountain, S. 1997. *Education for Conflict Resolution: A Training for Trainers Manual.* New York: UNICEF. United Nations Children's Fund. Education for Development.

Fountain, S., Starr, C., and Wolff, L. (Eds.). 1997. *Education for Peace and Conflict Resolution* (Canadian Edition). Toronto: UNICEF. Education for Development Committee.

Gerber, J. 2000. *Pour une éducation à la non-violence: Activités pour éduquer les 8-12 ans à une paix et à la transformation des conflits.* Brussels: Vie Ouvrière. Lyons: Chronique Sociale.

Gilhooley, J. and Scheuch, N.S. 2000. *Using Peer Mediation in Classrooms and Schools: Strategies for Teachers, Counselors, and Administrators.* Thousand Oaks, CA: Corwin Press.

Girard, K. and Koch, S.J. 1996. *Conflict Resolution in the schools: A Manual for Educators.* San Francisco, CA: Jossey Bass.

Girard, K. and Koch, S. 1997. *Resolución de conflictos en las escuelas. Manual para educadores.* Barcelona: Ediciones Granica.

Global Directory of Peace Studies and Conflict Resolution Programs. 2000. Fairfax, Virginia: COPRED, Consortium on Peace Research, Education and Development.

Gust, J., McChesney, J.M., Gechtman, R.R., and Gliken, A. 1997. *Improving Communication Skills:Interactive Thematic Units for Preventing Conflict.* Carthage, IL: Teaching and Learning Company.

Handbook on the Peaceful Settlement of Disputes between States. 1992. New York: United Nations.

Handbook: Resource and Teaching Material in Conflict Resolution, Education for Human Rights, Peace and Democracy. 1994. Paris: UNESCO. IPRA, International Peace Research Association.

Hendrich, D. Schwendenwein, U., and Teutsch, R. 1998. *Peace Education and Conflict Resolution: Handbook for School Based Projects.* Vienna: Federal Ministry of Education and Cultural Affairs, Department of Internal Relations and Exchanges.

Hopkins, S. 1999. *Hearing Everyone's Voice: Educating Young Children For Peace and Democratic Community.* Redmond, Washington: Child Care Information Exchange.

Hopkins, S. and Winters, J. 1990. *Discover the World: Empowering Children to Value Themselves, Others and the Earth.* Philadelphia, PA: New Society Publishers.

Jasmine, J. and Taggart, M.K. 1997. *Conflict Resolution.* Huntington Beach, CA: Teacher Created Materials.

Jessup, J.J. 1998. *An Encyclopedic Dictionary of Conflict and Conflict Resolution, 1945–1996.* Westport, CT: Greenwood Press.

Johnson, D.W. and Johnson, R.T. 1995. *Our Mediation Notebook* (3rd ed.). Edina, MN: Interaction Book Company.

Johnson, D.W. and Johnson R.T. 1995. *Reducing School Violence through Conflict Resolution.* Alexandria, VA: Association for Supervision and Curriculum Development.

Johnson, D.W. and Johnson, R.T. 1995. *Teaching Students to be Peacemakers.* Edina, MN: Interaction Book Company.

Johnson, D.W. and Johnson, R.T. 1999. *Como reducir la violencia en las escuelas.* Buenos Aires: Ed. Paidos Col. Paidos Educador.

Jones, B., Montgomery, M., and Morganti, M. 1998. *Hearing All Sides: Resolving Conflicts.* Upper Saddle River, NJ: Prentice Hall.

Jones, T.S. and Compton, R. (Eds.). 2003. *Kid's Working It Out: Stories and Strategies for Making Peace in Our Schools.* San Francisco, CA: Jossey Bass.

Jones, T.S. and Kmitta, D. (Eds.). 2000. *Does It Work? The Case for Conflict Resolution Education in Our Nation's Schools.* Washington, DC: Conflict Resolution Network.

Judson, S. 2000. *Aprendiendo a resolver conflictos. Manual de educación para la paz y la noviolencia.* Madrid: Los Libros de la Catarata, Colleccion Edupaz, No. 8.

Juvonen, J. and Graham, S. 2001. *Peer Harassment in School: The Plight of the Vulnerable and Victimized.* New York: Guilford Press.

Kamaluddin, L. 1996. *Conflict Resolution Education and Training in a Culturally Conditioned Environment: The Malaysian Experience.* Sydney, Australia: University of Sydney, Centre for Peace and Conflict Studies (Occasional paper, No. 96/5).

Keeney, S. and Sidwell, J. 1990. *Training and Implementation Guide for Student Mediation in Elementary Schools.* Albuquerque, New Mexico: New Mexico Centre for Dispute Resolution.

Kriedler, W.J. 1984. *Creative Conflict Resolution: More than 200 Activities for Keeping the Peace in the Classroom, K-6.* Glenview, IL: Scott Foresman.

Kriedler, W.J. 1997. *Conflict Resolution in the Middle School.* Cambridge, MA: Educators for Social Responsibility.

Kriedler, W.J. 1990. *Elementary Perspectives: Teaching Concepts of Peace and Conflict.* Cambridge, MA: Educators for Social Responsibility.

Kriedler, W.J. 1995. *Teaching Conflict Resolution through Children's Literature.* New York: Scholastic Professional Books.

Kriedler, W.J. 1996. *School-Age Adventures in Peacemaking.* Cambridge, MA: Educators for Social Responsibility.

Kriedler, W.J. and Whittall, S.T. 1999. *Early Childhood Adventures in Peacemaking.* Cambridge, MA: Educators for Social Responsibility.

Lantieri, L. and Patti, J. 1996. *Waging Peace in our Schools.* Boston: Beacon Press.

Le Baron, M. and Robinson, V.C. 1994. *Conflict Analysis and Resolution in Education: Culturally Sensitive Processes for Conflict Resolution.* Victoria, British Columbia: University of Victoria, Institute for Dispute Resolution.

Levin, D.E. 1994. *Teaching Young Children in Violent Times: Building a Peaceable Classroom.* Cambridge, MA: Educators for Social Responsibility.

Lieber, C.M., Lantieri, L., and Roderick, T. 1998. *Conflict Resolution in the High School: 36 Lessons.* Cambridge, MA: Educators for Social Responsibility.

Lim, Y.Y. and Deutsch, M. 1996. *Examples of School-Based Programs Involving Peaceful Conflict Resolution and Mediation Oriented to Overcome Community Violence.* New York: Columbia University, Teachers College. International Centre for Cooperation and Conflict Resolution and UNESCO.

Lincoln, M. 2002. *Conflict Resolution Communication: Patterns Promoting Peaceful Schools.* Lanham, MD: Scarecrow Press.

Luvmour, J. 2002. *Win-Win Games for All Ages: Cooperative Activities for Building Social Skills.* Gabriola Island, British Columbia: New Society Publishers.

Macbeth, F. and Fine, N. 1995. *Playing with Fire: Creative Conflict Resolution for Young Adults.* Philadelphia, PA: New Society Publishers.

Mashder, M. 1990. *Let's Cooperate: Activities and Ideas for Parents and Teachers of Young Children for Peaceful Conflict Solving.* London: Peace Education Project.

Mastellone, F.R. 1993. *Finding Peace through Conflict.* Amherst, MA: National Association for Mediation in Education.

McCann, J.T. 2002. *Threats in School: A Practical Guide for Managing Violence.* New York: Haworth Press.

Mertz, G. and Lieber, C.M. 2001. *Conflict in Context: Understanding Local to Global Security.* Cambridge, MA: Educators for Social Responsibility.

Miller, S. 1993. *Kids Learn about Justice by Mediating the Disputes of Other Kids.* Chicago: American Bar Association.

Miller-Lieber, C. 1994. *Making Choices about Conflict, Security, and Peacemaking. Part I: Personal Perspectives.* Cambridge, MA: Educators for Social Responsibility.

Muller, J.-M. 2002. *De la non-violence en education.* Paris: UNESCO and IRNC, Institut de Recherchir sur la Resolution Non-violente des conflicts.

Nathan, A. 1996. *Everything You Need to Know about Conflict Resolution.* New York: Rosen Publishing Group.

Noddings, N. 1993. *The Challenge to Care in Schools: An Alternative Approach to Education.* New York: Teachers College Press.

Palmer, J. 2001. Conflict resolution: strategies for the elementary classroom. *Social Studies 92*(2), 65–68.

Perlstein, R. and Thrall, G. 1996. *Ready-to-Use Conflict Resolution Activities for Secondary Students.* West Nyack, New York: The Centre for Applied Research in Education.

Porro, B. 1996. *Talk it Out: Conflict Resolution for the Elementary Classroom.* Alexandria, VA: Association for Supervision and Curriculum Development.

Prutzman, P. and Johnson, J. 1997. Bias awareness and multiple perspectives: essential aspects of conflict resolution. *Theory into Practice 36*(1), 26–31.

Prutzman, P., Johnson, J.M., and Fountain, S. 1998. *CCRC's Friendly Classrooms and Communities for Young Children: A Manual of Conflict Resolution Activities and Resources.* Nyack, NY: Creative Response to Conflict.

Prutzman, P., and Children's Creative Response to Conflict Program. 1988. *The Friendly Classroom for a Small Planet.* Philadelphia, PA: New Society Publishers.

Raider, E. and Coleman, S. 1992. *Conflict Resolution: Strategies for Collaborative Problem Solving*. New York: Columbia University, Teachers College. International Centre for Cooperation and Conflict Resolution.

La resolución de conflictos en el aula. 1999. Buenos Aires: Porro B. Paidos.

Resolving Conflict Creatively: A Teaching Guide for Grades Kindergarten through Six. 1993. New York: RCCP National Centre.

Resolving Conflict Creatively: A Teaching Guide for Secondary Schools. 1990. New York: RCCP National Centre.

Reyes Torres, F. 1994. *Democracia y conflicto en la escuela*. Santafé de Bogatá, D.C., Columbia: Instituto Para el Desarrollo de la Democracia Luis Carlos Galon.

Rozenblum de Horowitz, S. 1998. *Mediación en la escuela. Resolución de conflictos en el ambito educativo*. Buenos Aires: Editorial AIQUE.

Sadella, G., Holmberg, M., and Halligan, J. 1987. *Conflict Resolution: A Secondary School Curriculum*. San Francisco, CA: Community Board Programme.

Sadella, G., Holmberg, M., and Halligan, J. 1990. *Conflict Resolution: An Elementary School Curriculum*. San Francisco, CA: Community Board Programme.

Schilling, D. 1993. *Getting Along: Activities for Teaching Cooperation, Responsibility and Respect*. Spring Valley, CA: Interchoice.

Schmidt, F. 1994. *Mediation: Getting to Win Win!, Teacher's Guide*. Miami Beach, FL: Grace Contrino Abrams Peace Education Foundation.

Schmidt, F. and Friedman, A. 1991. *Creative Conflict Solving for Kids: Grades 3–4*. Miami Beach, FL: Grace Contrino Abrams Peace Education Foundation.

Schmidt, F. and Friedman, A. 1985. *Creative Conflict Solving for Kids: Grades 4–9*. Miami Beach, FL: Grace Contrino Abrams Peace Education Foundation.

Schmidt, F. and Friedman, A. 1990. *Fighting Fair: Dr. Martin Luther King, Jr., for Kids*. Miami Beach, FL: Grace Contrino Abrams Peace Education Foundation.

Schmidt, F. Friedman, A., and Marvel, J. 1992. *Mediation for Kids*. Miami Beach, FL: Grace Contrino Abrams Peace Education Foundation.

Schoenhaus, R.M. 2001. *Conflict Management Training: Advancing Best Practices*. Washington, DC: United States Institute of Peace.

Schrumpf, F., Crawford, D and Bodine, R. 1997. *Peer Mediation: Conflict Resolution in Schools* (Revised ed.). Champaign, IL: Research Press.

Scott, C.C., Gargan, A.M., and Zakierski, M.M. 1997. *Managing Diversity-Based Conflicts among Children*. Bloomington, IN: Phi Delta Kappa Educational Foundation.

A Selected List of UNESCO Practical and Reference Materials Related to Education for Peace. 2001. Paris: UNESCO, Education Sector, Division for the Promotion of Quality Education. (ED-2001/WS/12).

Sharan, S. 1994. *Handbook of Cooperative Learning Methods*. Westport, CT: Greenwood Press.

Siegal, L.A. and Lopez, L.M. 1995. *Establishing a Viable and Durable Peer Mediation Program: From A to Z*. Athens, GA: The Institute for Violence Prevention.

Slaby, R., Wilson-Brewer, R. and Dash, K. 1994. *Aggressors, Victims and Bystanders: Thinking and Acting to Prevent Violence*. Newton, MA: Education Development Centre.

Smith, M. and Sidwell, J. 1990. *Training and Implementation Guide for Student Mediation in Secondary Schools*. Albuquerque, New Mexico: New Mexico Centre for Dispute Resolution.

Spring, U. (Ed.). 2000. *Encyclopedia of Violence, Peace and Conflict*. San Diego, CA: Academic Press.

Starting a Conflict Managers Program. 1992. San Francisco, CA: Community Board Programme.

Suckling, A. 2002. *Bullying: A Whole School Approach*. London: Jessica Kingsley.

Talk It Out: Conflict Resolution in the Elementary Classroom. 1999. Alexandria, VA: Association for Supervision and Curriculum Development.

Teolis, B. 2002. *Ready-to-Use Conflict Resolution Activities for Elementary Students: Over 100 Step-By-Step Lessons and Illustrated Activities*. Paramus, NJ: Centre for Applied Research in Education.

Torrego Seijoo, J.C. (Ed.). 2000. *Mediación de conflictos en instituciones educativas. Manual para la formación de mediadores*. Madrid: Ed. Narcea.

Training High School Conflict Managers. 1996. San Francisco, CA: Community Board Programme.

Training Middle School Conflict Managers. 1996. San Francisco, CA: Community Board Programme.

Weil, P. 1990. *The Art of Living in Peace: An Education for Peace Manual for Teachers*. Paris: UNESCO.

Wichert, S. 1989. *Keeping the Peace: Practicing Cooperation and Conflict Resolution with Preschoolers*. Philadelphia, PA: New Society Publishers.

8.2.   Websites

ASPnet Associated Schools Project Network. Paris: UNESCO. Available at:
      http://portal.unesco.org/education/.
Association for Conflict Resolution. Washington, DC: The Association. Available at:
      http://www.acrnet.org/.
CADRE: Consortium for Appropriate Dispute Resolution in Special Education. N.P.: The Consortium.
      Available at: http://www.directionservice.org/cadre/index.cfm.
Centre for the Study and Prevention of Violence. Boulder, CO: University of Colorado, Institute of
      Behavioural Science. Available at: http://www.colorado.edu/cspv/.
C.I.R.C.M. Centre International de Résolution de Conflits et de Médiation. Montreal, Quebec: C.I.R.C.M.
      Available at: http://www.circm.com/.
Community Boards. San Francisco, CA: Community Boards. Available at:
      http://www.communityboards.org/.
Conflict Research Consortium. Boulder, CO: University of Colorado. Available at:
      http://www.conflict.colorado.edu.
Conflict Resolution Education Clearinghouse Project. Washington, DC: Tabula Rasa Institute. Available
      at: http://www.trinstitute.org/crecp.htm.
Conflict Resolution Network. Chatswood NSW: The Network. Available at: http://www.crnhq.org/.
Conflict Resolution Network Canada. Waterloo, Ontario: University of Waterloo, Institute of Peace and
      Conflict Studies. Available at: http://www.crnetwork.ca/front.asp.
Conflict Resolution/Peer Mediation (CR/PM) Research Project. Gainesville, FL: University of Florida,
      College of Education, Special Education. Available at: http://www.coe.ufl.edu/CRPM/
      CRPMhome.html.
CRI: Conflict Resolution Research Resource Institute. Tacoma, WA: The Institute. Available at:
      http://www.cri.cc/.
CRU Institute: Conflict Mediation Programs. Bellevue, WA: The Institute. Available at:
      http://www.cruinstitute.org.
Culture of Peace Website: Peace is in Our Hands. Paris: UNESCO. Available at: http://www.3.UNESCO.
      org/iycp/.
Educators for Social Responsibility. Cambridge, MA: ESR. Available at: http://www.esrnational.org/.
hrea.org: Human Rights Education Associates. Cambridge, MA: HREA. Available at: http://www.hrea.org/.
International Center for Cooperation and Conflict Resolution. New York: Columbia University, Teachers
      College, The Center. Available at: http://www.tc.columbia.edu/icccr/.
Morris, C. (2004) *Conflict Transformation and Peacebuilding: a Selected Bibliography.* Victoria,
      BC: The Peacemakers Trust. Available at: http://www.peacemakers.ca/bibliography/index.html.
National Center for Conflict Resolution Education. Urbana, IL: Conflict Resolution Inc. Available at:
      http://www.nccre.org.
National Youth Violence Prevention Resource Center. Rockvile, MD: The Center. Available at:
      http://www.safeyouth.org.
Non-violence Actualité: Centre de Ressources sur la Gestion Non-Violente des Conflits. Montargis, France:
      Le Centre. Available at: http://www.nonviolence-actualite.org.
Non-violence Education. In UNESCO: Education. Paris: UNESCO. Available at:
      http://www.portal.unesco.org/education/.
Ohio Commission on Dispute Resolution and Conflict Management. Columbus, OH: The Commission.
      Available at: http://disputeresolution.ohio.gov/index.htm.
Peace Education Foundation. Miami Beach, FL: The Foundation. Available at: http://www.peace-ed.org/.
RCCP National Center: Resolving Conflict Creatively Program. Cambridge, MA: Educators for Social
      Responsibility. Available at: http://www.esrnational.org/about-rccp.html.
Seeds of Peace: Empowering Leaders of the Next Generation. New York: Seeds of Peace. Available at:
      http://www.seedsofpeace.org/.
Teaching Students to be Peacemakers. Twin Cities, MN: University of Minnesota, Cooperative Learning
      Centre. Available at: http://www.co-operation.org/pages/peacemaker.html.
United States Institute of Peace. Washington, DC: The Institute. Available at: http://www.usip.org/.

Chapter 11

CONFLICT RESOLUTION IN A TROUBLED REGION: DEVELOPING INDIVIDUALS FOR INTERACTION

Valerie Jakar and Esther Lucas

It is our intention to describe projects that have been carried out in Israel aimed at bringing together Jewish and Palestinian young people for interaction. Palestine–Israel has been a troubled region for more than a 100 years and animosity dates back to long before the establishment of the State of Israel in 1948. Promoting a culture of peace is most difficult in areas of conflict (Colin Power in Campbell 2001). However the last few years have seen a real attempt at developing understanding among students, teachers and even parents of the two communities. The concerns identified by respondents in this study (as articulated in Items 37 and 53) are addressed here.

1. EDUCATION IN ISRAEL

The small country of Israel, founded in 1948, has a population of about 6 million, of which a fifth are Arabs (both Moslem and Christian), Druze, Circassians and Bedouin. The Arabs living in Israel are Palestinians with Israeli citizenship. They are a minority with sympathetic links to their Palestinian neighbours.

During the British Mandate 1918–1948 there was no compulsory education. Arabic replaced Turkish in the schools for boys, taken over by the British. There were some Christian schools run by missions, while Jewish education that covered all Jewish children was the responsibility of the Jewish Community.

The Ministry of Education was established in 1949. Education became free and compulsory for all citizens from kindergarten (age 5) to 14 and later 15. Today, students also benefit from free education even if not compulsory in grades 10 to 12.

Jewish and Arab state education is basically separate. Arabic is the language of instruction in Arab schools and Hebrew in Jewish schools. The Ministry of Education has recently recognised a number of bilingual schools where Arab and Jewish children study together. There are also some private Christian schools in the Christian Arab communities. In this chapter, the term *Arab* applies to Arab citizens and schools in Israel. *Palestinian* applies to citizens and schools in the Palestine Authority, and *Jewish* applies to Jewish citizens and schools in Israel.

2. TEACHER EDUCATION FOR CONFLICT RESOLUTION

In Israel today, teacher education can be separated into four parameters: pre-service, in-service, formal and informal (or voluntary).

J. Campbell et al. (eds.), Towards a Global Community, 179–198.
© 2006 *Springer. Printed in the Netherlands.*

2.1.   Pre-service

The agents of education in the pre-service domain are the Teachers' Colleges and the University Departments of Education. Most universities and all colleges are multicultural, with a mixed population of Hebrew, Arabic, Russian and Amharic native speakers; Jews, Christians, Moslems, Secular Israelis, Druse, Bahai and people from other nations or other language groups. There are some 'uninational' institutions, both Arab and Jewish for orthodox religious groups or for native Arabic speakers.

Each university or college has its ethos, which is reflected in the kinds of activities which predominate, both formal and informal, the types of research that are pursued, and the voices that are heard representing the establishment in the media. Thus, for example, Bar Ilan University is known for its devotion to Jewish religious studies but also for its prowess in the natural and social sciences. The Dr Joseph Burg Chair in Education for Human Values, Tolerance and Peace was recently awarded the prestigious status of an UNESCO Chair in Human Rights, Peace, Democracy and Tolerance. This Chair was named for the late Dr Burg who strove for pluralistic interpretations of Jewish Law and the tolerance and peace, which he believed that would bring.

Another example is the David Yellin Teachers' College, Jerusalem where Jewish, Muslim and Christian students study certain subjects together but others in single language groups! The Centre for Studies of the Work of Januscz Korczak* was established, following extraordinary efforts on the part of one of the teachers at the college to translate the (originally Polish) Hebrew text into Arabic. A number of peace and co-existence initiatives have been started there (see below) which have been strongly influenced by the teachings and interpretations of the teachings of Korsczak.

2.2.   In-service

In-service education for teachers is organised by the Ministry of Education or by private agencies with a particular agenda. The 'formal' element, cited above, relates to the curriculum of studies in the various establishments where there are compulsory and elective courses. The 'informal' parameter relates to courses, groups and 'clubs' available to the students as extra curricular activities and the voluntary groups of teachers which are established, usually at 'grass roots' level (for example, the various groups of teachers, of many disciplines, who regularly participate in the MECA encounters).[1] An additional element (or one which can be subsumed under the heading of 'in-service' education) is the in-service activities of the college/university staff: the professors, the instructors and the administrative staff.

At each of the above levels or parameters we see students, teachers, and their teachers, striving to develop and maintain mutual co-existence. They do this in a variety of ways, on occasions duplicating a project or pursuing a concept that has already been explored, but always finding out more about themselves and 'the other', which is, if one can be excused the (anti) pun, half the battle won! Many of the programmes claim to promote a reciprocal tolerance approach between two groups, and all have

---

[1]   See p. 183

'education' as their prime agenda. Cited below are just four examples of the teacher education endeavour, where mutual coexistence and/or conflict resolution studies are either the focus or the adjunct agenda for the programme. They represent the energy, enthusiasm and effort that many of the student teachers, teachers and teacher educators exert in order to resolve conflicts that exist and prepare for a better future.

2.3. Mutual Coexistence Project (for Pre-service Teachers)

A department for mutual coexistence has been set up at least two colleges of education (Beit Berl and David Yellin) where students elect to take courses on subjects such as Comparative Religion, East and West Philosophies and Multicultural Education. One obligatory course is the *du-kium* (mutual co-existence) course where equal numbers of Jewish and Arab students meet together once a week to discuss issues of importance to them as human beings, as representatives of their national groups, and as prospective teachers.

At David Yellin College, the programme moves from intensive discussion groups, which are matched for socio-economic and ethnic backgrounds, to active groups/pairs who run programmes or events at schools. In this programme, there are two leaders for each group (of approximately 24 participants), one being a Hebrew speaker and one an Arabic speaker. These leaders take a preparatory course in leadership and conflict resolution, and continue participating in 'reflection sessions' throughout the duration of the course. At approximately a third of the way through the year, the student teachers begin planning activities that can be accomplished in a dual-lingual situation in an elementary school. They then visit the school in question, observe the pupils, and, on return to their college environment, reflect upon the planned lesson, revise it (if necessary) and prepare it for the next occasion.

The student teachers work in pairs (one Arabic speaker and one Hebrew speaker) and visit both Jewish and Arab schools. Towards the end of the year long programme pupils from Arab and Jewish areas are brought together for the planned activities devised by the student teachers. On occasions, the parents are invited too (see also: The Traditional Creativity in School Communities Project). Thus cross-cultural communication is going on at a number of levels, from the organising professor, down (or up) to the children in the class. The pre-service teachers are gaining in experience and expertise in planning lessons where the content is meaningful to the pupils and also to society at large.

2.4. TETEC (Teachers English Through Experiencing Cultures) (In-service Education for Elementary School Teachers)

Following the success of the Traditional Creativity in School Communities Project, a group of advisers decided to set up a training course for teachers where English would be the medium of communication and learning. The goal is to create materials to be used in the classroom that pertain to learning about our own heritage or to the status, rights and plights of children in our era. An additional component of this venture is that two groups of teachers are working simultaneously and together; this is significant because one group is from the Jewish part of the city, and the other group is from the Arab part. They speak English at all times and encourage their pupils to use English for self-expression. Ostensibly, the mutual communicability is preferable to any other means of communications, but it has been found that there is a power differential, which cannot be resolved. The native speakers of Arabic are unable to speak English as fluently as the Hebrew speakers. This gives them a sense of inequality when that is the last sentiment one would want to evoke in those circumstances! This situation is in the process of being resolved.

3.   KNOWING THE OTHER—THE INFORMAL/VOLUNTARY INITIATIVE

Now completing its second year of regular meetings, the multicultural group of teachers/instructors, Jews and Arabs, at the David Yellin College are concerned with 'knowing the other' in order to promote mutual peaceful coexistence. In their meetings, the participants, specialists in languages, mathematics, science, pedagogy, philosophy of education, psychology and physical education, do not shy away from discussing 'hot topics' but rather explore them, recruiting experts to assist in the discussion sessions and information exchange.

4.   CONSORTIUM—VOLUNTARY, PROFESSIONAL DEVELOPMENT INITIATIVE

Funded by the Abraham Foundation, a group of teacher educators, from seven colleges of education around the country, assembled once a month to learn about programmes of conflict resolution, mutual coexistence and peace studies. This was with a view to finding out about the various programmes that were being conducted, and following that up with some proposals for collaborative programmes across college populations (Arab, Jewish, Christian, Druse, Israeli, Palestinian).

Participants learned about animal therapy, the life and teachings of Korczak, the workings and philosophies of *Neve Shalom* (Oasis of Peace), the Mutual Coexistence programme (see above) and bibliotherapy. All of the above contributed to the group's collective knowledge, which they then applied to programme planning for the coming academic year. Unfortunately, because of fiscal problems, the projected next stage (implementation of programmes and evaluation of same) was not completed, leaving some teacher-educators with a sense of loss, and others with a sense of challenge 'So *we'll do it alone*'!!

Of the four examples given, none have had 100% success, but all have been positive learning experiences. People have made lasting friendships, both collegial and social. Since these friendships have lasted, and generated more interest and enthusiasm for such programmes.

5.   CONFLICT RESOLUTION PROJECTS

Thousands of students have been involved in a great variety of mainly extra curricular projects. Some activities have developed through the support of international organisations. Many have developed through local initiative.

5.1.   Purpose of Conflict Resolution Activities

To confirm self identity and worth (Tseng 2002)
To confirm knowledge and appreciation of own community
To create respect for diversity
To communicate constructively
To enhance cooperation
To develop individual involvement and responsibility
To build a climate of peace

5.2.   Organisations and Projects

The following four projects *are described* in some detail:
- *Garden of Peace International, The Association for the Commemoration of Bat Chen.* <ofri1@inter.net.il> <bat-chen.israel.net/diary>
- *Peaceful Coexistence, the Ben Zvi-Tira Project.* Carmella Goldglass <goldglas@ barak-online.net.il>
- *The Israel Middle East Model United Nations (TIMEMUN)* <http://www.wbais. org/timemun> <http://www.timemun,org>
- *Seeds of Peace, Centre for Coexistence*, Jerusalem http://www.seedsofpeace. org

The following are *not described* and can be accessed via internet address shown:
- *Adam Institute for Democracy and Peace.* <http://www.adaminstitute.org.il>
- *Bet Hagefen, Haifa Youth Centre for Coexistence* <http://www.haifa.gov.il/beit-hagefen>
- *Crossing Borders, Bi-monthly regional youth magazine* <http://www.crossing border.org>
- *Givat Haviva, Jewish Arab Centre for Peace.* <http://www.mpdn.org/givat. htm>
- *Hand in Hand Bilingual Schools.* <http://handinhand12.org>
- *'Hello Peace' Phone call Project.* <http://www.hellopeace.net>
- *Hope Flowers School Bethlehem.* <http://www.mideastweb,org/hopeflowers>
- *Israel Boy and Girl Scout Federation.* <israel@scout.net>
- *Middle East Children's Alliance.* <http://www.mecaforpeace.org>
- *MidEast Web 'Pieces for Peace' Project*<http://www.mideastweb.org/ pieces4peace.htm>
- *Neve Shalom/Wahat Al Salaam, the Arab Jewish School and Peace School.* <http://www.nswas.com>
- *Pathways to Reconciliation of the Israel/Palestine Center for Research and Information.* <http://www.ipcri.org>
- *Reut Sadaka.* <http://www.Israelpages.co.il/reut>
- *The Traditional Creativity in School Communities Project.* Simon Lichman. <ccech@012.net.il>
- *UNESCO Associated Schools Project (ASPnet) in Israel.* National Coordinator YaelHarel. <learningtolivetogether@hotmail.com>
- *UNICEF Education for Development Projects in Israel.* <unicefil@zahav. net.il>

5.3.   Supporting Organisations

The major supporting organisations are: UNESCO, The Abraham Fund,[2]
The Peres Fund for Peace, The Adenauer Fund

5.3.1.   Activities of Three Selected Organisations

There are more than 60 non-governmental institutions, community centres and schools in Israel devoted to peace education. The following descriptions reflect the varied approaches of those selected.

The Garden of Peace—Association for the Commemoration of Bat-Chen

This Association was founded after Bat Chen a 15-year-old girl was killed by a suicide bomber in Tel Aviv in 1996. After her death, her mother found diaries and poems she had been writing secretly. Seven years after her death, memorial meetings took place, featuring exhibitions of students' diaries from schools involved in the project.

The Association is called The Garden of Peace, because 'Bat Chen' in Hebrew is the name of a garden flower. Full of charm like its Hebrew name, this white, pink or red daisy-like flower is an early bloomer that flourishes in semi-shade.

5.3.2.   Aims of the Association: Yes to Dialogue, No to Violence

–   To promote peace, co existence, tolerance and dialog among citizens of the region. (Abuateya, S. 2001)
–   To encourage meetings and dialog between Arabs and Jews.
–   To develop creative writing, especially diaries, in formal and informal educational frameworks.

5.3.3.   Activities

Distribution to educational institutions of a film and book about Bat Chen.
Distribution of extracts from Bat Chen's diary and poems.
Grants to participating schools and institutions.
Organisation of ceremonies and memorial days.

5.3.4.   Secret of the Diary—The Programme

The programme aims to introduce students to the diary genre as well as promoting coexistence through meetings of Arab and Jewish students in relation to the writing of diaries.

---

[2]   The Fund has just set up a new website in Hebrew, English and Arabic. See www.coexistencenet.org.

5.3.5.   *From Bat Chen's Second Grade Diary (translation)*

I've decided to keep a diary and tell about everything that happens to me in my life, whether I'm happy or sad. I've decided that keeping a diary will be a lovely souvenir of my childhood. Especially in hard times, there's someone to run to and tell, and that makes life much easier.

There's someone to pour out your heart to, someone to encourage you, without words. Really amazing!

Love, Bat Chen Shahak

5.3.6.   *From Bat Chen's Seventh Grade Diary (translation)*

There is a lot of unrest in our country.

It's very hard for me to make up my mind. One moment I'm for the left. Then suddenly the radio announcer says: Jews have been murdered. The terrorists have been captured, and I say: It could have been one of my family. All this hatred has lasted over 2000 years, and we and the Arabs all live in fear. I always say there are good Arabs too, but I only hear about the murders. I want peace and believe that it will come in the end, because peace is vital for the continuation of life.

Peace ('Shalom') is a beautiful word.

A word with a wonderful meaning.

A word of value and significance.

Every day and every hour

5.3.7.   *Secret of the Diary—Procedure*

Each student creates a portfolio that records his/her emotions and thoughts. Particular emphasis is given to students' emotions and thoughts subsequent to their encounter with the diary form.

First meeting. Questionnaires regarding participants and their interests in reading and writing are filled in and collected. Following brainstorming on associations with the word 'diary', opposites are invoked. Assignment: bring diaries to next meeting.

Second meeting. Excerpts from texts of different diaries' authentic and fictional are distributed. Individually or in pairs, students discover and describe diaries. They discuss one authentic and one fictional diary in groups, and prepare an identity card for each writer.

Third meeting.

Distribution of the book about Bat Chen and encounter with Bat Chen's writing
Preparation of an identity card for Bat Chen

Fourth meeting.
>   Distribution of Bat Chen's 7th Grade diary.
>   Discussion on why the diary was written in the 7th grade, probably to enable her to cope with possible difficulties in junior high.
>   Students choose text or sentence that they can relate to. Explanation of choice.

Fifth meeting.
>   Summarizing characteristics of writing a diary: It's not addressed to anyone. It doesn't have to be perfect. It's secret. No need to erase anything. There's no fear of criticism.
>   Questionnaires handed out a second time.
>   Suggestion that students write a letter to Bat Chen or her family.
>   Website address given. Students are encouraged to send feedback.
>   Screening of film: 'It's not Fair'.
>   Meeting with Bat Chen's mother.
>   The diary writer's dilemma is echoed in what Bat Chen wrote:

>>   'I tell it everything, without worrying that it will be discovered and there will be a slip of the tongue. I know the diary is a real friend. On the other hand there is always the possibility that the contents will be published, and perhaps one day you'll read it in the paper. Who knows'?

5.3.8.   What Students Write

The sessions outlined above are carried out in Jewish and Arab schools. Exhibitions, which are also encounters, display diaries, written in Hebrew, Arabic or English. An Arab 14-year-old girl writes 'We, the Moslems greet each other with the words "Peace be upon you". Peace, which is one of God's names and qualities, is a purpose for all of us. Our prophet, Mohammed, peace upon him, has commanded his fighters during war, not to hurt elderly people, not to kill women or children, not to uproot trees. That is our religion. That is how we are'.

5.3.9.   Letter to Bat Chen's Mother from a Pupil Involved in the Project: The Garden of Peace

Explanatory note. This letter has been translated from the Hebrew. Verse has been attempted where the pupil wrote in verse. The pupil is a junior high school girl called Liron.

>   Dear Ayelet,
>   Thank you for giving me hope
>   The dream for peace to help me cope
>   THANK YOU for showing me that Jews and Arabs can live together and get along.
>   When I first heard about the forum of families who met with Arabs, I though to myself:

How is this possible? Aren't they afraid? But now I see things differently, in a better perspective.

Peace has to be made with enemies.

Bat Chen is a special girl who saw everything in a way that makes things possible, and I was very moved to read and hear what she wrote.

When I was a little girl, I would write poems, which made it easier for me to live my life, and then, I stopped . . .

But after my conversation with you, when I returned home, I had a strong desire to write, and due to you, I am writing once again. I owe you the privilege of writing down again what I feel I would like to share with you a poem I wrote after our conversation. It's about Yitzhak Rabin.

Three shots that killed a man so marvellous
Turned peace into something barbarous
Rabin, we shall remember you forever
Forget a man like you, no never.
Every year I remember and I think, who cares
How can one kill a man just for different ideas?
If you were still alive, you'd represent our cause
Why solve things with violence? Make peace, forget the wars.
No murder, no more pain,
No bloodshed, no foe will remain.
Goodbye friend, we miss you no end.

I admire you for continuing with the peace process in spite of Bat Chen's death, caused by the conflict between Arabs and Jews, and that you manage to meet with Arabs and convey all their messages to us. And I admire you for publishing Bat Chen's diaries, because she wanted to write poems that would convey feelings, and that's exactly what she did.

Hoping to receive an answer from you.
Liron

5.3.10.   *Peaceful Coexistence: The Ben Zvi-Tira Project*

The Ben Zvi Jewish Junior High School in Kfar Saba and the Tira Arab Junior High School in Tira have an ongoing project that started in 1988. The cities of Kfar Saba and Tira are situated in the 'bottleneck' of Israel between the coast and the West Bank. They serve over 100,000 people of both communities. The two schools are members of the Associated Schools Project of UNESCO (ASPnet)[3] and have been commended and supported by UNESCO for their activities on the national and international level.

---

[3]   See p. 183

The project has continued uninterrupted through all the present troubled period, with students, teachers and parents meeting regularly even during terrorist attacks. Teachers and parents have realized that coexistence has to be nurtured daily at all levels in the two communities. The project has involved more students and members of the community each year. Principals of other schools and the Ministry of Education have shown interested in this experience.

The target groups taking part each year are 800 (400 from each school) students of the 8th and 9th grades aged 14 and 15. About 100 parents also take part. Teachers receive training in the schools and are assigned specifically to carry put the project. Recruiting students to the project is an integral part of the two schools' curricula.

5.3.11.   General Objectives

1. Planting the seeds of coexistence as early as possible through educational activities in the schools. (Fountain 1995; Best Practices 2003)
2. Ensuring a natural acceptance of the situation and developing respect and tolerance towards each other's differences.
3. Involving more students, teachers, parents and members of the community and hence reaching more people in both communities.

5.3.12.   Stages of Development

Stage one—the principals. The two principals get acquainted and express commitment to the coexistence idea.

Stage two—the teachers. Staff members of the two schools get to know each other and agree upon one educational base for the project. The warm relations between the teachers serve as a model for the students Staff members begin designing the syllabus of the coexistence encounters.

Stage three—preparation of the students for the encounters. The syllabus of the preparatory stage includes:
- Principles of democracy
- Democratic culture
- Majority v. minority
- History of the Israel-Palestine conflict
- Conflict resolution and mediation

Stage four—student committee encounters. The student committees of each school meet, get acquainted, and make provisional plans for the encounters.

Stage five—class encounters. The encounters consist of 'intimate' meetings between two classes at a time. They meet alternately in Kfar Saba and Tira, both in school and at students' homes for ice-breaking games, breakfast, artistic creation, outdoor activities and town visits.

Stage six—entire age-group encounters. 200 students from each school, altogether 400, meet for joint activities in nature, tree planting, hikes, artistic programmes and lectures by experts.

Stage seven—parents meet. Parents' meetings, which began 4 years after the start of the project, and take place once a month, have been very successful. Numbers have grown considerably. Meetings include lectures by experts, discussions, festive meals and artistic programmes by the children.

Stage eight—the community gets involved. Both mayors of Kfar Saba and Tira take part in peak events of the project. They express support and encouragement.

5.3.13.   *Joint Activities*

– Sessions in the classrooms dealing with prejudice and stereotyping.
– Mutual visits between students of both schools.
– Home visits by parents of both schools.
– Annual tree planting with hundreds of students participating.
– Parents' and pupils' joint family picnic days.
– Participation in international events, e.g., as delegates to Germany, Global Village Project, etc.

5.3.14.   *Topics Dealt With*

– Group involvement
– Exploration of learning skills
– Family roots
– Know your country, trips and excursions
– Reading encouragement
– Holidays and national days
– Peaceful coexistence.

5.3.15.   *Evaluation*

Evaluation takes place at the end of every school year through questionnaires and interviews with students and parents. Results have shown that coexistence encounters improve emotional attitudes and eradicate prejudice.

6.   THE ISRAEL MIDDLE EAST MODEL UNITED NATIONS: TIMEMUN

Starting in 2000, a model UN has taken place in Israel annually.

6.1.   *Objectives*

– To enable students of different backgrounds and religions to meet and discuss local and international problems

- To enable students to understand how the UN General Assembly works
- To make students aware of the attitudes of different countries, and to be able to take on roles
- To assist students in writing reports
- To give students an opportunity to talk English

6.2. Population

Two-hundred and fifty students from grades 8–12 took part in TIMEMUN for 4 days in January 2003, at the American International School in Israel. Sixteen public, private and international schools and their Jewish, Arab, and international students participated together with their teachers who acted as Advisers.

6.3. Preparation

Students spent months preparing for TIMEMUN. Each delegate was supplied with a Delegates' Handbook, containing: instructions to the students on behaviour and etiquette, a detailed schedule of events, summaries of issues to be discussed, rules of procedure, explanations of how to write a resolution and lists of phrases to assist students in producing documents correctly. There were also short biographical details of the students serving as executives. Students were reminded in the Handbook that they were no longer high school students, but delegates and diplomats of their assigned country. It was their job to represent their country's best interests, even if these policies conflicted with their personal views. The students lived up to all expectations. Much of the planning, and decision making regarding the work of the commissions was carried out by the students themselves.

6.4. Model UN

Students were divided among 31 delegations: Angola, Armenia, Azerbaijan, Bulgaria, Cameroon, Chile, Egypt, France, Germany, Guinea, India, Iran, Iraq, Israel, Japan, Jordan, Lebanon, Mexico, North Korea, Norway, Pakistan, Palestine National Authority, Republic of China, Russian Federation, Saudi Arabia, South Africa, Spain, Syria, Turkey, United Kingdom and the United States.

TIMEMUN had eight Commissions:
1. The Security Council
2. Human Rights
3. Regional Cooperation
4. Disarmament
5. ECOSOC (Economic and Social)
6. Environment
7. Territorial Dispute
8. Mediation (Conflict Resolution Forum).

Students could use the *Issue Summaries* in the Delegates' Handbook as background information for debates and resolutions. A team of Advisors (teachers) corrected the resolutions as they were written and OK'd the final drafts for printing.

Students took on the roles of chairpersons and dealt with any infringement of order. Executives (chairpersons) carried out their responsibilities efficiently, and delegates maintained their roles consistently. Students were deeply involved in the issues.

6.5. Mediation Commission

The Mediation Commission was a new venture. It had not been part of previous MUNs. The other seven commissions demanded role-play, but in the Mediation Commission students expressed their own opinions and no Advisers or visitors were present. This commission was trained by the Adam Institute for Democracy and Peace (Israel). At the closing ceremony, a 12th grade student, who was one of the facilitators and had helped to organise this, his third Model UN, reported on his experience 'For the for the first time at a Model UN, a committee operated', he said, 'where formal dress was not a requirement, nor did the participants have to prepare policy statements. There were no formal debating rules, and no resolutions were passed'. He described how difficult it was at first to contain the storm of emotions, of rage, fear, disappointment and bewilderment. He learnt that to resolve conflicts one has to bring the conflict out into the open, expose it and confront it. He realized that looking at needs rather than positions was perhaps the focal point of conflict resolution. 'Instead of asking what we want, we should ask ourselves why we want it and how else we can answer those needs. The students did not reach full agreement, but', he claimed, 'they learnt skills, made friendships and through pain and emotion and re-evaluation of basic "truths", their commission was real education for coexistence and peace'.

6.6. Resolutions

The resolutions produced by the other commissions were often innovative. The Environment Commission, for instance, urged among other suggestions that the developed world support a pro-peace project of constructing desalination plants so that water can be shared between Israel and Palestine. The Territorial Disputes demanded the removal of all troops from Jammu and Cashmere and suggested that India and Pakistan hold a peace summit in South Africa. The Disarmament Commission called upon all Member States to support international efforts to prevent terrorist sponsoring nations from acquiring weapons of mass destruction and requested the Secretary General to compile a report on measures already taken by international organizations. The ECOSOC Commission urged Member States to enhance supervision over Internet webmasters and licensed pornography distributors.

6.7. Interviews with Students (Lucas 2003)

The students interviewed, said the MUN had been a great experience. An Arab 12th grader from an international school was attending her 4th MUN, one in Turkey and three in Israel. Asked which MUN she had liked best, she said the first one in Turkey had been most inhibiting, but she liked it best because of its formality. On the other hand TIMEMUN had been best for informal friendship making. When asked why she came, she said her aim was to attempt to solve problems, to be aware, to think, to learn what had been done. She claimed she had indeed learnt so much. She had talked about things than had never been discussed before She found the human encounter most worthwhile, and had 'tons of' stories to tell. She admitted that some parents had been afraid to let their children come to TIMEMUN, and other families where she lives considered her school 'snobs'.

Several girls claimed they came to improve their English. One girl in 12th grade, who belongs to Seeds of Peace, an organisation that brings Arab and Jewish young people together at camps and meetings, had attended such a meeting in the US 2 years ago. She also attends local coexistence sessions. It makes her life much richer and it means a lot to her to meet different people. She gets much parental support. Her hobbies are swimming and dancing and she intends to study law.

An 11th grade student from an international school in Jerusalem, who commutes from Bet Jalla near Bethlehem, where he was obliged to celebrate Christmas at home, was full of praise for TIMEMUN. He had come at the suggestion of his English teacher, and found everything interesting. It was a new experience, and he had learnt about the UN. He had already formed definite views about the UN and did not agree with the veto. Why should one country have more power than others? He appreciated his new friendship with Israelis whom he had hardly ever met before.

Also a member of Seeds of Peace, a 12th grader in an Arab school, had met Jewish students from Jerusalem and had been to coexistence meetings in the USA three times. He enjoys discussing issues of peace, tolerance and education and would like to be a camp staff member with Seeds of Peace. His aim in coming to TIMEMUN was to meet people.

A Jewish 11th grader from a local school, who was at an MUN for the first time, was somewhat reserved at the beginning. He was even slightly cynical, wondering what use a student conference of this kind could do. By the end of the 4 days, he was cooperating fully in his role as chair of the Human Rights Commission. He had made new friends and had realized the value of his role in this assembly. He is now looking forward to participating in TIMEMUN 2004.

Students came to TIMEMUN on the recommendation of their teachers. They came, eager to learn about the UN and the problems that the UN has to deal with. They came to meet other students, and because international schools took part, they met many different nationalities. Those not in 'English speaking' schools came to improve their English. They worked hard, and had a lot of fun, including an evening of dancing.

6.8.   Support

TIMEMUN was supported by UNESCO and the American International School.

The General Assembly was opened by: the ambassadors of the United States and India, The Deputy UN Special Coordinator for the Middle East Peace Process, local dignitaries and the organising teachers. The closing session was addressed by the Director General of the Israel National Commission for UNESCO and the students. 'If our leaders cannot meet and reach a solution, we can do the job for them' said a student.

7.   SEEDS OF PEACE CENTRE FOR COEXISTENCE, JERUSALEM

Seeds of Peace, a non-profit and non-political organisation, was founded in 1996 and received the UNESCO Peace Prize in 2000. While helping teenagers in regions of conflict learn the skills of peacemaking, the Centre for Coexistence in Jerusalem focuses on the Arab Israeli conflict.

7.1.   Core Goals

1. Inspiring motivation in Israeli and Palestinian youth to humanize the 'other' and perceive each other free of hatred, bias and prejudice. (Abuateya, S. 2001)
2. Developing concrete knowledge about the other and the conflict.
3. Building the specific skills of leadership and communication needed to have an impact on their own societies as well as on each other.
4. Creating an interpersonal network of real people that they will work with in the future to build two coexisting nations.

7.2.   Population

Participants are equal numbers of Palestinian (from Israel and Palestine) and Jewish students. Seeds from all areas meet locally and abroad, mainly at the Centre's camp in the USA. Total participation runs into the hundreds.

7.3.   Methods

Methods include: intensive dialogue locally and abroad, public presentations, creative expression, leadership training and empowerment, enhancing and deepening knowledge and awareness on specific issues, experiential learning, supporting social contact nurturing mutual relations. The programme is multi-tiered for school students, schools graduates and leaders. Activities continue all through the year and are specifically designed for Palestinian and Israeli Seeds with some overlapping.

7.4.   General Activities

7.4.1.   Seeds of Peace Camps

At camps, mainly in the USA, Seeds from different Arab and Jewish communities, meet in order to get to know each other and gain a better understanding of each other's experiences. They examine critically why enemy imaging continues and who stands to benefit from the practice. They discuss how they can change the attitudes of people who do not have the same experience. They read essays written by former campers and discuss changes in viewpoints expressed by these Seeds. The camps are based on experiential learning, since conflict resolution is a process that needs to be understood at the personal level.

7.4.2.   Advanced Coexistence Programme

Twice a month five different coexistence groups of 16–29 Arab and Jewish Seeds (in all 90 Seeds) meet for an advanced dialogue on all the issues pertaining to the Israel Arab conflict. The advanced programme builds on the skills and knowledge participants have gained in their introductory coexistence groups at camp.

7.4.3.   Winter Workshop at Kibbutz Yahel in December 2002

- More than 120 'Seeds' from eight different summer camps worked together. Seeds from 2001 to 2002 were participants. Those from 1998 to 1999 were Coaches, and Seeds from 1994 to 1997 served as staff members, leading the discussions and implementing the programme.
- Seeds from 2002 held coexistence discussions with their year round coexistence groups.
- Seeds from 2000 to 2001 presented Seeds of Peace to the area school attended by five local kibbutzim, a concrete manifestation of leadership.
- Everyone participated in a leadership discussion about the people they thought had the greatest positive impact on global, personal and communal levels. They discussed how they wanted to be remembered, how they wanted the world to be different because they were in it.
- Seeds chose a Leadership Workshop, where they could either work on a project designed to have a positive impact on others, or they could help develop a new skill important to them as future leaders. Seeds taught each other Hebrew and Arabic, learned some of the basics of mediation and negotiation, created a memorial to be given to Israeli and Palestinian parents whose children have been killed in the conflict, learned and practiced skills of public speaking and delivering presentation, and wrote messages of hope and courage to 'Seeds' who they knew were experiencing painful times.
- Sand dune play! A Yahel Seminar tradition: playing and rolling and tossing each other in the soft desert sand.
- The first ever Seeds of Peace Talent Fire, round the bonfire, where the performances were funny and serious. A highlight was a Hebrew and Arabic rap performed by an Arab and Jewish student that they composed together in the bus on the way down.
- Colour Games (aka Pomelo Games)! An 18-h event of team games led by the Coaches from Israel, West Bank and Gaza. They set a moving example of teamwork and cooperation.

7.4.4.   Holiday of Holidays Festival

Seeds of Peace plays a central role in the City of Haifa's multi-religion and multi-ethnic festival. Seeds create a booth at the festival where they interact with and engage hundreds of members of the Haifa community, explaining the goals and values of Seed of Peace, face painting scores of youth and assisting them in creating a mural of hand prints. As part of the celebration, Seeds have built a giant cement turtle in the garden of the library of Beit Hagefen, an Arab-Jewish community centre. Local children climb and play on it together.

7.4.5. Language Workshops

Although living side by side, many Israelis and Palestinians cannot communicate in their native languages. Seeds of Peace is launching a programme with Seeds teaching each other the basics of Hebrew and Arabic.

7.4.6. Cultural Exchanges

When Seeds have an opportunity to see and experience each other's realities, there is profound impact. Dozens of Jewish, Moslem and Christian Seeds have experienced holiday hospitality at each other's homes during Ramadan, Chanuka and Christmas, learning about the other's religions and customs in the warmest possible way, building a deeper level of trust and personal connection at the same time.

7.4.7. Bring a Friend Events

Seeds return from camp with a great desire to spread their experiences to their communities, families and friends. This is one of the main reasons for the existence of the Centre. Bring a Friend events are held in the spring, designed to give Seeds and intimate opportunity to meet peers from the other side, begin to know them as people, and have a chance to hear views and opinions while expressing their own.

7.4.8. School Presentations

Seeds talk about Seeds of Peace in their classroom. They bring other Seeds and Seeds of Peace staff with them to introduce their classmates to their friends from 'the other side'. 'Seeds' gain pose and self-confidence as they speak in front of large groups of peers, while learning how to deliver their message in a way their audience will hear with receptive interest. Interested classes follow up their presentations with a trip to the Centre where they can continue their meaningful dialogue.

7.4.9. Model UN

Seeds from different communities took part in The Israel Middle East Model UN, representing Palestine.

For Seeds from the West Bank and Gaza Regional Check in Meetings held in the West Bank and Gaza are designed for participants to share want they have been facing in recent months and how they have met the challenges and obstacles they confront, what discourages and what inspires them. The meetings are an important way for the Seeds to stay connected to the staff, the organization and its vision and to each other. The meetings are regional because of travel restrictions facing Palestinians and because of mixed ages. Check in meetings are held in Ramallah, Gaza and a number of other cities.

7.5.   Team Projects

7.5.1.   Facilitation Training Team

Inspiring Seeds to lead is at the heart of the programme. Those who have completed both an introductory and advanced coexistence programme are eligible to enrol in facilitation training. Through observation, role play, discussion of theory and practice and supervised hands-on experience, Seeds learn the skills to facilitate meaningful dialogue.

7.5.2.   Performance Team

Palestinian and Israeli Seeds have jointly produced a puppet show script that embraces values of tolerance and respect. The project now in its third year, includes puppet building, set painting, developing pre and post show interactive activities rehearsing and performing the show. Each year the show is seen by some 600 people.

7.5.3.   Community Service Team

Serving as role models for Jewish and Arab children, Seeds volunteer at an after-school-centre in a disadvantaged neighbourhood in Jaffa, a mixed Jewish-Arab city. The Seeds are thrust in genuine positions of leadership as they guide them through their homework and the values of coexistence, tolerance and mutual respect.

7.5.4.   Education Team

Ten Arab and Jewish Seeds lead school and other presentations, helping the newer Seeds gain the skills and confidence they need to deliver their message effectively to different audiences.

7.5.5.   Outreach/Family and Friends Team

This group plans and executes events designed to promote Seeds of Peace in the community and created opportunities for friends and families of Seeds to have meaningful encounters with each other. They are responsible for the Holiday of Holidays festival and the Bring a Friend events.

7.5.6.   Summer 2003 Special Activities

Mother tongue/leave your mark. Leaders for peace learn to communicate with each other in each other's languages, and create something artistic together.

Bring a friend. Members show non-Seed friends what Seeds of Peace is all about.

Media seminar. Three day seminar at Oasis of Peace (Feuerverger 2001, Lucas 2001) exploring issues involved in covering conflict and how different forms of media can be used to bring about reconciliation and tolerance. Meetings with Palestinian and Israeli media experts and crate samples of own multi-media.

Jerusalem/What's Cooking? Exploring Jerusalem with various tours and discussions and getting a taste (literally) of each other's food.

Human Rights Seminar at Oasis of Peace. (Feuerverger 2001) Exploring human rights through discussions. What are human rights? How are they most often violated? What can Seeds do to help ensure the human rights of both sides?

Celebrate the Summer. Seeds come together with family and friends for a morning festival with local kids in Jerusalem and an afternoon/evening to appreciate the talents of local Arab and Israeli musicians and performers. Talents are shared at an extra-ordinary End of the Summer event.

When booking for these events, Seeds are informed that their energy, leadership and creativity are needed.

7.5.7. The Olive Branch

The Bi-annual magazine is written by Seeds from 23 countries. Not only do Israeli and Palestinian Seeds develop as writers, they also learn international perspectives on relevant issues by Afghans, Bosnians, Cypriots and Indians, who are all like themselves, active members of Seeds of Peace.

8. CONCLUSION

The Coexistence programmes appear to be a means of helping to reduce tension between Arabs and Jews despite the present violence. A survey carried out by the University of Haifa's Centre for Research on Peace Education in 2003 among Jewish and Arab teenagers, showed more positive feelings towards the other community by those that had taken part in peace programmes than did young people who had not taken part.

The survey[4] was commissioned by the Abraham fund, and covered 123 Jews and 129 Arabs between the ages of 14 and 18. 177 of them had participated in coexistence programmes. Those who took part were more willing to learn the language of the other community, and expressed more readiness to act as ambassadors and recommend joint meetings to their friends. The findings were considered significant because some of the meetings took place after the violent events of October 2000. The research concluded that participation in coexistence programmes prevent negative feelings. In fact, the positive influences that the study measured testify to the power of these programmes.

---

[4] See <www.coexistence.org/?oid=1925>

9.   REFERENCES

Abuateya, S. 2001. Adolescents' behavior and political conflict: the case of Palestinian students. *New Era in Education 82*(1), April, 18–21.

Best Practices of Non-violent Conflict Resolution In and Out of School—Some Examples. 2003. Paris: UNESCO.

Campbell, J. (Ed.). 2001. *Creating Our Common Future, Educating for Unity in Diversity.* UNESCO Publishing/Berghahn Books, Paris.

Feuerverger, G. 2001. *Oasis of Dreams: Teaching and Learning Peace in a Jewish Palestinian Village in Israel.* New York: Routledge Falmer.

Fountain, S. 1995. *Education for Development.* Hodder & Stoughton, UNICEF.

Jakar, V. 2001. *Developing Curriculum, Pedagogic Strategies, and Mutual Understanding Through Holism.* Paper presented at the Ethnographic Forum, University of Pennsylvania, Philadelphia, February.

Jakar, V. 2002. *Pickles and Proverbs.* Paper presented at the First TESOL Eastern Mediterranean Conference (INGED, TESOL-Greece, & ETAI), Middle Eastern Technical University, Ankara, Turkey.

Lucas, E. 2001. Review of Feuerverger: Oasis of peace. *New Era in Education 82*(2), August, 58–59.

Lucas, E. 2002. *Education for Development Manual.* Jerusalem: Israel Committee for UNICEF.

Lucas, E. 2003. TIMEMUN for hope: The Israel Middle East Model United Nations. *New Era in Education 84*(1), April, 36–37.

Snow, C., Met, M. and Genesee, F. 1989. A conceptual framework for the integration of language context in second/foreign language instruction. *TESOL Quarterly 23*(2), 201–216.

Stoller, F. 2002. *CBI: A Shell for Language Teaching or a Framework for Strategic Language and Content Learning?* Paper presented at Annual TESOL Convention, Salt Lake City, April.

Tseng, Y.-H. 2002. A lesson in culture. *ELT Journal 56*(1), January, 11–21.

Chapter 12

EDUCATING WORLD CITIZENS: A CURRICULUM FOR CITIZENSHIP EDUCATION

Rob Gilbert

In the Western political tradition, the history of citizenship has been intimately bound up with the nation state as the site of civil and political power. This concept of citizenship emphasises that when a person becomes a member of a state, either by birth or naturalisation, a set of legal rights and obligations comes into play; this relationship is the defining core of citizenship.

In Australia, for instance, a government inquiry illustrated this idea in the following way.

> Citizenship is the legal bond between an individual and a state which establishes that the individual legally is a member of a state. Citizenship is conferred on an individual by a state ... The status brings with it rights which can be enjoyed and obligations which need to be fulfilled ... Citizenship is the mechanism by which states differentiate between those who acquire rights as a citizen and those who are treated as aliens. (Joint Standing Committee on Migration, 1994, pp. 11–13)

The history of citizenship education has been equally national in character. Educational programmes based on this concept of citizenship tend to emphasise the history of the state and its institutions, especially parliament. Such programmes may laud the state as a source of protection of the rights of citizens, and promote the moral duty of citizens in return to be loyal to the state and its institutions. This often leads to an uncritical glorification of the state in which its history is presented as a continuous story of progress in the name of democracy and the people. It can also lead to the boredom of a descriptive history of abstract institutions based on a deficit model of student knowledge (Osler and Starkey, 2003)—an approach which has given civics and citizenship education such a bad name in the past.

This approach to citizenship is flawed, for it is an inadequate basis for the kinds of connections among people which are implied by the democratic ideal. If this approach is to be anything more than uncritical indoctrination into a particular national tradition, the proponents of national identity as the base for citizenship must find a moral basis for selecting the traditions to be promoted as the collective national memory. Without this, there can be no way of identifying the *democratic* rights and obligations, which need to be fulfilled.

However, the advocates of this exclusive national concept of democratic citizenship face a dilemma. The dilemma is that any genuine search for national traditions

J. Campbell et al. (eds.), Towards a Global Community, 199–207.
© 2006 *Springer. Printed in the Netherlands.*

which will promote the welfare of all their people can be satisfied only by universal humanitarian and democratic principles; but these must then undermine any attempt to promote the welfare of the nation's members over the welfare of those outside it. In other words, the principles of democracy cannot be argued only for a select group. National identity may be an important basis for explaining the attempts by a certain collectivity to promote human welfare (if that has been its aim), but in a time of increasing globalisation, the moral high ground will more and more be the territory of the internationalists.

This becomes an important criterion by which to test the theories and practices of education for citizenship. Promoted as they are by nation states, and historically grounded in such a strong tradition of grand narratives of progress through the story of the nation (Gilbert, 1992; Lyotard, 1984), traditional programmes in education for citizenship will surely find the concept of world citizenship difficult to accept and even more difficult to reconcile with a nationalist agenda.

However, citizenship as an international phenomenon is increasingly recognised. Not only are international agencies and agreements becoming more important, it is also now possible to speak of a global civil society engaging in global citizen action. In issues like international finance, trade, human rights, development, the environment, and landmine eradication, campaigns have been based on citizen alliances which extend beyond national boundaries and interests (Edwards and Gaventa, 2001).

> The broadening of citizen action into the global sphere recognises a new contemporary reality in which power relations at local and global levels are increasingly intertwined and in which 'governance involves more than the state, community involves more than the nation, and citizenship involves more than national entitlements and obligations'. (Gaventa, 2001, p. 275; Scholte, 1999, p. 22)

In short, the notion of education for global citizenship, or what has been called cosmopolitan citizenship (Delanty, 2000; Osler and Starkey, 2003) is a logical consequence of both the democratic ideal and the developing reality of citizens' experiences.

There are signs that students themselves are registering this development. Osler and Starkey (2003, p. 252) report an interview study with students in the United Kingdom in which young people 'demonstrated multiple and dynamic identities, embracing local, national and international perspectives'. Grundy and Jamieson (2003) report a survey of the extent to which young European adults were familiar with the idea of global citizenship. In Spain, over 50% of young people surveyed said that they thought of themselves as a global citizen 'always' or 'often'; almost half the German respondents said the same, although the British respondents were quite low on this measure.

The recognition of a global dimension of citizenship is an increasing trend among researchers and commentators, extending to young people themselves. It is important therefore to ask what education for citizenship in this new context might mean. The survey which was the stimulus for this volume is an important contribution to answering this question. What follows is an analysis of the survey results and its implications for curriculum development. Drawing on a range of research and development in education for citizenship theory and practice, the analysis outlines a form of education for global or cosmopolitan citizenship.

1.   THE WORLD EDUCATION FELLOWSHIP SURVEY

As related elsewhere in this volume, the survey conducted by the World Education Fellowship identified thirteen items, which met benchmarks for 'high desirability', 'high priority' or both. These items are a valuable indication of the range of outcomes to which citizenship education should aspire. The items are as follows:

Item 1: Individuals who have senses of trust, 'connectedness' to others, autonomy and initiative and are able to enter into mutually supportive relationships.

Item 2: Individuals who have commitments to 'universal values' such as un-selfishness, love for others, truth, honesty, integrity, forgiveness, tolerance and the like.

Item 6: Individuals who accept moral responsibility for their decisions and actions.

Item 19: Individuals who are aware that violent conflict, retaliatory attacks and the like, are inappropriate ways of resolving disagreements.

Item 27: Individuals who approach nature with a sense of responsibility to the Earth's resources and habitats.

Item 29: Individuals who have a respectful attitude to the rights of others and are prepared to listen to the viewpoints of others.

Item 30: Individuals who have a special concern for the disadvantaged, the excluded, the marginalised, minorities, children.

Item 31: Individuals who are tolerant of diversity in all its forms (social, cultural, economic, political, ethnic, religious, etc.), subject to basic human rights being honoured.

Item 34: Individuals who are committed to human rights and social justice, including a reasonable standard of living for all people.

Item 35: Individuals who have a commitment to sustainability of Earth, caring and preparing for the quality of life of future generations and are willing to change their lifestyles to protect the environment.

Item 37: Individuals who have an over-whelming preference in social and political interactions for conflict resolution through negotiation rather than conquest, denigration or withdrawal.

Item 53: Individuals who are able to, and do, collaborate with others—listen, talk through issues patiently and flexibly and contribute to plans and actions to bring these to fruition.

Item 55: Individuals who are able to, and do, engage in collaborative democratic exercises to alleviate poverty, counter corruption, ensure equity in distribution of resources, etc.

To construct a curriculum which might attain these goals, it is useful to relate them in some systematic way. Running through the items above are three quite different kinds of educational goals with distinctive implications for curriculum and teaching. To develop a curriculum to implement such a vision, educators need to address each of these threads, their differences and how they relate to each other. It is possible to structure the connections among the identified items in terms of three key foci

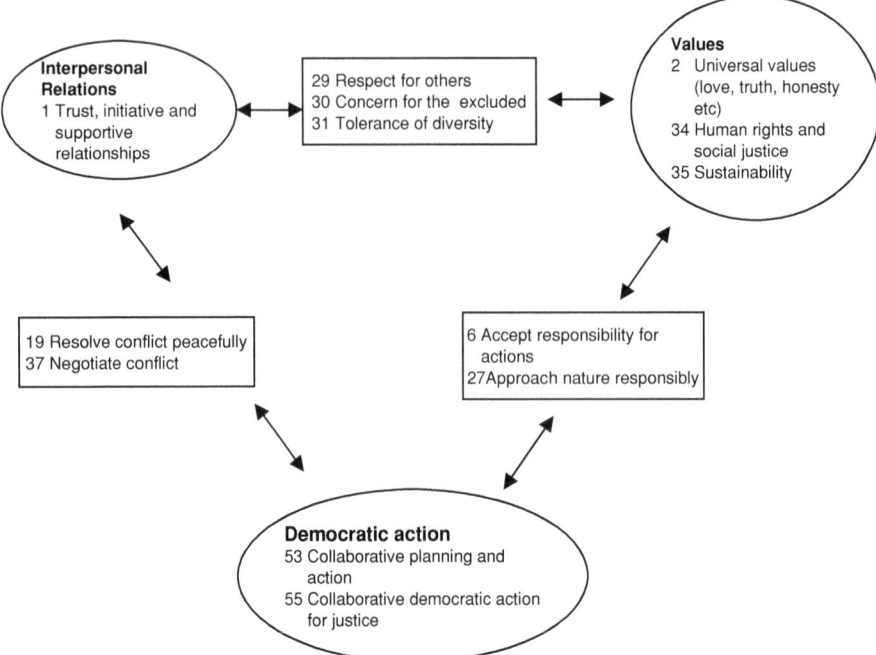

Figure 12.1: A Map of Curriculum Requirements for World Citizenship

and overlaps among them, as illustrated in Figure 12.1. The following discussion considers the three foci of interpersonal relations, values and democratic action, and important issues for curriculum development and teaching which arise from them.

2.   INTERPERSONAL RELATIONS

The first focus relates to interpersonal relations, as described in item 1:

Item 1: Individuals who have senses of trust, 'connectedness' to others, autonomy and initiative and are able to enter into mutually supportive relationships.

Development of a sense of trust and connectedness to others implies recognition of the common humanity shared by all people, and an understanding of how differences arise from this common base. This involves recognising the different levels of culture in which human experience is created (Kalantzis and Cope, 1984). For instance, birth, death, relationships, family are universal features of human culture and are celebrated as central to the experience of all people; the need for shelter, sustenance, security and care are also universal. At a second level are the political and economic institutions which organise these experiences, such as the dominant economic and media organizations or technological and commercial practices which influence the lives of the world's people across a huge range of spatial, cultural and national dimensions. At the most local level, there are the specific cultural practices through which traditions of difference and meaning are expressed, and in which the dynamics of cultural change and exchange are played out. Understanding this system of similarity and difference will be an important part of a global citizenship education, going well beyond the conventional focus on the nation as the key to the experience of citizenship.

Related to this item is the important process of empathy. Empathy is part creative act (in being able to imagine the experience of another and their possible reaction), part cognitive skill (in being able to critically assess the relation between a person's experience, its context and their likely perspective on that experience) and part attitude or predisposition (the willingness to put aside stereotypes and culturally based assumptions to genuinely entertain the possibilities of the other's point of view). It is a key part of intercultural understanding and a sense of connectedness. There is an important literature on empathy (Verducci, 2000), and its relationship with a commitment to supporting others (Ruiz and Vallejos, 1999). While empathy is most directly developed through direct relationships with others, strategies based on media and virtual interactions will also be important in programmes for global citizenship.

However, this item does not restrict itself to the conceptual understanding of culture, or the cognitive and affective aspects of empathy. It links these as necessary parts of the ability to act autonomously, take initiative and enter into supportive relationships with others. In curriculum and teaching terms, this implies the experience of cooperative group work, leadership skills, intercultural communication, and other social skills. A number of programmes have proposed ways to address these skills. The classic programme developed by Newmann, Bertocchi and Landsness (1977) illustrates what is involved here, emphasising interpersonal dynamics as a part of communication skills and a sense of efficacy related to civic participation.

As Figure 12.1 illustrates, the focus on relations with others is connected in important ways with the other key foci of values and democratic action. Relating to others with respect (Item 29) and tolerating diversity (Item 31) are both abilities which need to be learned and practised, as well as values to which students need to be committed. Similarly, concern for the disadvantaged and excluded implies valuing the rights of the weak and dispossessed, but also relating to others in ways which are welcoming and inclusive.

Interpersonal relations also links with democratic action, especially in resolving conflict and negotiating agreement in ways which are peaceful and which enact the democratic rights of all participants.

3. VALUES

In addition to interpersonal relations, a second focus on values can be identified in the survey results. A commitment to certain values is an essential element of a number of the items, namely

Item 2: Individuals who have commitments to 'universal values' such as unselfishness, love for others, truth, honesty, integrity, forgiveness, tolerance and the like.

Item 34: Individuals who are committed to human rights and social justice, including a reasonable standard of living for all people.

Item 35: Individuals who have a commitment to sustainability of Earth, caring and preparing for the quality of life of future generations and are willing to change their lifestyles to protect the environment.

Values exist in at least three ways. They are (a) concepts which need to be understood, (b) preferences or commitments to be expressed and prized and (c) principles or tenets to be followed in behaviour and action.

For instance, social justice values are based on a belief that all people share a common humanity and therefore have a right to equality of opportunity and a fair allocation of community resources. Social justice also implies that people must not be discriminated against, nor their welfare and wellbeing constrained or preju- diced by their background or group membership. These values apply to how people are treated, how resources are allocated and to the need to promote fairness by eliminating discrimination on the grounds of 'race', gender, class, ethnicity, ability, etc.

This will involve understanding, reflecting on and applying such value concepts as equity and equality, anti-sexism, anti-racism, human rights and respect for diversity. Understanding these principles and their associated terms is an important objective for teaching, and this is best done by having students use the terms in discussing issues.

Once the meanings of democracy are understood, teaching and learning focus on how the concept can and should be applied to important issues in society and the students' experiences. Here the key question is 'What should be done'? It is important to note that this involves going beyond the formation of individual personal opinion which is the focus and end point of so much classroom discussion. At least as important, however, and in practice the ultimate issue, is the question of collective decision making. In other words, the question is not merely 'What do I believe?' but rather 'What should we do?' Seen in this way, values education becomes one of decision making in social context, clearly the most authentic approach.

In reflecting on social justice values in topics for study, students explore such questions as
- What are people's needs in this situation and to what extent are they being met?
- Are some people disadvantaged in this situation?
- What needs to be done to promote the welfare of all in this situation?
- How can we promote social justice in our own situations and globally?

Similarly, in reflecting on values of democracy in any issue or event, students would explore such questions as
- What are the democratic rights of people relevant to this situation?
- How might they be understood from a range of perspectives?
- How are people's rights supported or limited by the traditions, rules, institutions and actions in the situation?
- What needs to be done to maximise democratic rights in situations like this, and what responsibilities are implied?
- How can we promote these rights and responsibilities in our own situations and globally?

The last question in each set illustrates that understanding the ideas associated with social justice and democratic process needs to be related to experience and ac- tion in everyday life. Values of social justice lead, for instance, to treating others fairly and respectfully, promoting fairness to others in various situations and institutions, practising anti-sexist and anti-racist strategies and valuing diversity. Democratic val- ues lead to community involvement, active citizenship, willingness to negotiate with and respect the rights of others and commitment to free, open and inclusive ways of making decisions. These can be illustrated and modelled in the way students relate to each other, how classrooms and schools operate, as well at the broader institutional level beyond the school, and there is a considerable literature on how this might be done (Gilbert and Hoepper, 2001; Halstead and Taylor, 2000). In the context of global citizenship, community organizations focusing on global issues, such as Amnesty International or Oxfam, are valuable contexts for learning ways to promote these values. Important developments are also taking place in the various internet communities engaged in similar work, including those focused on world youth, such as the TakingITGlobal site (TakingITGlobal.org).

4.   DEMOCRATIC ACTION

As discussed above, the culmination of values education is applying value decisions to experience and action, as stated in items 53 and 55:

Item 53: Individuals who are able to, and do, collaborate with others -listen, talk through issues patiently and flexibly, and contribute to plans and actions to bring these to fruition.

Item 55: Individuals who are able to, and do, engage in collaborative democratic exercises to alleviate poverty, counter corruption, ensure equity in distribution of resources, etc.

Newmann, Bertolucci and Landsness (1977) outline community service and citizen action projects as important steps to promote democratic participation and action, and strategies for developing democratic action are now well established in education for citizenship. For instance, the Council of Europe Education for Democratic Citizenship project notes that

> Whether and how the concepts and human/democratic values will be used depends to a great extent on the development of certain skills, such as:
> A) Basic skills
> Skills of critical and argumentative thinking
> Creative and productive skills
> Problem-solving skills
> Assessment and evaluation skills
> Knowledge application/procedural skills
> Moral reasoning skills
> B) Specific skills involved in social conduct
> Participative skills
> Multiple communication skills
> Co-operative or teamwork skills
> Debating, negotiating and compromising skills
> Intercultural skills
> Conflict-prevention and conflict-resolution skills
> Mediation and facilitation skills
> Assertiveness skills
> Democratic leadership skills
> Lobbying skills
> (Duerr, Spajic-Vrka and Martins, 2000)

As Figure 12.1 shows, the link with values involves, first, accepting oneself as a responsible agent (Items 6 and 27), and then collaborating with others to promote democratic action in local to global spheres. This requires a process of reflecting on one's own behaviour and how priority might be given to the value, linking with others who are committed to the value, and seeking organizations and other forms of assistance to help express the value through action (Lemin, Potts and Welford, 1994).

In the context of global citizenship, democratic action requires new forms of communication and participation. Linking with others will be done on a much larger scale, primarily with information and communication technologies, and through international organizations. As Clark points out, the old peace movement slogan of 'Think globally; act locally' can now be revised to 'Think locally and globally; act locally and globally together' (Clark, 2001, p. 18).

5.   CHALLENGES FOR EDUCATION FOR GLOBAL CITIZENSHIP

Reforming learning in the 21st Century will involve visions of how people will live their lives, of the kinds of communities they will inhabit, and the kinds of relationships they will have with each other at local, national and global scales. The changing global context raises a range of crucial issues which can only be addressed within a global curriculum framework (Gilbert, 1997).

The growth of the transnational company and the disaggregation of national economic power has put in question corporate arrangements between the state and the national private sector, and along with it the power and authority of national governments themselves. Many young people are directly linked to this global system through their consumption patterns, a key dimension of life whereby many young people find pleasure, identity and forms of expression as well as utility. Consumption becomes a link with the global economy, and a means of showing how economic processes affect people's daily lives. In the global context, it raises important issues of social justice and sustainability.

An important aspect of this is the international culture industries. The information revolution is among the most pervasive forms of social change experienced by the present generation. In the developed economies, the growth of the culture industries is a key aspect of contemporary social change, and no country or culture is free of this influence. In particular, the culture industries are an important part of the experiences of young people, and therefore a potential site for education for global citizenship.

Equally important are issues of sustainability. Environmental education has in recent times offered valuable models of what citizenship education might be. Addressing important current concerns, environmental educators have been able to combine a focus on knowledge, experience and commitment to action in ways which parallel the approaches discussed here. Further, environmental concern leads to a view of nature as global or holistic, a perception promoted by the media which have generated an imagined community of all societies inhabiting one earth.

Further evidence of globalisation is increased migration, and other movements of people as refugees, migrant workers and the representatives of international government and corporations. The democratic rights of such minority groups and individuals are important issues for global citizenship. The massive increase in the refugee populations of the world is the most spectacular and lamentable indication of this. There are clear signs of an increasing tension between identity based on territorial exclusion and that produced by the experience of globalisation. Education for citizenship will need to acknowledge this tension, by connecting citizenship to the reality of the global village, rather than seeing it only as something to be feared by the nation state.

The issues listed here are among the most pressing issues for national and international policy, and are sure to be long-term challenges to the world community. They emphasise the need for a global perspective on development, the environment and human rights and welfare. If education for citizenship is to prepare young people to operate effectively in this changing context, the ideals of global citizenship must be at its centre.

6.   REFERENCES

Clark, J. 2001. Ethical globalisation: the dilemmas and challenges of internationalising civil society. In: Edwards, M. and Gaventa, J. (Eds.) *Global Citizen Action*. Boulder, CO: Lynne Rienner Publishers.

Delanty, G. 2000. *Citizenship in a Global Age*. Buckingham: Open University Press.

Duerr, K. Spajic-Vrka, V. and Martins, I. 2000. *Strategies for Learning Democratic Citizenship*. Strasbourg: Council of Europe. http://www.coe.int/T/e/Cultural_Co-operation/Education/E.D.C/ Documents_and publications/ (Accessed 21/8/2003).

Edwards, M. and Gaventa, J. (Eds) 2001. *Global Citizen Action*. Boulder, CO: Lynne Rienner Publishers.

Gaventa, J. 2001. Global citizen action: lessons and challenges. In: Edwards, M. and Gaventa, J. (Eds) *Global Citizen Action*. Boulder, CO: Lynne Rienner Publishers.

Gilbert, R. 1992. Citizenship, education and postmodernity. *British Journal of Sociology of Education* 13(1), 51–68.

Gilbert, R. 1997. Issues for citizenship in a postmodern world. In: Kennedy, K. (Ed.) *Citizenship Education and the Modern State*. London: Falmer, pp. 65–82.

Gilbert, R. and Hoepper, B. 2001. The place of values. In: Gilbert, R. (Ed.) *Studying Society and Environment: A guide for teachers*. Katoomba, NSW: Social Science Press.

Grundy, S. and Jamieson, L. 2003. *Are We All Europeans Now? Local, National and Supranational Identities of Young Adults*. Paper presentation at the British Sociological Association Annual Conference, York. http://www.ed.ac.uk/sociol/youth/Presentations.html (Accessed 4/8/2003).

Halstead, J. and Taylor, M. 2000. Learning and teaching about values: A review of recent research. *Cambridge Journal of Education* 30(2), 169–202.

Joint Standing Committee on Migration. 1994. *Australians All: Enhancing Australian Citizenship*. Canberra: Australian Government Publishing Service.

Kalantzis, M. and Cope, B. 1984. *Multicultural Education and the Meaning of 'Culture'*. Stanmore: Social Literacy Project, pp. 31–42.

Lemin, M., Potts, H. and Welsford, P. (Eds.). 1994. *Values Strategies for Classroom Teachers*. Melbourne: Australian Council for Educational Research.

Lyotard, J.-F. 1984. *The Postmodern Condition: A Report on Knowledge*. Manchester: Manchester University Press.

Newmann, F., Bertocci, T. and Landsness, R. 1977. *Skills in Citizen Action: An English-Social Studies Program for Secondary Schools*. Madison, WI: Citizen Participation Curriculum Project.

Osler, A. and Starkey, H. 2003. Learning for cosmopolitan citizenship: theoretical debates and young people's experiences. *Educational Review* 55(3), 243–254.

Scholte, J. 1999. *Global Civil Society: Changing the World?* Centre for Study of Globalisation and Regionalisation Working Paper No. 31/99. Warwick, UK: University of Warwick.

Ruiz, P. and Vallejos, R. 1999. The role of compassion in moral education. *Journal of Moral Education* 28(1), 5–17.

Verducci, S. 2000. A conceptual history of empathy and a question it raises for moral education, *Educational Theory* 50(1), 63–80.

Chapter 13

EDUCATING FOR CITIZENSHIP IN A GLOBAL COMMUNITY: WORLD KIDS, WORLD CITIZENS AND GLOBAL EDUCATION

Joseph Lo Bianco

(Dedicated to Jack Campbell, a great inspirer)

1. NEW TIMES AND WORLD KIDS

Over the past few decades broad and deep changes in society have made themselves felt in a succession of curriculum reform movements. Changes in the fundamental technologies of society, in gender relations, in the ethnic, national, linguistic and religious composition of populations sharing the same geo-political space, changes in personal and social values, in mobility across space, in rapidity of communication across great distances, and, not least, in the nature and patterns of work, have found their way into claims that schooling should 'reflect' new realities.

In critical and cultural studies the term New Times (Morely and Chen, 1996, citing Stuart Hall) is invoked to describe these phenomena, characterised by complex and often contradictory trends and patterns. Globalisation is a key word guiding these theorisations of New Times, but globalisation is far from unidirectional, stable or even consistent. As a result, New Times give forth multiple and complex literacies (Cope and Kalantzis, 2000; Street, 1995), multiple and complex citizenship (Janoski, 1998; Kymlicka, 1995; Schuck, 1998), multiple and complex notions of constitutional arrangements for society (Tully, 1997), new consumerist articulations of childhood universality, and even 'World Kids' (Luke, 1990; Luke and Luke, 1999) alongside World Music, World Cuisine, World Movies and World Clothes.

Globalisation also has its own history (Hopkins, 2002) and the present patterns are the result of longer travels of forms of identity away from their sources of origin to attract adherents in distant places. Today we see that old forms of human community and old forms of human rivalry are joined to entirely new forms of community and new forms of antagonism. Some modern fundamentalisms look not at all like modernity but throwbacks to primordial divisions of humanity into rival groupings incapable of dialogue. Other kinds of modern identification look very new and are unimaginable before 'the network society' (Castells, 1996), or the hi-tech, bohemian, culturally hybrid 'urban space' (Florida, 2002). These ties between the global and the local, linked by 'networks', essentially situate a specific site in relation to distant sites, distant in time and space, and thereby connect local to extra-local identities through 'flows' of visual images, people, education, economies, ideas, behaviours and knowledge (Appadurai, 1990), at a time of vast population mobility (Castles and

J. Campbell et al. (eds.), Towards a Global Community, 209–226.

Miller, 1998). That new kinds of identity are possible at all indicates that community is 'imagined' as much as it is actually lived out in daily interactions (Anderson, 1991).

What essentially we are seeing is the supplementing of the 'old categorisations' of human groupings, (faith, nation and 'race'), with new ones. These new identity formations are often unique personal compositions, drawing on vastly greater semiotic possibilities that global connections make possible. They are often shifting and multiple, and may give prominence to personal style, professional category, gender or sexuality, physical or recreation activity. In addition also are combined with multiple political citizenship. In what is an apparent fragmentation (Hall, Held and McGrew, 1992) of the ways to be human traditionalists worry that the public space, the public identity of larger collectivities, is eroded in the slide of personal attachments and local identities. However, as modern fundamentalisms remind us, the contemporary, post-modern, world recreates the larger collectivities of the past even as it devises original creations. Such contradictions under conditions of globalisation appear to be the most tangible sign of New Times.

These contradictions of the global moment in history invoke localisation, globalisation and regionalisation simultaneously. These are co-occurring phenomena that interact with each other (Bauman, 1998; Giddens, 1999), and this interaction demands new kinds of understanding of human identification processes. Some identities are relational, only evident when salient contrasts come into play. Sharp among the contradictions is the national state. As new states are born in the mould of 19th Century European style national states, based on ethnicity, language and bounded territory, in Europe itself the national state is ceding space and sovereignty to the transnational European Union. The national state, therefore, is both persisting and dissipating (Smith, 1995). Globalisation is both a distinctively economic phenomenon, essentially prominent in the integration of financial markets and trading economies (Henderson, 1999), but also a cultural phenomenon, whose structure and texture identifiable in narratives of local and shifting identity (Appadurai, 1990). New notions of culture, identity and community are required to understand these changes (Anderson, 1991; Tully, 1997).

Children around the world are socialised increasingly by common stocks of knowledge and models of behaviour, principally consumer identities embedded in cultural products, such as films and music inscribed with models of identity and behaviour. These are extraneous to families and traditional kinds of local socialisation. For many this suggests a galloping homogeneity across old divisions of national culture and history, so that children everywhere will wear baseball caps backwards and say 'Yeah Right'! to express scepticism, or 'cool' to positively value the worth of things. Much of this socialisation influence is unmediated by adults.

However, this apparent homogenous trend, when applied locally creates hybrid forms, as the standard influence interacts with local practices. In this way even common shaping of cultural futures contributes to diversity and difference. As we know these homogenising patterns are also resisted, and this resistance can give rise to revival of dormant traditions. The Slow Food movement that commenced in Italy in reaction to the introduction of MacDonald's and other fast food outlets is an excellent case in point. Slow Food is now a huge international network of food and wine producers, restaurateurs and their supporters who assert the value of local produce, tradition and lingering over meals. This kind of resistance both subverts and inflects homogenising patterns, gives life to local values and meanings, and makes more complex the impact of globalisation, by making localisation one of its manifestations. These local instantiations of extra-local cultural influences actually diversify rather than homogenise.

Families accommodate, sometimes resisting, sometimes embracing, this media-delivered, and largely English language mediated, cultural shaping of the young. Also ambiguous is the response of political and economic systems, rejecting while embracing. All the while young people access new knowledge and embrace new patterns of identity and shaping independently of the structures of formal schooling, and institutional authorisation.

Whether they deny it in speech, or embrace it in political and economic structures, all social formations and the leaders of society in some way or other accommodate to the extra-local origin of local influence. The most dramatic instance of this is the contrast between the almost complete integration of the global financial system into an almost seamless interdependence. A daily encountered example of this is the fact that so many Australian people know the Hang Seng Index, or the Nikkei Index. Stock market performance in a small number of networked cities impacts directly on retirement incomes and plans in many parts of the world. Sadly, we need to set against this transnational awareness and interdependence the simultaneous, bitter recovery of ancient grievance across national space and history in the conflicts of religion, antistate struggle, and terror of the first few years of the 21st Century.

Agitation for curriculum reform is influenced by these deep and wide changes, but this paper discusses curriculum reform in a narrower perspective, related only to differences of ethnicity and national culture, what is commonly called international education, multicultural education and cross-cultural education and not the many other kinds of difference that have become prominent in the New Times.

1.1. New Citizenship

A reflection of New Times has been the more complex work that the words *citizenship* and *literacy* are required to do in forging our understanding of the world we live in.

Citizenship used to mean carrying the passport of a given country, voting in its national elections, paying taxes to its administration authorities and being prepared to serve that polity, potentially paying 'the ultimate price'. These duties, and their related responsibilities, assumed a broadly homogenous population makeup, and more dense relations within states than across them. Neither of these assumptions holds today. Countries everywhere are vastly more ethnically, religiously and culturally diverse than ever, and global communications make horizontal connections across countries within interest and professional or family connections as dense and sometimes denser than intra-national ones. As a result, many countries provide dual and multiple citizenship, even in the formal sense, so that paying taxes, voting and residence are dispersed beyond one state for growing numbers of people. The term citizenship is also qualitatively more complex. Citizenship is invoked in discussions of participation, used to mean specifiable stocks of knowledge, skills and capabilities that education systems should produce to enable citizens to contribute in 'substantive', rather than simply formal, ways of governance, public policy and national debate.

The most evolved experiment along these lines is the European Union, which, while it is far from a coherent transnational polity, has made remarkable strides in that direction. Like many Europeans though, mobile and educated populations of many other states expect and demand participatory citizenship practices. In recent years this has been manifested in the legal concession of dual or multiple citizenship (Kymlicka, 1995). Studying this kind of development Janoski's (1998) survey of the meaning of contemporary citizenship, identifies four general types of rights that citizens now claim. These are *legal rights* (e.g. rights to equal treatment, expressive rights such as freedom of speech, right to own property); *political rights* (right to vote, right to hold office, right to form or join a political party); *social rights* ('enabling' rights such as access to health care, 'opportunity rights' such as access to education); and *participation rights* (rights to job security, collective bargaining) (pp. 31ff).

European integration is found most concretely in the mobility entitlements of the EU. It is a right of all citizens of the EU to seek employment, education or recreational and residential opportunities across the Union. In a 1995 policy the European Commission set the objective of all EU citizens being proficient in three European languages to facilitate this citizenship right. The EU often uses the language of extended citizenship in these kinds of declarations, and links curriculum reform to their realisation:

> Proficiency in several Community Languages has become a pre-condition if citizens of the European Union are to benefit from the occupational and personal opportunities open to them in the border-free single market. This language proficiency must be backed up by the ability to adapt to working and living environments charac-terised by different cultures. (European Commission, 1995, p. 67)

In a mirror image of EU citizenship regulations, on April 9, 2002 the Australian Minister for Citizenship and Multicultural Affairs announced the repeal of Section 17 of the Citizenship Act of 1948 (Hardgraves, 2002), which had precluded multiple citizenship. What had been instituted as a device for arresting potential disloyalty was discarded as a consequence of '*the reality of global labour markets*' and interna-tional consistency. This, as Schuck (1998) shows, is a growing pattern; increasingly plural populations means plural citizenships, with a considerable language policy implication, globalising the structure and experience of a 'homeland' and 'diaspora' for most language and ethnic groups.

Like citizenship, whose more complex forms schools are now to inculcate in learners, literacy is a vastly expanded entity, understood in multiple ways from the straightforward ones of reading and writing, to the more complex, socially situated and variable notions of literacy favoured by many academic researchers and literacy educators. Freebody and Luke (1990) set out four 'resources' that sustain effective personal literacy. These resources are an ability to *break the code* of texts; an abil-ity to participate in the *meanings of texts*; an ability to *use texts functionally* and an ability to *analyse texts critically,* by asking questions about the ideologies they carry. Extending this is the notion of multiple literacies, or *multiliteracies* (Cope and Kalantzis, 2000), which combine text forms, computer and digital literacy, with their multimodal combinations of the visual, the textual, audio and other symbolic systems, with communication modality, the insights of 'New Literacy Studies' (Street, 1995), in which out-of-school, or university, literacy events and practices are connected with the uses and values of literacy within educational institutions. Literacy is also metaphorically associated with all other areas of learning so that learners are expected to be socially, culturally, internationally, politically, artistically and in many other ways 'literate'.

2.   CURRICULUM REFORM

Western education systems have been engaged with a continual series of curriculum reform movements since the 1970s. Mostly these seek a greater symmetry between the way society is composed and educational practice and many aim to modify the cultural messages and lessons that are overtly imparted in education.

Almost invariably, socially oriented curriculum reform of this kind does not limit its ambitions to altering what learners know, the cognitive realm, but, ultimately, to bringing about new kinds of human subjectivity, impacting on the emotional, affective, attitudinal realms. Education reform is inevitably ambitious in this way, despite many cautionary writings that schools and schooling reflect society as much as shape it. However, because formal schooling is principally concerned with the realm of cognition, aiming to influence attitudes, values and behaviours that are social in nature requires work in the wider context of mass popular culture, and institutions and media, as major and lasting change can only be achieved if it works in tandem with out-of-schooling social trends. In decades past this was understood as operating with the 'hidden curriculum', that part of educational practice that was unplanned, non-overt, implicit in the practice of education, as distinct from the overt and explicit domain of what is taught and imparted in education.

The massive expansion of learning outside the domain of formal institutions and processes of instruction, especially in employment, and in the non-formal domain of entertainment and recreation, where learning is enveloped in play, game, simulation, 'reality' improvisation mean that the hidden/overt distinction must be discarded as too simplistic. Perhaps the greatest change relevant to our notion of difference here is that which invokes identity beyond just the immediate location of the learner, identity and attachment to places, polities, political and cultural histories and traditions in addition to the specific location.

Curriculum reform movements often arise at different socio-cultural and political junctures, responding often to crises in human social or political relations, and name and are named to reflect their times. For sake of simplicity I will refer to these collectively as efforts to *pluralise the cultural perspectives imparted by formal education*. This pluralisation is itself of various kinds. Some actively political, others more strictly pedagogical; some cognitive, some deal with the realm of feelings, affect, emotion and identity.

What is common to the movements for transforming curriculum that I have grouped together is their intention to pluralise, to extend the enculturation practices, the secondary socialisation functions of education, away from citizenship based on prescriptive nationality towards civic notions of plural citizenship. Traditional notions of citizenship invoke the ethno-linguistic networks of identity and solidarity on which many or most national states are based (Billig, 1995; Connor, 1994), in idealised form if not in actuality. Civic kinds of citizenship (Kymlicka, 1995) seek instead to establish social bonds on the basis of equal participation in public life, without the surrender of differences, or the assumption of common backgrounds and identities.

Essentially the kind of dualism, or multiplicity, of citizenship claims being discussed involves a displacement of identity away from exclusive attachment the local setting, the local state or nation, to others, who may be present in the local setting as an ethnic or linguistic minority, an immigrant population or an indigenous population, but not necessarily. This new spread of attachments is best understood as diasporic in which there are homelands and dispersed populations in a diaspora. Diasporic patterns of distribution of identities are not new, but are massively extended under the conditions of globalisation in which vast population mobility (Castles and Miller, 1998).

This separation between political membership of states, where citizenship is civic and not dependent on ethnicity, and states whose membership is determined by ancestry or blood, or bonds of ethnic, linguistic or religious commonality, is a critical one for curriculum reform movements that want to pluralise the enculturation function of education. Most states respond to the demands for the recognition of cultural histories different from the dominant one either through various levels of repression or assimilation, in which education systems play a critical role, or through token concessions to difference while demanding local loyalty, or, through a third strategy in which local attachment and loyalty is required and all differences are packaged into a set of learnings about tolerance of differences. This is a cultures-general approach in which direct and possibly conflicting loyalties of minorities are suffused under a generic policy of cultural differences contrasted to the dominant loyalty demands of the host society.

This strategy is often politically successful because the other loyalties that minorities might nurture are residual and often not active, superficial and not deep, and transient. In addition these other loyalties are often to traditions of culture, or languages, rather than statehood or nationalism. Finally, these other loyalties are of many kinds: some are to minorities within the national state, others are to proximal states, or to distant others, or to minorities in other states, or ideologies of traditions repressed in other states. A culture-general approach to minority attachments in which educational practice teaches about and around these traditions works effectively in many countries in dispersing loyalties across many groups, in geographically scattered distribution, and in which a hierarchy of loyalty is established so that these identifications are made subordinate to local loyalty and treated as marginal difference.

2.1.   International Education

Education for cultural difference of this kind is not new. Perhaps the first practice of its kind was 'International Education' (Hayden, Thompson, and Walker, 2002).

During the late 19th Century and early 20th Century many intellectuals knew a global age was coming and tried to prepare for it. Although Fox (2001) associates the emergence of the International Baccalaureate with the 'aftermath of World War II and the tragedy of Hiroshima' (p. 65), with the express purpose of 'promoting international understanding and world peace' (p. 65), Thomas (2001) traces international education movements back to the late 19th Century in Scandinavia, other parts of Europe and the United States, locating international education within a broader movement of Education for Peace.

Writers on international education have had to try to elucidate what are the key values that underlie their work, one identifying eight 'value characteristics' (McKenzie, 1998, pp. 245–246), as follows: (1) world mindedness; (2) open mindedness; (3) the promotion of a sense of global interdependence; (4) the promotion, conjointly, of a sense of individual and cultural self-esteem; (5) the promotion of a commitment to world peace and development; (6) a relish for the withering of prejudice; (7) a passion for learning as process and product and, (8) respect for, and tolerance of other cultures and cultural diversity, leading possibly to 'interculturality'.

The narrower identities of nation, state and heritage that require citizens to be willing to 'give up their lives if necessary in the service of their countries' (Thomas, 2001, p. 104), are the alternative to the wider identities that Education for Peace aims to inculcate. As Hopkins shows even that most contemporary of social movements, globalisation, has a history, with precedents in most parts of the world and most walks of life. In many parts of the world we can identify antecedents to these kinds of pluralisation, to cite only two, the multicultural and multilingual orientation of India's only Buddhist Emperor Ashoka, in the 3rd Century BC, the Roman senator Cicero, who, a short time later, was conceiving of loyalties and attachments as extending beyond local ones, to more abstract entities of humanness. The most pervasive universalistic claims, however, are found in religious traditions; which mostly advocate universality though a spiritual humanity, and precede formal attempts in secular education to devise attachments to extra-local identities.

But most education, especially the variety that emerged strongly in the wake of industrialism, imperial expansion of European powers and formal kinds of exclusive rights owes its present character to the national state. The 19th Century in Europe is often called the century of the nation state, giving birth to many new states based on nationality. As a result many saw the national state as the most evolved organisational form, the apex of a development in political structures that was the mirror of biological evolution. But national states by definition elevated certain kinds of religious, ethnic and linguistic practices and characteristics to count as state approved and aimed to assimilate, or obliterate, difference. Education systems were the primary instrument for the inculcation of national attitudes, identification and loyalty; and all aspects of schooling were implicated in this goal, what knowledge was taught, which emotional attachments were encouraged, and what behaviours approved. These domains of feeling, doing, and thinking (Olser and Starkey, 1996) form recurring focuses for curriculum reform movements, teacher education, and professional development, materials production and general advocacy of change to make education systems contribute both sentiment and skill to transnational education.

2.2. Multicultural Education

If curriculum reform for International Education has not been terribly successful it has been less controversial than its domestic counterpart, multicultural education, at least in the United States, where it has become enmeshed within the wider politics of cultural literacy, the celebrated culture wars of the 1980s and 1990s. The exemplary exponent of cultural literacy discourse was E.D. Hirsch whose position was that: '*Linguistic pluralism enormously increases cultural fragmentation, civil antagonism, illiteracy, and economic-technological ineffectualness*' (Hirsch, 1988, p. 91). Bernstein's (1994) work similarly expresses the connection between multiculturalism and language education policy and the wider social compact, treating the idea that there might be Cherokee taught in public schools to incredulous ridicule (p. 244) and seeing it as a kind of '*act of rebellion against white, Anglo-cultural domination*' with a '*multicultural animus against European culture and its derivatives*' (p. 245).

The understandings of multicultural education that these views express contrast dramatically with Nieto's (2000, p. 313) understanding of multicultural education as '. . . a philosophy, a way of looking at the world, not simply a programme or a class or a teacher'. According to Nieto there are seven 'basic characteristics' of this kind of multicultural education: 'anti-racist education, basic education, important for *all* students, pervasive, education for social justice, a process and critical pedagogy' (emphasis in original, p. 305).

The demand for this kind of multicultural education, and the impact that it has on writers like Hirsch and Bernstein who fear national dissolution, results from immigration. As national states began to admit new residents concern shifted towards multiculturally oriented education reform. Concern with broadening of international trade stimulated concern for cross-cultural training in business and had a washback onto education in the form of cultural diversification, learning about different others. In parts of the world where regional organisations have come to be strong cultural pluralisation takes the form of transnational elements in education.

Based in very specific conditions and settings where conflict rages, or has raged, and in the post-conflict setting education takes its place as a site of reconciliation and social renewal.

Often the term becomes an adjective modifying 'literacy' so that we have Asia literacy, social literacy, cultural or arts literacy, multicultural literacy etc. There have been many studies and research efforts systematising these approaches and classifying them in various ways.

Political campaigning for cultural pluralisation others takes the form of advocacy on behalf of historically excluded or silenced others. Some have been more assertive such as antiracist education, or counter racist perspectives in schooling. Some have targeted specific subject areas such as history in settings where there are contested expectations or interpretations of history, others have aimed to counter gender stereotyping and are therefore cross-curricular. Some curriculum movements follow new ways of organising political space, such as the moves for Europe wide perspectives in schooling brought forth by the Council of Europe, or the European Union. Others are weaker kinds of regionalism in an institutional sense, but no less powerful in other ways, such as Asian Studies in Australia. Reconciliation with indigenous peoples in new world settings often involves similar kinds of cultural reconstruction such as Indigenous education studies in the US or Canada or some Latin American countries, or Australia. In some settings political history is also reconciled with modifications to school curricula, like the new kinds of education planning in Sri Lanka, or in South Africa after apartheid.

2.3.   Language Education

Foreign languages have often been invoked as representing a critical, sometimes the sole, part of the curriculum to be devoted to pluralising curricula. Languages themselves have traversed several stages (Lo Bianco, 2002; Risager, 1998). In thinking about the pluralisation of curriculum, from the time when it was assumed that languages were spoken by distant others, in which each language represented a bordered cultural space, such as a national state, with its secure history and literature, art forms and ways of life. This was the *foreign-cultural* approach that essentially assumes a single culture for a single country in a specific territory and isolated from the learners' culture. The aim tended to be to teach admiration for and knowledge of this culture, but it was seen to be an essentially foreign entity. The approach has been losing ground since the 1980s.

Replacing this practice was the *intercultural* approach, based on contrasting the target culture and the learners' culture, noting similarities and disimilarities. In some parts of Europe and in much of North America this appears to be the main approach today. A third alternative has been the *multicultural* approach. This approach is found in societies with many different cultures and languages. It seeks to impart common and shared knowledge within respect for and maintenance of differences. Some forms of multicultural approaches seek hybrid connections between the existing cultures and see culture as a set of practices that members of these societies can add to existing notions of culture. This is the emerging approach in multiethnic societies. Globalisation however has challenged all of these ways to understand culture in language education and today what is coming to be called the *transcultural* approach is adopted. This tends to see cultures as interacting, not tightly bounded by national states, cultures that are 'available' to learners in digital and virtual form, in which learners can access selections and aspects of, rather than the authorised versions depicted by authoritative bodies or texts or individuals.

In this sequence of change we can see distilled what has happened more widely in national culture. All this raises the need for openness to the new ways that a learner can gain information independently of the mediation of schools, teachers and textbooks. Indeed this autonomy of access is independent of almost any adult structures or people at all and often proceeds without any direct guidance. These processes also change the literacy itself, in that the 'consuming' of new information is fused with its production, so that 'reading about' another place, becomes a process of assembling from vast amounts of available information a perspective or take that the learner constructs. This is not so much 'reading about' as 'assembling', or even 'authoring'.

2.4.   Cross-Cultural Training

Unlike multicultural education, foreign language education or international education, cross-cultural training occurs largely outside of mainstream school contexts. It is instructive to consider cross-cultural training in this context because of its rapid growth in recent years and because of its intimate connection with globalization.

Since World War II socio-political and economic trends have combined with civil and human rights movements to elevate the practical importance of cross-cultural awareness and competence. As a result international aid and development; global commerce and transnational governance have embraced similar kinds of curriculum reform practices, mainly short-course cross-cultural training, which are growing rapidly across the world today.

This growth is closely tied to five major global trends. Different traditions and practices of cross-cultural training can be found in North America, North Asia and Western Europe as a result of the differential impact of these trends.

- First, is the expansion of the world role of the United States after the Second World War, especially its prominence in the security architecture of the Pacific Rim region;
- Second, is the impact of new thinking about universal human rights, identifying a class of rights that transcends state sovereignty. The stimulus for much of this came from the creation of the United Nations in 1946, but there was also an influence from the early 1960s Civil Rights Movement in the United States, and especially the 1964 Civil Rights Act, the forerunner of similar legislation in other parts of the world;
- Third, has been the rapid growth of international economic integration in recent decades, and in particular the emergence within this economic globalization of several Confucian based societies in north Asia as great global trading powers;
- Fourth, has been the growth of regional, or geography-based, transnational political alignments, the so-called supra-national blocs, particularly the European Union;
- Fifth, has been the emergence of the transnational corporation.

The main cross-cultural training practices and methods respond to the needs of international business, trade and commerce. The greatest single contributor to cross-cultural training innovations and practice in recent years has been the transnational corporation. Major corporations operating across the globe have invested heavily in cross-cultural, less often in multilingual, training, and the professional literature shows many innovations in thinking about culture and its teaching have come from the corporate management needs of executives in transnational companies.

In the corporation the dominant mode of cross-cultural preparation prefers to describe itself as *training*, rather than *education* or *teaching*, and stresses a practical 'results-oriented' approach. Much of it takes place in and through English and itself grew out of the expanded world role of the United States since 1945. This new role required American society and government agencies to take an interest in the societies where its commercial, strategic and political interests were engaged. Seeking to win hearts and minds was also part of the politics of Cold War tension, which made cultural and linguistic competence a strategic investment.

2.4.1. Training for Volunteers

Contributing to this growth in cross-cultural training were vigorous new organisations created by the US to facilitate its new world role. These often aimed to involve young Americans in volunteering educational, health, medical and social assistance in development contexts across the world. *The Peace Corps*, founded by President John F. Kennedy in 1961, is the best-known example. The need to prepare these volunteers, more than 170,000 in the Peace Corps alone, for their often demanding postings usually meant learning languages rarely taught in mainstream education, sometimes small tribal languages without writing systems. Tackling these languages required a focus on spoken discourse as the main aim of learning. Cultural knowledge was central to this task, culture no longer adequately thought of as literature, aesthetics, and formal history. The result was a need to focus on culture in communication, taught to western-educated English speaking learners whose social backgrounds contained few shared cultural assumptions with their target communities. To meet these acute challenges US agencies drew on the vast American ethnographic tradition and specifically the work of anthropologists such as Edward Hall. Hall's 1959 book entitled *Silent Language* identified ways in which culture and communication infused each other; in later work (1966), he extended this interest into a range of para-linguistic and non-linguistic dimensions of communication, such as the role of physical space (proxemics) on communication effectiveness; while later still (1981) he inaugurated the concept of high context and low context cultures.

Hall's ideas found their way into pre-departure culture training programmes for Peace Corps volunteers, although his treatment of culture and language as inseparable was gradually set aside as a growing number of such programmes were designed without an integral component of language learning.

Among the many innovations that resulted were simulations, the use of drama, role-plays, perception exercises and a myriad of other participation activities to stimulate noticing of the pervasive effects of culture on our lives. The general aim was to assist learners to see ordinary events; but also time, values and history; as culture-shaped. Via immersion in activities, often quite elaborate ones, participants encountered and resolved misunderstanding, conflict and tension. In these ways participants were forced to examine their own behaviours and reactions against common stimuli, looking to identify differences of perception, moral judgment, interpretation, belief about causation and responsibility. Sophisticated methodologies evolved in which learners were led to notice and describe such differences. Among the vast array of practices that emerged some dealt with patterns of belief from the cosmological scale (life, death and law), others with events of history, whether contested or uncontentious; and more mundane cultural practices, such as food, divisions of the day, and many others, were revealed as being culturally shaped. In these courses processes of relativising perceptions and values oscillated between focussing on specific target cultures (e.g. Americans and Filipinos) to focusing on 'cultures in general'.

2.4.2.   Extended to Business

As international trade accelerated during the 1970s, these activities found their way into training programmes for international business. The emergence of the transnational corporation meant that many executives from western and other developed countries would have staff drawn from many parts of the world, and would be negotiating and conducting commerce on a global scale. The content and practices of volunteer training programmes were adapted to the specific needs of business executives. During the 1980s a further change was underway: research and thinking began to extend the notion of culture away from ethnicity or national differences, to include categories and practices of the business enterprise itself. The internal identity affiliations and corporate groupings (finance, planning, customer relations, clients, owners and shareholders, managers and workers) now came to draw on the language and discourse of culture.

In these ways the ideas of 1960s style inter-cultural training found fertile new ground as perception, worldview, attitudes and values were seen to reflect occupational, or professional, categories, in extending past usage away from ethnic and national differences alone. Researchers, course designers and trainers also added new informing disciplines. Alongside the traditional sources of anthropology and pedagogy, psychology and especially the branches of psychology that deal with influence through socialisation ('social' psychology), and functional theories of management, came to have direct influence.

In north Asian business contexts there was a marked influence of US precedents as Japan, and then Taiwan and South Korea, became formidable industrial and technological powerhouses, however, in many cross-cultural activities designed in these countries history and psychology were very prominent sources of ideas and content. By contrast European inter-cultural studies originated from the domestic institutions created to overcome the turmoil of the Second World War. Specifically, various affiliated agencies of UNESCO, as well as the Council of Europe, and eventually the European Union, came to shape cross-cultural training practices. Unlike the North American and North Asian cross-cultural training context however, languages retained a clear presence in such programmes, and in thinking about inter-cultural education the role of languages remains politically sensitive to this day. Nevertheless, it has also been clear from the early 1990s that within the curricula of the major business schools across Europe English-mediated cross-cultural training has gained a strong presence.

The proliferation of courses produced interesting experimentation and professional cross-fertilisation. Few practitioners and theorists adopt pure or pristine methodologies and literally thousands of activities and techniques have been devised and circulate among its practitioners. Despite this apparent eclecticism it is possible to discern among the body of practices used by cross-cultural trainers, professionals and non-professionals alike, some broad 'families of methods', suggested below.

3.   APPROACHED TO TEACHING ABOUT DIFFERENCE

3.1.   Cognitive or Didactic

An early but continuing approach to intercultural training has been to expand the knowledge base of the learner through providing extensive information about a culture participants are studying, or a country to which they are to be posted, or about cultures in general. This approach focuses on reading material about the culture, its history, values, achievements, difficulties, locations, language, religion, worldview etc. Usually the trainer adopts a direct teaching role, sometimes even lecturing trainees, or just providing and discussing facts and information. Cognitive-based approaches remain prominent today because they are easy to prepare and deliver, and remain useful because knowledge is inevitably a component of attitudes and beliefs.

However, there are problems with cognitive-didactic training. First, there is often too much information, and much of it is not always directly relevant to learners.

More importantly cross-cultural education does not just aim for people to *know* about other cultural and ethnic groups, but to develop positive pre-dispositions and emotions towards them, skills in living with differences, competence and confidence with diversity. In more recent years critical analysis has contributed to how culture is understood, problematising the rather homogenous representations of the past. Cognitive approaches also suffer because they are less inclined to allow learners to retain their own perspectives and values and individual moral compass and cannot theorise a way to reconcile a learner perspective from a target culture perspective. In addition, knowledge is a poor predictor of what people feel, and do, and alone cognitivism is inadequate for the goals of contemporary cross-cultural training. Finally, a cognitive approach provides little space for language study.

3.2. Functional-Experiential or Pragmatic

In this approach trainees are set objectives to achieve, practical tasks that they should accomplish in the new culture, and their performance is assessed to see whether they attain the aims set for them. The stress is less on learning new information than on gaining practical skills in how to live and function in a new culture in an effective way, solving daily problems and dealing with ordinary life.

These approaches are valuable because the experiences are often close to reality, and involve all the senses, including critical faculties. This approach can be directly related to learners' needs and to the specific society and setting where the training takes place. The training can be pre-departure and post-arrival, in situ. However there are also some major problems. Training along these lines can be very challenging to prepare and deliver and time for debriefing is essential to prevent negative experiences due to inadequate knowledge from shaping, perhaps permanently, attitudes and beliefs about the target culture. Participants can feel threatened and experience failure, sometimes generating unexpected and negative emotional responses.

3.3. Affective or Person-Centred

This approach focuses on the feelings and attitudes of trainees. Instead of supplying large quantities of material about the new culture, or about cultures in general, or of locating the learner in the new environment and setting them goals to accomplish, affective methods focus on self-growth. Activities are organised to interact with the target culture but these are accompanied by constant perception checking, the monitoring of judgments and feelings about the other culture and its members.

This approach is valuable because of its attention to varying perspectives to common stimuli, and to engaging trainees emotionally. However affective approaches have major limits. Self-understanding is only a preliminary stage in learning about others. Affective learning does not always lead to positive intercultural changes or better understanding of new information. Depending only on personal affective modifications can have the result of making participants resent the constant focus on other ways of doing things and other ways of seeing the world, feeling their own perspectives are being undermined. Some affective techniques are personally confrontational when the aim is to challenge what trainers feel to be deep-rooted, but denied, racism.

Many approaches to cross-cultural training claim to combine cognitive and affective experiences, often by using functional-experiential methods. The aim is that trainees acquire knowledge, develop positive attitudes through self-monitoring, in direct engagement with different practices of culture. The stress on real-world practical experiences with different cultures supplements book learning and direct teaching. In this trainers seek to overcome the disadvantages of excessive focus on knowledge, or excessive focus on feelings and attitudes, or too much dependence on self-discovery via pragmatic engagement with problems.

Occasionally a 'combined approach' espouses the idea that critical perspectives are needed so that the voices of disadvantaged, or marginalized, groups be heard rather than idealised representations of the target culture.

4.   PEDAGOGICAL DILEMMAS

Before the electronic revolution of the 1990s curriculum reform movements often debated the merits of whether to seek to become represented on timetables as a discrete area of learning (as a subject) or to seek to have the new perspectives they advocated dispersed across the whole curriculum. Concentration in a named subject was seen to have the advantage of prominence, or presence, announcing the success of advocacy. Being present across the whole curriculum was seen to have the advantage of being a naturally reinforced part of the entire educational experience of learners.

Becoming a named and timetabled subject may bring the recognition of prominence, but this can be a temporary, or even counterproductive, outcome as far as the knowledge and attitudes of the learners is concerned. Subject ranking and hierarchies work to punish areas of learning and social change movements are often stigmatised in this way. The alternative approach of 'infusing' all curricula with the perspectives and content of the curriculum reform area runs risks too. For a start it is a much harder thing to achieve, and is vulnerable to loss of focus, superficiality of treatment, of being diffused too thinly, and ultimately of being sidelined. Perhaps most problematical is the dimension of the task. If you aim for your curriculum area to be a perspective, or a theme, that characterises all learning, such as ensuring that learning does not exclusively privilege western epistemological frames, or European ways to think and do things, the changes required are great and dispersed. Changes are required to teacher attitudes, to how knowledge is organised and delivered, indeed to the entire culture and organisation of schooling. As a result many curriculum reform advocates support a combination of transverse and direct change, wanting to be present both overtly and subtly. This combined approach wants the advantages of status that being a subject will give, and the naturalisation of the message the curriculum reform movement is after.

There is an even deeper dilemma than how curriculum reform should be represented on timetables and in curricula. This dilemma is about the pedagogy of change, or how to teach for change. Few teachers, teacher educators or researchers, believe that purely cognitive approaches are adequate to bring about the deep change that these pluralisations of curricula seek. Cross-cultural education and training, for example, often aims to combine cognitive approaches with affective methodologies, with challenges to the emotions and feelings of learners towards other cultures and national traditions.

Radical curriculum reform movements around various kinds of 'social literacy' aim to change history teaching, teaching about society and citizenship, and even literacy and English education. Believing that education must play a role in lessening the reproduction of social class, material inequality and privilege these curriculum reform movements are often influenced by post-colonial theory and animated by new sociologies of education that link the material-economic world to the symbolic or ideological dimensions of society.

Foreign language teaching sometimes takes a similarly ambitious approach, seeing culture as inextricably part of all language teaching, an 'invisible' dimension of becoming a bilingual, and needing to be addressed explicitly and overtly (Lo Bianco and Crozet, 2003), and language teaching as a critical part of multicultural, but unequal, societies under conditions of globalisation (Block and Cameron, 2002).

Globalisation has produced massive revival of interest not only in language education, but also in new kinds of language education that made culture learning a central goal. An example is the extensive series from the publisher Multilingual Matters, *Languages for Intercultural Communication and Education*, an activity reflected by other large publishing houses, and reflecting the huge energy that is being devoted all across the world by teachers and researchers to raise issues of intercultural awareness and competence in and through second language teaching. These efforts overwhelmingly demonstrate that bilingualism, when it accompanies taught cross-cultural skill that is deliberately taught, can be effective in producing lasting kinds of intercultural capability and insight. Essentially these efforts aim for deep change in how 'otherness' is depicted but also how opportunity is distributed and how societies operate given that multiethnicity is an economic dimension of many societies as population mobility accompanies economic globalisation.

In this regard the Common European Framework of Reference for Languages (COE, 2001) explicitly associates the project of European integration, population mobility, improved working relations etc, to enhanced second language education within a culturally explicit programme with related changes to history and citizenship education.

5.   EMPATHY AMD CULTURE

The review of approaches to teaching about difference in the context of globalisation continually refer back to culture, and to subtle aims of education and training practice that aim to change the subjectivity of learners, not just what they know. Andrew Lohrey (1998) argues that underlying any hope of achieving these goals is to bring about change to the emotional and psychological state of empathy. For Lohrey empathy both the outcome of such teaching, and a method used to teach any syllabus that aims to bring about such change.

For Lohrey there are two steps that are essential in teaching empathy. The first is to identify and recognise distinctions and the second is to integrate these distinctions into a larger whole. In sequence this involves recognizing individual differences and then integrating these into larger groupings, (school or class groups, families etc); then recognizing these differences and in turn integrating them into broader patterns of culture and community. Finally, these differences are recognized and integrated into even broader patterns of economy and society, which in turn are seen to be distinct from other economy-society patterns but are integrated at a higher level into wider and deeper common patterns of humanity.

To teach empathy via these two steps of identifying distinctions but then merging them into larger wholes Lohrey argues that a conscious effort is needed to extend the boundaries held by learners. Boundaries are usually of two kinds: *cognitive* boundaries (what we know about ourselves and others), and *identity* boundaries (what we attach ourselves to and how we feel about such attachments). In Lohrey's view empathy breaks down in societies when there is too much emphasis on unity (which leads to pressure for assimilation); or when there is too much emphasis on differences (which leads to pressures for separation); or when there are rapid or severe swings between too much unity and too much difference (Lohrey, 1998, pp. 8–9).

Allied to this view of empathy and its role in global education ideals is a required new sense of what constitutes culture. Contemporary understandings of culture stress that cultures are not uniform, monolithic and unchanging entities. Cultures comprise internal stresses and conflicts, and are asymmetrical, meaning that not all members of any particular culture share all its attributes. Cultures change, and through internal dissent, political disputation, inequality and challenge, but also external influences such as economic globalisation, migration, the Internet, tourism and other contemporary influences cultures change and evolve, and form hybrid mixtures, characterised by domination and resistance as well as participation and community.

Constitutional scholar James Tully (1997) has declared the present phase in world history the 'Age of Diversity', a time when despite homogenising pressures within globalisation diversity and difference are flourishing and challenging many societies to take account of differences of world view and culture as in no previous period. From education systems to constitutional arrangements societies everywhere are dealing with difference, however well or badly. This intensity of focus on difference requires us to understand that cultures are not '*separate, bounded and internally uniform*' but '*overlapping, interactive and internally negotiated*' (Tully, 1997, p. 10). It follows that identities are multiple and shifting and that education for empathy, and empathy in education, are requirements for the globalised World Kid and for world citizens. The profoundly unequal arrangements of the economic order do not displace the agitation for the recognition of difference, but demand instead that radical agendas for education that aim to lessen the material disparities of the economic order recognize that differences are persisting and even growing, even under global conditions.

6.   CONCLUSION

The World Education Forum initiative of Jack Campbell takes its place within a noble history of innovation and theorization for education that aims, explicitly and with moral grounding, for invoking cognitive as well as affective changes to human identity. It is unique however, in its processes. Whereas dialogue and empathy are central features of the outcome of all claims for making curricula, in the case of WEF, it was also a central feature of the process of its formulation, and, indeed, of the individual who inspired it.

7. REFERENCES

Anderson, B. 1991. *Imagined Communities: Reflections on the Origin and Spread of Nationalism.* London: Verso.

Appadurai, A. 1990. Disjuncture and difference in the global economy. In: Featherstone, M. (Ed.) *Global Culture: Nationalism, Globalization and Modernity.* London: Sage, pp. 295–311.

Bauman, Z. 1998. *Globalization: The Human Consequences.* New York: Columbia University Press.

Bernstein, R. 1994. *Dictatorship of Virtue: Multiculturalism and the Battle for America's Future.* New York: Knopf.

Billig, M.1995. *Banal Nationalism.* London: Sage.

Block, D. and Cameron, D. 2002. *Globalization and Language Teaching.* London and New York: Routledge.

Castells, M. 1996. *The Rise of the Network Society.* Cambridge, MA: Blackwell:.

Castles, S. and Miller, M.J. 1998. *The Age of Migration: International Population Movements in the Modern World.* London: Macmillan Press.

COE. 2001. *Common European Framework of Reference for Languages: Learning, Teaching, Assessment.* Strasbourg: Modern Languages Division, Council of Europe and Cambridge, UK: Cambridge University Press.

Connor, W. 1994. *Ethno Nationalism: The Quest for Understanding.* Princeton: Princeton University Press.

Cope, B. and Kalantzis, M. 2000. *Multiliteracies: Literacy Learning and the Design of Social Futures.* London: Routledge.

European Commission. 1995. *White Paper on Education and Training—Teaching and Learning—Towards the Learning Society.* Brussels: European Union. COM (95), 590.

Florida, R. 2002. *The Rise of the Creative Class: And How Its Transforming Work, Leisure Community and Everyday Life.* New York: Basic Books.

Fox, E. 2001. The emergence of the international baccalaureate as an impetus for curriculum reform. In: Hayden, M. and Thompson, J. (Eds.) *International Education, Principles and Practice.* London: Kogan Page, pp. 65–77.

Freebody, P. and Luke, A. 1990. Literacy programmes: debates and demands in cultural context. *Prospect* 5, 7–16.

Giddens, A. 1999. *Runaway World.* London: Profile.

Hall, E.T. 1959. *Silent Language.* New York: Doubleday.

Hall, E.T. 1966. *The Hidden Dimension.* New York: Doubleday.

Hall, E.T. 1981. *Beyond Culture.* New York: Doubleday.

Hall, S., Held, D. and McGrew, T. (Eds.). 1992. *Modernity and Its Futures.* Milton Keynes, UK: Polity Press and Open University.

Hardgraves, G. 2002. Minister for Citizenship and Multicultural Affairs, Media Release, Changes to Citizenship Laws, April 9, (H36/2002), Parliament House, Canberra.

Henderson, H. 1999. *Beyond Globalization. Shaping a Sustainable Global Economy.* West Hartford, CT: Kumarian Press.

Hirsch, E.D. 1988. *Cultural Literacy: What Every American Needs to Know.* New York: Vintage Books.

Hopkins, A.G. 2002. *Globalization in World History.* London: Pimlico.

Janoski, T. 1998. *Citizenship and Civil Society.* Cambridge: Cambridge University Press.

Kymlicka, W. 1995. *Multicultural Citizenship.* Oxford: Oxford University Press.

Luke, C. 1990. *Constructing the Child Viewer: A History of American Discourse of Television and Children, 1950–1980.* Praeger: New York.

Luke, C. and Luke, A. 1999. Theorizing interracial families and hybrid identities: an Australian perspective. *Educational Theory* 49(2), 223–249.

Lo Bianco, J. 2002. *Multicultural Education and English: A Training Manual.* Colombo, Sri Lanka: The British Council and National Institute of Education.

Lo Bianco, J. and Crozet, C. 2003. *Teaching Invisible Culture: Classroom Practice and Theory.* Melbourne: Language Australia Publications.

Lohrey, A. 1998. *How to Teach Empathy.* Hobart: University of Tasmania.

McKenzie, M. 1998. Going, going, gone. . . global!. In: Hayden, M., Thompson, J. and Walker, G. *International Education in Practice, Dimensions for National and International Schools.* London: Kogan Page, pp. 242–253.

Morely, D. and Chen, K.H. 1996. *Stuart Hall: Dialogues in Cultural Studies.* Routledge: London.

Nieto, S. 2000. *Affirming Diversity. The Sociopolitical Context of Multicultural Education.* New York: Longman.

Olser, A. and Starkey, H. 1996. *Teacher Education and Human Rights*. London: Fulton.

Risager, K. 1998. Language teaching and the process of European integration. In: Byram, M. and Fleming, M. *Language Learning in Intercultural Perspective-Approaches Through Drama and Ethnography*. Cambridge: University Press, pp. 242–254.

Schuck, P. 1998. Plural citizenships. In: Pickus, N. (Ed.) *Immigration and Citizenship in the Twenty-First Century*. Lanham, MD: Rowman & Littlefield, pp. 149–191.

Smith, A.D. 1995. *Nations and Nationalism in a Global Era*. London and New York: Polity Press.

Street, B. 1995. *Social Literacies*. London: Longman.

Thomas, P. 2001. Education for peace: The cornerstone of international education. In: Hayden, M. and Thompson, J. (Eds.) *International Education, Principles and Practice*. London: Kogan Page, pp. 103–119.

Tully, J. 1997. *Strange Multiplicity, Constitutionalism in an Age of Diversity*. Cambridge: Cambridge University Press.

NOTES ON CONTRIBUTORS

Jack Campbell was Emeritus Professor of the University of Queensland, a graduate of the Universities of New Zealand (B.A., M.A. Hons., Senior Scholar) and London (Ph.D.), and has held appointments at the Universities of Otago, Sydney, Kansas, Illinois, Uppsala and Queensland and has chaired 12 state, national and international inquiries on education. He has served as President of the Queensland WEF Section, President of the Australian WEF Council (twice) and Vice-President of WEF International, is an ANZAAS Mackie Medallist, and in 1994 was appointed an Officer of the Order of Australia.

Colin Power is graduate of the University of Queensland (B.Sc., B.Ed., Ph.D.) where he began his academic career, and he is currently an Adjunct Professor of Education. From 1989 to 2000, he served as UNESCO Deputy Director-General and Assistant Director-General for Education, and such, he was responsible for all of its education programmes and initiatives from 1989 to 2000. Previously, he Professor of Education at Flinders University of South Australia. Colin Power is author or co-author of 13 books and over 250 published works on education, and continues to play an active role in many professional associations, including WEF. Currently, he chairs the Commonwealth Consortium for Education and the Board of the Institute of Educational Research, Policy and Evaluation, and serves as editor-in-chief of *Educational Research for Policy and Practice*. In 2002, he was awarded an Order of Australia, Alumus of the Year of the University of Queensland, and an Honorary D.Lit. from the University of Sydney.

Nick Baikaloff is a graduate of the University of Queensland (B.Ed. St., M.Ed. Admin.), specializing in Curriculum. After working on course design in the TAFE Sector of Education, he was appointed to the Faculty of Education, Griffith University where he investigated, and taught, 'contemporary issues' in education. He has been on WEF Councils at State and National levels for over two decades, including several terms as President of Queensland Section. He has a particular interest in enhancing national and international links among WEF members.

Richard Bawden is a graduate of Universities of London (B.Ag.Sc. Hons.) and Queensland (Ph.D.). Recently, he has been appointed as distinguished Professor, College of Agriculture and Natural Resources, Michigan State University. Prior to this, he was Dean of the Faculty of Agriculture and, latterly, Director of the Centre for Systemic Development at the University of Western Sydney. In January 2000, he was appointed a Member of the Order of Australia for services to agricultural education and rural development.

Abraham Blum was born 1928 in Switzerland and lives since 1950 in Israel. He is Professor Emeritus at the Hebrew University of Jerusalem. After many years as

J. Campbell et al. (eds), Towards a Global Community, 227–230.
© 2006 *Springer. Printed in the Netherlands.*

secondary school teacher and teacher trainer, he became one of the founding members of the Israel Curriculum Centre, where he was responsible for curricular development in Agriculture and Environmental Studies. He directed the Yahas environmental education curriculum project and was involved in UNESCO's efforts to promote Integrated Science Teaching.

Rob Gilbert is a Professor of Education at James Cook University of North Queensland with primary responsibility for secondary school social science curriculum studies. His research interests are in social science curriculum; education and social justice, gender and citizenship; youth culture and education; qualitative research methods and doctoral research training. He has published widely in these fields, including an edited collection entitled *Studying Society and Environment: A guide for teachers* (Social Science Press, 2001), and, with Pam Gilbert, a book on boys and schooling entitled *Masculinity Goes to School* (Allen and Unwin, 1998).

Margaret Henry B.A., Dip.Ed., M.Ed. St., Ph.D., OAM, WEF Clarice McNamara Award. After training as a teacher and researcher, she began her educational career in programmes encouraging urban indigenous families to play a more enjoyable, satisfying role in their children's learning. She taught at primary level, took part in an evaluation of Australian programmes for disabled children, and turned to the growing field of child care, setting up short courses to increase the confidence and competence of child care personnel, at a time when these did not exist in Australia. For the last 18 years of her professional life, she lectured on early development and family-professional relationships in the School of Early Childhood at Queensland University of Technology.

Valerie S. Jakar, Ph.D., grew up in England, where she was involved in social action from an early age. She qualified as a music teacher and a remedial studies specialist for schools, and after gaining further professional advancement in E.S.L., E.F.L., counselling and Reading Development, she addressed her energies to teaching EFL in Israel. Doctoral studies in the USA (University of Pennsylvania) provided her with ethnographic research skills which enabled her to investigate second language acquisition in various situations. Dr. Jakar's abiding interest in sociolinguistics is put into practice professionally as lecturer and teacher counsellor/adviser in Israel, where she has lived for the past 20 years. She strives to promote human rights awareness, in her teaching and in all other domains of her life.

Judy Lawley, B.Soc. Science, Diploma in Guidance and Counselling, Dip. Teaching. As a Rotary International Paul Harris Peace Studies scholar, she completed an M.Sc. in comparative social policy and research at Oxford University in 1998, and as recipient of a Churchill Fellowship, she visited Canada and the USA. Her background is in social work, social research, school counselling and she was the first New Zealand project manager on local government/national government initiatives to connect social services for better outcomes. As well, as project manager for 'Living Values', she experienced first-hand the very wide range of ways schools are tackling values education and citizenship. She is presently a City Councillor in Auckland, New

Zealand, where she promotes better government through partnerships and humane connections.

Joseph Lo Bianco holds the Chair of Language and Literacy Education at The University of Melbourne, was formerly Director of the National Languages and Literacy Institute of Australia. He has worked on language policy, peace education, literacy planning, bilingualism and multicultural education in several countries, including Australia, Sri Lanka and Scotland. His recent books include *Australian Policy Activism in Language and Literacy*, with R. Wickert, 2001; *Voices from Phnom Penh, Development and Language*, 2002; *Teaching Invisible Culture: Classroom Practice and Theory*, with C. Crozet 2003; and *Language Policy in Australia, Council of Europe*, 2004. For his research and policy work in language and literacy Professor Lo Bianco has been elected Fellow of the Australian Academy of the Humanities and Fellow of the Australian Council of Educators, and has been awarded the Order of Australia and the title of *Commendatore nell'ordine di merito della repubblica Italiana*.

Diva Lopes da Silveira is a graduate (State University of Londrina, 1972); M.A. (Ball State University, 1975); Ph.D. (Polytechnic of Central London, 1984) and Distance Education Specialist (London University, 1990). A Senior Lecturer at the Federal Rural University of Rio de Janeiro (UFRRJ, 1975–1995), she has researched the issues of Socialisation; Scientific Initiation; Environment, Chaos and Education and created/systematised concepts about learning, evaluation, solidaristic/chaotic para-transdisciplinarity and talents timely initiation. She has published various articles in scientific journals, written book chapters and presented papers at the universities: Oxford, 1979; Tübingen, 1993, 2003; Ulm, 1996; Sydney, 1996; Muscat, 1997; Cape Town, 1998; OISE/UT, 1999; Namibia, 2000; South Korea, 2001; London, 2002. Currently (2001–2003), she also participates in the Animal Ethology Studies (UNESP); and teaches/researches/supervises graduate/post-graduate students at the UFRRJ, University Centre of Barra Mansa and UNESP.

Esther Lucas was born in Finland and lived in England for almost 30 years. Her extensive educational achievements were undertaken, sequentially, at: University College, London, in 1936; Courses Sorbonne, Paris; University of Vienna; Oxford University; Tel Aviv University; and Dr. Phil. from Lueneburg University, in 1990. Her career path included: Research Assistant at the Royal Institute of International Affairs, and Foreign Office Research Department, London; the Preparatory Commission of the United Nations, and she was present at the first Security Council and General Assembly meetings in London; in Israel, she was Kibbutz Member, Head of English at High School, Lecturer School of Education TAU, and Lecturer EFL Teacher Training College. Her affiliations with International Organizations and Associations are extensive and include the UNESCO and UNICEF.

David C. Woolman, Ph.D., is a Professor and Director of the Curriculum Resources Centre at Rhode Island College. He has taught cultural foundations of education, history and peace studies. His research interests are curriculum, international education, peace education and social studies. He has implemented a post-colonial

African history curriculum as a teacher educator in Nigeria, co-directed a Fulbright curriculum project on modernization in the Arab Republic of Egypt, assisted in developing a multilingual resource centre for teachers of recent immigrants, worked on a team that wrote standards-based social studies guidelines for Rhode Island, and designed internet-based resource guides for teachers. His publications have focused on African education reform, educational reconstruction, environmental education, international understanding, peace education, social studies and the role of education in post-colonial societies.

Lightning Source UK Ltd.
Milton Keynes UK
UKHW010238290519
343482UK00003B/199/P